Skyhorse Publishing books may be purchased in bulk at special discounts for sales promotion, corporate gifts, fund-raising, or educational purposes. Special editions can also be created to specifications. For details, contact the Special Sales Department, Skyhorse Publishing, 307 West 36th Street, 11th Floor, New York, NY 10018 or info@skyhorsepublishing.com.

Skyhorse® and Skyhorse Publishing® are registered trademarks of Skyhorse Publishing, Inc.®, a Delaware corporation.

Visit our website at www.skyhorsepublishing.com.

10 9 8 7 6 5 4 3 2 1

Library of Congress Cataloging-in-Publication Data

Ventura, Jesse.

They killed our president : 63 reasons to believe there was a conspiracy to assassinate JFK/Jesse Ventura with Dick Russell and David Wayne.

pages cm

ISBN 978-1-62636-139-3 (hardcover : alk. paper) 1. Kennedy, John F. (John Fitzgerald), 1917-1963—Assassination. 2. Conspiracies—United States—History—20th century. I. Russell, Dick. II. Wayne, David, 1963-III. Title.

E842.9.V44 2013

364.1522092—dc23

2013024922

Printed in the United States of America

THEY KILLED OUR PRESIDENT

63 Reasons to Believ
There Was a Conspira
to Assassinate JFK

Jesse Ventura
WITH DICK RUSSELL AND DAVID W

I
V
T
V
pa
IS
19
II.
E84
973

Prin

Skyhorse Publishing

Back when I was a little kid, there used to be an old TV show that we'd watch every Saturday morning called *Superman*. That show always started out by announcing that he "fights a never ending battle for truth, justice, and the American way."

These days I think you'd almost have to actually *be* Superman to break through the gridlock of lies and cover-ups surrounding the JFK assassination.

But I'm "old school" and I still believe. So this book is dedicated to (you guessed it):

Truth, Justice, and the American way.

Also:
Gerald Posner
Vincent Bugliosi
Bill O'Reilly
(they need to read this)

Table of Contents

SECTION TWO
THE COVER-UP 149

SECTION THREE
THE WITNESSES   249

SECTION FOUR
THE WHY, WHO, AND HOW   279

The Katzenbach Memo

We're going to begin with the "Smoking Gun" related to the tragedy of November 22, 1963.

What you're about to read is a verbatim copy of a Justice Department memo from the then-acting Attorney General of the United States, Nicholas Katzenbach, to new President Lyndon Johnson's aide, Bill Moyers. It was written shortly after Lee Harvey Oswald was murdered by Jack Ruby and is the clearest documentation that exists, to this day, of our government's intent to cover up the truth—for whatever reason—behind the assassination of President John Fitzgerald Kennedy.

November 25, 1963 MEMORANDUM FOR MR. MOYERS
It is important that all of the facts surrounding President Kennedy's Assassination be made public in a way which will satisfy people in the United States and abroad that all the facts have been told and that a statement to this effect be made now.

1. The public must be satisfied that Oswald was the assassin; that he did not have confederates who are still at large; and that the evidence was such that he would have been convicted at trial.

2. Speculation about Oswald's motivation ought to be cut off, and we should have some basis for rebutting thought that this was a Communist conspiracy or (as the Iron Curtain press is saying) a right-wing conspiracy to blame it on the Communists. Unfortunately the facts on Oswald seem about too pat—too obvious (Marxist, Cuba, Russian wife, etc.). The Dallas police have put out statements on the Communist conspiracy theory, and it was they who were in charge when he was shot and thus silenced.

3. The matter has been handled thus far with neither dignity nor conviction. Facts have been mixed with rumor and speculation. We can scarcely let the world see us totally in the image of the Dallas police when our President is murdered.

I think this objective may be satisfied by making public as soon as possible a complete and thorough FBI report on Oswald and the assassination. This may run into the difficulty of pointing to inconsistencies between this report and statements by Dallas police officials. But the reputation of the Bureau is such that it may do the whole job. The only other step would be the appointment of a Presidential Commission of unimpeachable personnel to review and examine the evidence and announce its conclusions. This has both advantages and disadvantages. I think it can await publication of the FBI report and public reaction to it here and abroad.

I think, however, that a statement that all the facts will be made public property in an orderly and responsible way should be made now. We need something to head off public speculation or Congressional hearings of the wrong sort.

Nicholas deB. Katzenbach
Deputy Attorney General

(R) – ITEM IS RESTRICTED

To see the entire document, please visit the following website:
maryferrell.org/mffweb/archive/viewer/showDoc.do?absPageId=756877

Introduction

AUTHOR'S NOTE: There are many video clips I will be referring to, which will convey some fascinating information. To make it easier for you to WATCH ALONG AS YOU READ, I've put all the links online at "Jesse Ventura—The Official Facebook Page": facebook.com/OfficialJesseVentura.

This case has so much blatant evidence that totally blows the doors off the official version of the tragedy that took place fifty years ago in Dallas that it's ridiculous. I've listed 63 solid reasons in this book which—from a standpoint of criminal law—is 62 more than I really need to prove reasonable doubt. One solid point is all it takes to convince a jury; and you're about to see dozens of them. This proves a conspiracy to assassinate the 35th President of the United States—period.

That's really how I looked at this case—like an attorney taking it to court. And I can tell you straight up that there is *no way* they would convict my client in this case; with the knowledge and the witness testimony that now exists, Lee Harvey Oswald would have been found innocent of doing this crime.

In fact, since Bill O'Reilly apparently thinks he knows so much about the JFK assassination, I'd like to publicly challenge him to answer my 63 points. Or—if Mr. O'Reilly is "too busy" to come up with so many responses—how about a public debate? Let's do it. Let's set it up! *I'll be there, Bill.*

This book even comes with a guarantee. I don't just *say* it was a conspiracy—I show the *evidence*, and far beyond any reasonable standards of proof. I guarantee you that there is more than sufficient evidence and that, after examining it, any reasonable person will be convinced of that fact.

I've also decided to break with convention and begin this book with some conclusions because I know that's what people want and—especially in this case—truly deserve. So bear in mind that proof for these conclusions resides in the pages that follow.

John F. Kennedy was murdered by a conspiracy involving disgruntled CIA agents, anti-Castro Cubans, and members of the Mafia, all of whom were extremely angry at what they viewed as Kennedy's appeasement policies toward Communist Cuba and the Soviet Union. President Kennedy sought peace and was viewed by these groups as a cowardly traitor by not giving in to their overwhelming call for war. Those groups—it should be clearly noted—are precisely the same groups that Attorney General Robert F. Kennedy concluded were responsible for his brother's death, after conducting his own private investigation.[1]

Please note, by the way, that these are not just *my* opinions or conclusions:

- The U.S. House of Representatives investigated the assassination and concluded that JFK "was probably assassinated as the result of a conspiracy."[2]
- Robert Kennedy and First Lady Jackie Kennedy sent word to Moscow via special envoy right after the assassination that JFK was killed by "a large political conspiracy" and that he was "the victim of a right-wing conspiracy . . . by domestic opponents."[3]
- The head of the U.S. Secret Service confirmed that on the evening of the assassination he briefed Robert Kennedy that his brother had been

---

[1] Talbot, David, *Brothers: The Hidden History of the Kennedy Years* (Free Press: 2007), xiii, 6, 8–12, 21, 278–279, 323–331.

[2] United States House of Representatives, "Report of the Select Committee on Assassinations, U.S. House of Representatives, Ninety-fifth Congress, second session" 1979: archives.gov/research/jfk/select-committee-report/

[3] Fursenko, Aleksandr & Naftali, Timothy, *"One Hell of a Gamble": Khrushchev, Castro & Kennedy, 1958–1964: The Secret History of the Cuban Missile Crisis* (W.W. Norton: 1998) 344–345.

killed by three to four shooters and that the Secret Service believed that JFK was the "victim of a powerful organization."[4]

- Senior members of the United States Senate who investigated the case concluded that the CIA and FBI played troubling roles in the JFK assassination cover-up, that "the fingerprints of intelligence" were all over Lee Harvey Oswald, and that the "accused assassin was the product of a fake defector program run by the CIA."[5]
- Senator Richard Schweiker concluded that "the CIA was involved in the murder of the president."[6]

And if you haven't heard about the above facts from your mainstream media source of news, I would submit that right now you should be asking yourself, *why not?*

The political imperatives at the time of the assassination were obvious to all concerned. "The point was to stabilize the country after the assassination—let's get on with the ship of state. . . . It would become clear that if one wanted to remain a member in good standing in Washington political and social circles, it was wise not to say anything intemperate about the assassination."[7] So, quite predictably, officials supported the official government version.

To make matters worse, mainstream media immediately backed up the official government version, even if it took a reporter like Dan Rather lying about the backward movement of President Kennedy's body after the shots. He told a national TV audience that the fatal shot drove his head "violently forward" even though the film footage that Mr. Rather was referring to had shown exactly the opposite to be the case.[8] Mainstream media *continues* their endorsement of the original official version by their overwhelmingly ardent support of books that support that version—like *Reclaiming History* and *Case Closed*—and their tendency to dismissively label as "conspiracy theories" any scholarly-researched efforts that point out the numerous inconsistencies in the government's case.

---

[4] Talbot, *Brothers*, 14; Hepburn, James (Hervé Lamarr), *Farewell America: The Plot to Kill JFK* (Frontier: 1968), 301.

[5] Talbot, *Brothers*, 377–382.

[6] Ibid, 383.

[7] Ibid, 290.

[8] Ventura, Jesse & Russell, Dick, *American Conspiracies: Lies, Lies, and More Dirty Lies that the Government Tells Us* (Skyhorse Publishing: 2010), 38.

Members of the U.S. military were also involved in the conspiracy, specifically in feeding false information on Lee Harvey Oswald, the "patsy" who was set up to take the blame for the President's assassination.[9] Their purpose was to instigate an invasion of Cuba, their arch enemy since it had gone communist under Castro, and to militarily engage communism openly in Vietnam and around the world—even including our nuclear-armed superpower enemy of that era, the Soviet Union—in stark contrast to President Kennedy's clearly enunciated policy shift toward détente with our enemies.[10]

Kennedy's shifting policies toward peaceful solutions *completely alienated* the Military-Industrial Complex from Kennedy. JFK was at war with his own national security structure, and no one knew that fact more clearly than he and his trusted inner circle who have documented those facts in the historical record.[11]

If you want to get a real feel for what Jack Kennedy was up against, watch three movies that vividly portray it:

The Manchurian Candidate, a book that President Kennedy helped get made into a film because it documented the dangers about brainwashing, right-wing extremists, and the real possibility that they could be combined to assassinate a president; *Dr. Strangelove,* in which the character of the crazy nuclear-war-hungry general was actually based on General Curtis LeMay, the Chief of Staff for the U.S. Air Force who was in charge of the nation's huge fleet of bombers armed with nuclear weapons at the time and was savagely anti-Kennedy in meetings of the National Security Council; and *Seven Days In May*, a film about a military takeover of the government that was made because President Kennedy convinced Hollywood producers that if it was made it might actually *prevent* a coup from taking place. And to give you an idea of how important it was to him to get that last film made, JFK told his Hollywood friends that he

---

[9] Scott, Peter Dale, *Deep Politics and the Death of JFK* (University of California Press: 1996), 258.

[10] Douglass, James, *JFK and the Unspeakable: Why He Died and Why It Matters* (Touchstone: 2008); Scott, *Deep Politics;* James P. Hosty Jr. & Thomas Hosty, *Assignment Oswald: From the FBI agent assigned to investigate Lee Harvey Oswald prior to the JFK assassination* (Arcade Publishing: 1997).

[11] Talbot, *Brothers*, 41, 44, 50–53, 64–71, 95, 103, 106–108, 146, 163–174, 189, 207–212, 217–230, 253–254.

and his family would even abandon the White House whenever they needed to film there.[12]

The opinion of General Tommy Power—the man who assisted and then followed General LeMay as chief of our Strategic Air Command—provides us with a glowing example of the men who were "advising" President Kennedy:

> Restraint? Why are you so concerned with saving *their* lives? The
> whole idea is to *kill* the bastards. Look. At the end of the war, if
> there are two Americans and one Russian, we win![13]

So the Military-Industrial Complex was clearly at war with President Kennedy over the direction of U.S. foreign policy.[14] In his farewell address to the nation just prior to President Kennedy taking office, President Dwight D. Eisenhower warned the nation of the rising and threatening power of the vast U.S. war machine which he called the "Military-Industrial Complex." Eisenhower stated that it was a serious threat to our Democracy and sorely needed addressing. His warning was straight and bold—and bear in mind that he was speaking not only as the Commander-in-Chief of the Armed Forces, but as a highly successful five-star General in the U.S. Army during World War II and the Supreme Commander of Allied Forces in Europe. He was no stranger to war or why wars should be fought.

In his farewell address, he defined the new problem that was facing us; not the foreign enemy, but our totally new *domestic enemy*:

> Our military organization today bears little relation to that known
> by any of my predecessors in peacetime, or indeed by the fighting
> men of World War II or Korea.

> Until the latest of our world conflicts, the United States had no
> armaments industry. American makers of plowshares could, with
> time and as required, make swords as well. But now we can no lon-

---

[12] Ibid, 148–151: curtis-lemay.tripod.com/

[13] Kaplan, Fred, *The Wizards of Armageddon* (Stanford University Press: 1991), 246, emphasis in original.

[14] Talbot, *Brothers*, 41, 44, 50–53, 64–71, 95, 103, 106–108, 146, 163–174, 189, 207–212, 217–230, 253–254.

ger risk emergency improvisation of national defense; we have been
compelled to create a permanent armaments industry of vast pro-
portions. Added to this, three and a half million men and women
are directly engaged in the defense establishment. We annually
spend on military security more than the net income of all United
States corporations.

This conjunction of an immense military establishment and a
large arms industry is new in the American experience. The total
influence—economic, political, even spiritual—is felt in every
city, every Statehouse, every office of the Federal government.
We recognize the imperative need for this development. Yet
we must not fail to comprehend its grave implications. Our toil,
resources and livelihood are all involved; so is the very structure of
our society.[15]

And then he got very specific and dramatic about the extreme gravity of our
situation:

In the councils of government, we must guard against the acquisi-
tion of unwarranted influence, whether sought or unsought, by the
military-industrial complex. The potential for the disastrous rise of
misplaced power exists and will persist.

We must never let the weight of this combination endanger our liberties or democratic processes.

We should take nothing for granted. Only an alert and knowledgeable citizenry can compel the proper meshing of the huge industrial
and military machinery of defense with our peaceful methods and
goals, so that security and liberty may prosper together.[16]

---

[15] President Dwight D. Eisenhower, "Presidential Address to the Nation," January 17, 1961:
npr.org/2011/01/17/132942244/ikes-warning-of-military-expansion-50-years-later
[16] Ibid.

That threat became readily apparent to President Kennedy as he battled his own national security structure at every step of the way. In every crisis, JFK had to fight his own CIA and Joint Chiefs of Staff to avoid an all-out state of war.

He first had to fight over the Cuban "Bay of Pigs" invasion, then the Berlin Crisis of 1961, then the Cuban Missile Crisis, his efforts at a nuclear test ban treaty and drastic arms reductions, and finally his efforts at détente with Cuba, Vietnam, and the entire Soviet Bloc. By 1963, he had so alienated the military-corporate war machine that he—quite rightly—was in actual fear of a coup openly taking place against his Administration or of being murdered. Robert Kennedy and others shared and voiced those same fears.[17]

But even though the Cold War has now been over for two decades, military spending has actually increased. Some is clearly necessary for our defense. However, especially since we lack an enemy anywhere even near us militarily, some military spending seems utterly ridiculous. Here's an example of the cost of *one project* of the Pentagon for a new airplane called the F-35 Lightning II. Originally budgeted at $178 billion for a fleet of these new fighter jets, costs ballooned—by 2011—to a new estimate of $325 billion.[18] And, as usual, they'll certainly cost a lot more than that by the time they're actually airborne. Would you like to know how necessary that plane is, as a component of our nation's security? Here's how *The New York Times* put it:

> The F-35 is simply not needed. Only one American fighter plane
> has been shot down by an enemy aircraft in nearly forty years. Our
> fighter aircraft are already a full generation ahead of nearly every-
> body else's. Off-boresight targeting technologies [which are what
> the Pentagon says makes the F-35 special] can be adapted to exist-
> ing aircraft, giving them an enduring edge.[19]

So, in a word: unnecessary. And that's just *one example* of dozens where taxpayer money is spiraling down the Pentagon's golden drains. In the meantime, we really could have used $325 billion to assist our declining education system and repair our nation's failing infrastructure.

---

[17] Talbot, *Brothers*, 41, 44, 50–53, 64–71, 95, 103, 106–108, 146, 163–174, 189, 207–212, 217–230, 253–254.

[18] Arquilla, John & Fogelson-Lubliner, "The Pentagon's Biggest Boondoggles," March 13, 2001, *The New York Times*: nytimes.com/imagepages/2011/03/13/opinion/13opchartimg.html

[19] Ibid.

But over a period of time, that military-corporate complex—which evidently now runs this country—has whittled away at our status quo, changing our national priorities. Issues like our health and our education have, to a large extent, *lost out* in that battle; bullets and bombs have won.

It wasn't always that way. During the Cuban Missile Crisis, President Kennedy overruled the military masters who actually—even *openly*—sought a nuclear exchange with the Soviets. Kennedy stopped them. It was extremely difficult to rein them in, but his Administration succeeded in that effort. So the Pentagon did not have that same dominating influence over the Kennedy Administration.

Peace really *did* have a chance; a long, long time ago.

That all seemed to change right at the time of the death of John F. Kennedy. President Eisenhower warned us about the real powers that needed standing up to. President Kennedy stood up to those Powers That Be; and was murdered.

That's why his death is so important: Because that's when everything changed.

That's why it still matters, even today.

Jesse Ventura
Autumn, 2013

SECTION ONE

The Evidence

President Kennedy, per the government's version, was assassinated by a lone gunman, Lee Harvey Oswald, who acted entirely on his own, firing three shots from his "sniper's nest" on the sixth floor of the Texas School Book Depository building, from behind the President's motorcade with a Mannlicher-Carcano 6.5 millimeter Italian rifle that was owned by the assassin. Only three shots were fired and they all came from the rear, after the motorcade had passed the window of that building.

Approximately forty-five minutes after killing President Kennedy, the same assassin then shot and killed Dallas Police Officer J. D. Tippit in a different section of town and was then arrested inside a nearby movie theater. The Warren Commission, a body of elite officials entrusted with the official investigation, "found no evidence that Oswald was involved with any person or group in a conspiracy to assassinate the President"; "there was no evidence to support the speculation that Oswald was an agent, employee, or informant of the FBI, the CIA, or any other governmental agency"; "No direct or indirect relationship between Lee Harvey Oswald and Jack Ruby" (the Dallas nightclub owner who murdered Oswald two days after the assassination) and "no evidence of conspiracy, subversion, or disloyalty to the U.S. Government by any Federal, State, or local official."[20]

The official government version of the JFK assassination is incorrect and that's a fact that has already been proven—you just haven't heard it yet from any of our government's gatekeepers in the mainstream media. I plan to prove that to you far beyond any reasonable questions of doubt.

Because, just for openers, those official conclusions above mean that *there were no shots from the front and that there were three gunshots and three gunshots only.*

Well guess what, folks? That simply isn't true. And that's not just some opinion of mine—that can and *has* been proven scientifically. So please keep reading, because I won't just give you some good reasons or theories that raise the possibility that they're wrong—I'll give you 63 points that *prove* it and will give you a pretty good idea of who the real perpetrators were.

---

[20] "Report of the President's Commission on the Assassination of President Kennedy," September 24, 1964: home.comcast.net/~ceoverfield/warren.html

1

Frontal Gunshots

The forensic evidence is the crucial part of any crime scene investigation, as you've no doubt witnessed firsthand on TV shows like *Law & Order* and *CSI*. Forensic evidence is not about people's opinions or anybody's freaking theories. It's about logical and scientific explanations of what actually happened—and you do that by examining the primary facts of evidence. So let's look at the medical determinations; the blood spatter evidence and the photographic testimony.

President Kennedy was rushed to Parkland Memorial Hospital in Dallas immediately after the shooting, and his body was taken on a stretcher from the limousine into the emergency room where a group of surgeons were ready and waiting to do whatever was humanly possible to save his life. It should be noted that Parkland was not just an emergency room, but an actual trauma center, where the doctors were experienced in the treatment of gunshot wounds.

In Trauma Room One, Dr. Malcolm Perry immediately performed an emergency tracheotomy, which is a standard trauma procedure to ensure that the victim can get air into their lungs. That procedure is accomplished by making a small incision in the lower front portion of the victim's throat and then inserting a breathing tube.

Now let me just stop here for a second and ask you this: If you were a physician and you were entrusted with the trauma care of the President of the United States who had just been shot, don't you think that you would vividly recall the *exact* specifics of precisely what took place? Well, so did they.

Dr. Malcolm Perry noted that there was already a smooth "wound of entrance" on the lower front area of President Kennedy's throat.[21] The Warren Commission, in their usual manner of obfuscation, managed to later get that same doctor to say things from which other inferences could then be drawn by that room of Washington lawyers. But if you look back at the actual words of Dr. Malcolm Perry—taken directly from the Parkland Press Conference on the afternoon of the President's death—Dr. Perry clearly describes that hole he observed in the throat as "a wound of entrance"; then again as "an entrance wound"; and also states that "the bullet was coming at him."[22] Anyone experienced with wounds—and Dr. Perry was *very* experienced—can differentiate an entry wound from an exit wound. A wound of entry is small, like the circumference of the bullet, and has what could be termed a smooth appearance, while an exit wound is much larger, caused by the "blowout" damage of the bullet before it exits the body, and its exit after causing its damage then leaves a wound that is rough and jagged. So, in precisely detailing his exact actions on that memorable day, Dr. Perry noted that the bullet hole in the front of President Kennedy's throat was a smooth wound of entry, and hence, because of what could be called the entry wound's convenient location in the correct portion of the throat, he enlarged that already existing wound slightly with his scalpel in order to make an incision sufficient for placement of the breathing tube. In addition to the entry wound he observed in the front of President Kennedy's throat, Dr. Perry also noted a massive blowout exit wound at the right rear of the President's skull.

Other doctors also observed the huge exit wound at the back of the head. And they too observed that since it was the President of the United States whose wounds they were observing, they weren't about to make a mistake about that *or* to forget it anytime soon.

---

[21] Fetzer, James H., Ph.D., *Assassination Science: Experts Speak Out on the Death of JFK* (Open Court, 1998). Also see: John Simkin, *The Education Forum*, "Dr. Malcolm Perry R.I.P. (1929–2009)," retrieved 14 April 2013: educationforum.ipbhost.com/index.php?showtopic=15105

[22] Ibid.

The medical consensus from all the doctors who treated President
Kennedy's wounds in Dallas clearly confirms the massive exit wound
at the back of the head.[23] In all, at least eight of the treating physicians
at Parkland Hospital confirmed on record that there was a huge *exit*
wound at the rear of the President' head.[24] The names of these doctors
were:

Dr. Malcolm Perry[25]

Dr. Charles Crenshaw[26]

Dr. Charles J. Carrico[27]

Dr. Richard Dulaney[28]

Dr. Ronald Jones[29]

Dr. Robert McClelland[30]

Dr. Paul Peters[31]

Dr. Kenneth E. Salyer[32]

The exit wound at the back of the head was also confirmed by:

FBI Special Agent Frank O'Neal[33]

Secret Service Special Agent Clint Hill[34]

---

[23] Belzer, Richard & Wayne, David, *Dead Wrong* (Skyhorse: 2013), 97–98.

[24] Horne, Douglas P., *Inside the Assassination Records Review Board: The U.S. Government's Final Attempt to Reconcile the Conflicting Medical Evidence in the Assassination of JFK* (Douglas P. Horne: 2009).

[25] Fetzer, Ph.D., *Assassination Science;* Simkin, *The Education Forum*, "Dr. Malcolm Perry": educationforum.ipbhost.com/index php?showtopic=15105

[26] Aguilar, Gary L., M.D., "John F. Kennedy's Fatal Wounds: The Witnesses and the Interpretations From 1963 to the Present," August 1994, *Electronic Assassinations Newsletter*, assassinationweb.com/ag6.htm

[27] Ibid.

[28] Ibid.

[29] Ibid.

[30] Ibid.

[31] Ibid.

[32] Ibid.

[33] Ibid.

[34] "Warren Commission Testimony of Secret Service Agent Clint Hill," March 9, 1964, *JFK* Lancer: jfklancer.com/CHill.html Also see: Douglas P. Horne, "SHAME ON

Emergency Room Nurse Audrey Bell[35]

Radiographer Jerrol Custer[36]

Autopsy Technician Floyd Riebe[37]

Autopsy Technician Paul O'Connor[38]

BOTH OF YOU CLINT HILL AND CHRIS MATTHEWS," at John Simkin, *The Education Forum*, retrieved 14 April 2013: educationforum.ipbhost.com/index php?showtopic=19068

[35] *History Matters Archive,* "ARRB Bell Interview," retrieved 11 Feb. 2012: historymatters.com/archive/jfk/arrb/medical_interviews/audio/ARRB_Bell.htm

[36] Aguilar, M.D., "Fatal Wounds."

[37] Ibid.

[38] Ibid.

Secret Service Agent Clint Hill—who later "changed his mind"—seemed exceedingly clear about the matter when he originally testified. At the time, *testifying* right after the assassination when one would think his memory would be vividly fresh, he described to the Warren Commission:

> The right rear portion of his head was missing. It was lying in the rear seat of the car. His brain was exposed. There was blood and bits of brain all over the entire rear portion of the car. Mrs. Kennedy was completely covered with blood. There was so much blood you could not tell if there had been any other wound or not, except for the one large gaping wound in the right rear portion of the head.[39]

So don't look now, but there seems to be a very large elephant in the room, folks. If our government can take a very clear statement like that and try to spin it a different way in a lame attempt to prove that it isn't true, then that's a serious indication that something is really rotten in Denmark and that, for some reason, dark forces are at work here.

The entry wound that *caused* all that massive damage at the back of the President's head was *also* clearly observed by the doctors:

---

[39] "Warren Commission Testimony of Secret Service Agent Clint Hill," *JFK* Lancer; and Horne, "SHAME ON BOTH OF YOU CLINT HILL AND CHRIS MATTHEWS"

Multiple witnesses, who were medically and otherwise credible, confirmed that they clearly saw an entry wound in the FRONT of President Kennedy's head, in his upper right forehead at the hairline.[40]

Now let's look at the blood evidence. Experts can look at blood spatter and determine from that what took place.

Sherry Fiester was a Certified Senior Crime Scene Investigator and Court-Recognized Expert in Crime Scene Reconstruction and Blood Spatter Analysis. She conducted an extremely detailed and professional reconstruction of the crime scene and here is the point-blank conclusion of that study:

The head injury to President Kennedy was the result of a single gunshot fired from the front of the President.[41]

That sure sounds pretty damn solid to me. She *did* say "front," didn't she?

Additional blood spatter evidence is further indicative of a shot from the front. There were two Dallas motorcycle officers riding flank-left-rear to the President's car, meaning that the placement of the outriders were slightly behind the rear wheels of the limousine on the left hand side of the car. The officers were Bobby Hargis and B. J. Martin, and their windshields were sprayed with the blood and brain matter of President Kennedy. It has been established that the limo had slowed considerably after the first shots—some said almost to a complete stop—so the dramatic spatter backwards and to the left of the car was *not* the result of the forward motion of the vehicle, but the result of directional gravity from the source of the shot, which would place the gunshot as coming from the right-front of the car. Bobby Hargis was riding closest to the car, behind it on the left side, and this is how he described what happened:

When President Kennedy straightened back up in the car the bullet hit him in the head, the one that killed him and it seemed like his head exploded, and I was splattered with blood

---

[40] Horne, *Inside the ARRB*, emphasis in original.

[41] Gutierrez Fiester, Sherry, *JFK Homicide: Forensic Reconstruction, Bloodspatter Analysis in the Kennedy Murder: Proving a Frontal Headshot* (JFK Lancer: 2010, DVD). jfklancer.com/catalog/gutierrez/index.html Also see: Sherry P. Fiester, *Enemy of the Truth: Myths, Forensics, and the Kennedy Assassination* (JFK Lancer: 2012).

and brain, and kind of a bloody water . . . well, at the time it
sounded like the shots were right next to me.[42]

Officer B. J. Martin, who was riding even farther to President Kennedy's
left, in tandem with Officer Hargis, was also sprayed with blood and brain matter immediately after the head shot to the President.[43]

So the blood spatter evidence *also* shows us that shots came from the
front; all proving through forensic findings that President Kennedy was
actually struck by *at least two bullets from the front*—one in the right side
of his forehead and one in the throat. And, since we know that shots also
came from the rear of the motorcade, *any shot from the front* is proof of a
conspiracy, as shots from both the front and rear necessitate that there were
multiple shooters. Case closed. But hang on, because we've still got 62 more.

The Warren Commission tried to explain away that blood spatter and
backward movement of the President's body with some medical semantics,
which I'll get into on the next entry. They *had* to come up with something,
because it turned out that there was a home movie made of it that day that
vividly depicted the violent backward motion and the backward spray of
blood and brain matter.

---

[42] Hargis, Robert "Deposition of Robert Hargis," 18 April, 1964

[43] Fiester, *Forensic Reconstruction*

2

Zapruder Film

When there is a film of a crime, it's a prime piece of evidence known as photographic testimony. In fact, in the case of the JFK assassination, the photographic testimony is what's known as *prima facie* evidence, vividly testifying about what actually happened without ever uttering a word.

A film was taken of the assassination of President Kennedy as the shots were fired. It was a home movie made by a man named Abraham Zapruder and has since become known simply as the Zapruder Film. The footage graphically confirms the fatal head shot and the fact that this came from the front of the limousine.

In this video, you can see that President Kennedy's entire body is driven sharply backward and to his left, as the result of taking a high-velocity round directly through his head. It appears to enter his head in direct conformity with the medical testimony in Dallas which recorded a small entry wound in the President's upper right side of his forehead, near the hairline.

The footage is very graphic, but if you think you can handle it, it can and should be viewed. It's currently available online at youtube.com/watch?v=jWHdEeHNbXY. (Remember that you can also go to my website at facebook.com/OfficialJesseVentura to view all the videos from the book.) The clips seem to get taken down from the Internet every once in a while but then are put back up by other assassination researchers. So if that link is invalid when you go to check, just Google "Zapruder film enhanced" and you'll find it. You'll see President Kennedy first reacting with shock to the bullet that hits him in the throat, and then—just as his wife and First Lady Jackie Kennedy is looking directly at him to see what is wrong—the kill-shot hits him high in the right side of his forehead and rips off a large portion of his head, rapidly driving his entire body backward and to his left. But be forewarned, this is something you'll never forget after you've seen it.

That footage by Abraham Zapruder so clearly depicted what happened that it was "shielded" from the public's view for many years. Media mogul C. D. Jackson, the power behind *Time-Life, Inc.*, purchased the rights to that film for a large sum of money and basically kept it under wraps. It was finally shown to an American television audience by author Robert Groden in 1975; and the audience literally gasps at the dramatic evidence of a head shot from the front. You can watch that one online, too, and you will undoubtedly share the shock of that audience: youtube.com/watch?v=4DwKK4rkeEM.

So the government had some explaining to do and they knew it. They came up with an elaborate medical explanation about a bullet having severed the neck vertebrae of the President and because he was held upright by a brace he wore to support his back, it created a "jet force" that blew the matter from his head backwards, even though he was shot from the rear. *Nice try*. But that dog can't hunt, people. Military veteran and former combat sniper, Craig Roberts, exhaustively researched the issue and determined that the government version was just what it sounds like—a bunch of bunk.

> With his extensive combat experience, Roberts is scathing about
> the mysterious 'jet force' that supposedly blows Kennedy's head
> backwards, towards Oswald, in the famous Zapruder home
> movie of the assassination. 'In that film,' says Roberts, 'we see
> Kennedy take a shot from the front.'[44]

Roberts further determined that the shot also had to be from an exploding bullet—what's known as a "frangible" round—due to the technical behavior of

---

[44] Badrich, Steve "Postcards from the Labyrinth: Thirty Years After, J.F.K. Researchers Gather in Dallas," (NameBase Newsline, No. 4, Jan.–Mar. 1994), the-puzzle-palace.com/files/NEWSLINE.194

the impact. So now, instead of the crap from the Warren Commission, listen to somebody who actually knows what he's talking about:

> Some of the supporters of the Warren Commission . . . stated that the bullet came from the rear because the eruption of brain matter and blood came out of the front of the president's skull.

> I saw something else. In a head shot, the exit wound, due to the buildup of hydrostatic pressure, explodes in a conical formation in the down-range direction of the bullet. Yet in the Zapruder film, I could plainly see that the eruption was not a conical shape to the front of the limo, but instead was an explosion that cast fragments both up and down in a vertical plane, and side to side in a horizontal plane. There was only one explanation for this: an exploding or 'frangible' bullet. Such a round explodes on impact—in exactly the manner depicted in the film.[45]

---

[45] Roberts, Craig, *Kill Zone: A Sniper Looks at Dealey Plaza* (Consolidated Press, 1994), 89–90.

3

U.S. Secret Service Agents

It may come as a shock to learn that many of the Secret Service special agents who were right at the scene of the shooting felt certain that shots which hit President Kennedy *came from the front*. What's even more shocking is that it has been so little publicized that most people are completely unaware of their conclusions. But that's actually what they thought—in fact, they stated this with certainty. But don't take my word for it. Let's look at exactly who they were and exactly what they said.

Forrest Sorrels was the Special-Agent-in-Charge of the Dallas district for the Secret Service. Special Agent Sorrels was one of the higher ranking Secret Service agents in Dallas that day and was riding in the lead car of the President's motorcade, just a bit ahead of the limousine carrying President Kennedy. SAIC Sorrels was in the back seat of the lead car on the right side. At the time of the gunshots, he was looking out the right rear passenger window. Here's what he said about it:

> I looked towards the top of the terrace to my right as the sound
> of the shots seemed to come from that direction.[46]

---

[46] Sorrells, Forrest, "Secret Service Report of Special Agent-In-Charge Forrest V. Sorrells," 28 November, 1963.

That sounds pretty clear to me, don't you agree? By the way, that terrace area that Special Agent Sorrels is describing as where the shots had come from is *precisely* the area that the government and their stooges mockingly refer to as the grassy knoll, as in "grassy knoll conspiracy kooks." Funny, it doesn't sound so kooky when it's an experienced high-ranking Secret Service agent who was right on top of the murder scene telling us where he thought the shots came from. Notice that he doesn't say that they came from behind him, where Oswald was located; he says that the shots—*plural*—came from the right side, and he was *ahead* of the President's car at that moment.

But wait, there's more! Here's another Secret Service agent who was in a different position from which to gauge the shots. Lem Johns was Shift Leader of the Secret Service Vice Presidential Detail. He was in the car with Vice-President Johnson which was two cars behind Kennedy. What Lem Johns remembered was in accord with Special Agent Sorrels:

> The first two [shots] sounded like they were on the side of me towards the grassy knoll.[47]

Here's another one. Special Agent Paul Landis, part of the White House Detail, was riding right in the Secret Service Follow-Up car which was immediately behind President Kennedy. So remember that he was immediately *behind President Kennedy*—the agents in the Follow-Up car had a bird's eye view of President Kennedy in the backseat of the car right in front of them and are trained to be alert to any possible danger arising around them. Here's what he said:

> My reaction at this time was that the shot came from somewhere towards the front.[48]

Well, gee whiz folks, none of that lines up with the official version, does it? I thought our government told us that the shots came from the rear? But here are three Secret Service agents who were *right there* in the best locations, and they're telling us something completely different. What's the deal? Who are we supposed to trust, highly professional Secret Service agents expertly trained in

---

[47] *House Select Committee on Assassinations*, "Interview of Special Agent Thomas L. Johns," 8 August, 1978.

[48] Landis, Paul "Statement of United States Secret Service Special Agent Paul E. Landis," 27 November, 1963.

gunfire, or a bunch of Washington lawyers in white shirts who write long books in legalese? I think I'll go with the Secret Service agents on that one.

That's a matter of great importance. The first focus of those Secret Service agents was on the area that had been *in front* of the limousine because—in their professional opinions—that's where they thought the shots came from.[49] And it wasn't just the Secret Service who thought that either, as the next fact proves.

---

[49] Palamara, Vincent Michael, *Survivor's Guilt: The Secret Service and the Failure to Protect the President* (TrineDay: 2013).

4

Grassy Knoll

The upper area from the road on Dealey Plaza known as the grassy knoll in particular was the area that a great majority of witnesses to the shooting were immediately fixated on. Dozens of them went rushing up the hill because they thought that was the location that was the source of the gunfire.[50] The Warren Commission tried to minimize that fact by focusing the majority of testimony they placed on the historical record on select witnesses who did *not* think shots came from that location. So—although it was very misleading—the Warren Commission did not conclude that the grassy knoll was the beehive of activity that it actually was.[51]

But as the testimony of one Dallas police officer vividly illustrates, the grassy knoll actually *was* the area that everyone immediately ran toward. Motorcycle Officer Clyde Haygood was riding one of the motorcycles flanking President Kennedy's car. He was riding right-flank, just slightly to the rear of the President, on the right side of the limousine. And his testimony is

---

[50] Groden, Robert *The Search for Lee Harvey Oswald: A Comprehensive Photographic Record* (Penguin: 1995).

[51] Brown, Walt, Ph.D., *The Warren Omission: A Micro-study of the Methods and Failures of the Warren Commission* (Delmax: 1996).

illuminating; the railroad yard that Officer Haygood refers to was located up the hill of the grassy knoll:

QUESTION: What did you do after you heard the sounds?

OFFICER HAYGOOD: I made the shift down to lower gear and went on to the scene of the shooting.

QUESTION: What do you mean by 'the scene of the shooting?'

OFFICER HAYGOOD: . . . I could see all these people laying on the ground there on Elm. Some of them were pointing back up to the railroad yard, and a couple of people were headed back up that way, and I immediately tried to jump the north curb there in the 400 block, which was too high for me to get over.

QUESTION: You mean with your motorcycle?

OFFICER HAYGOOD: . . . And I left my motor on the street and ran to the railroad yard.

QUESTION: . . . Did you see any people running away from there?

OFFICER HAYGOOD: No. They was [sic] all going to it.[52]

Officer Bobby Hargis, the one who had his windshield splattered after the shots, also parked his motorcycle unit and ran up the grassy knoll.[53] The Dallas Chief of Police, Jesse Curry, personally believed that a gunman did indeed fire from the grassy knoll.[54] Chief Curry was riding in the lead car of the motorcade, immediately ahead of President Kennedy. What the Warren Commission *should*

[52] Haygood, Clyde, "Testimony of Clyde A. Haygood to the President's Commission (Warren Commission)," 9 April, 1964: jfkassassination.net/russ/testimony/haygood.htm

[53] Curry, Jesse E., *Retired Dallas Police Chief, Jesse Curry, reveals his personal JFK Assassination File* (self-published: 1969).

[54] Palamara, Vincent Michael, "Important early book by a principal in the case," January 9, 2006: amazon.com/Retired-Dallas-reveals-personal-assassination/dp/B0006CZR8M

have done was to look at what law enforcement officials on the scene actually did. As soon as the shots rang out, Chief Curry grabbed the police radio and said the following:

> Get a man on top of that Triple Underpass and see what happened up there.[55]

It should be noted that the triple underpass was the area that was *in front* of the motorcade at the time of the gunshots and was connected to the railroad yard next to the grassy knoll.

The Sheriff of Dallas County, Bill Decker, was also in that lead car. What did he do, responsible people might ask? He immediately grabbed his police radio and stated the following:

> Have my office move all available men out of my office into the railroad yard to try to determine what happened in there and hold everything secure until Homicide and other investigators should get there.[56]

Funny, huh? If you read the report of the illustrious Warren Commission, they make it sound like it was the Texas School Book Depository building that was the immediate focus of attention. But it wasn't.

In fact, in the moments right after the gunshots, most of the attention of law enforcement personnel was focused on the area that had been in front of the motorcade at the shooting: the triple overpass, the railroad yard near it, and the grassy knoll area which had been to the right and front of President Kennedy as the shots rang out.

The Book Depository building, home of the famed "sniper's nest" on its sixth floor, only became a focus of major attention later. Eyewitness to the assassination, James Tague, made the following very cogent observation:

> If you go back to Dealey Plaza at 12:30 and get the photographs and police tapes, there was really no action taken on the School

---

[55] Galanor, Stewart, "The Art and Science of Misrepresenting Evidence: How the Warren Commission and the House Select Committee on Assassinations manipulated evidence to dismiss witness accounts of the assassination," retrieved 14 April 2013: historymatters.com/analysis/Witness/artScience.htm

[56] Ibid.

Book Depository for seven minutes. True, there were a couple of policemen who said they rushed in, which looks good on a sergeant's report, but it didn't happen that way. In those seven minutes, I think Oswald may have assisted in letting people into the building by saying they worked there or whatever. During that time, they could have moved an army in and out of the Texas School Book Depository.[57]

---

[57] James Tague, "Eyewitness Statement of James Tague," retrieved 14 April 2013: karws.gso. uri.edu/jfk/History/The_deed/Sneed/Tague.html

5

Previous Plots against President Kennedy

President Kennedy was being stalked. Contrary to the general notion of great shock at the President's assassination manifested in the Report of the Warren Commission, it was a known fact that in 1963, Kennedy's life was in danger from serious threat levels that had been positively identified by the United States Secret Service.[58]

The conspiracy plot against President Kennedy in Chicago was very real,[59] and the Secret Service was acutely aware of it.[60] Former Secret Service Agent Abraham Bolden wrote an entire book about that plot and its implications.[61]

The conspiracy plot against President Kennedy in Tampa, Florida, was also very real.[62] The Secret Service was also aware of that plot.[63]

---

58 Palamara, *Survivor's Guilt.*

59 Waldron, Lamar & Hartmann, Thom, *Ultimate Sacrifice* (New York: Carroll & Graf, 2005).

60 Palamara, *Survivor's Guilt.*

61 Bolden, Abraham, *The Echo from Dealey Plaza: The true story of the first African American on the White House Secret Service detail and his quest for justice after the assassination of JFK* (Crown: 2008).

62 Kelly, William, "The Tampa Plot in Retrospect," July 7, 2012: jfkcountercoup.blogspot. com/2012/07/tampa-plot-in-retrospect.html and Waldron & Hartmann, *Ultimate Sacrifice*

63 Palamara, *Survivor's Guilt.*

Those facts have been documented substantially in several books including *Ultimate Sacrifice*, a good place to begin if you wish to research those points in great detail. In both of those cases—Chicago and Tampa—the conspiracy plot was virtually identical to the conspiracy plot that finally killed JFK in Dallas, a short time after those first two attempts. It was a set-up, with plans for multiple shots from a high-powered rifle, complete with a patsy who was framed to take the blame by being set up as a "lone nut" who was a disenchanted soldier with a strange background; and the patsy was tied to the crime by falsely manufactured evidence, just like Oswald was a few weeks later.[64]

Right after that serious plot against the President's life in Chicago was averted, and just prior to JFK's trip to Tampa—only four days before he was shot dead in Dallas—authorities became aware of another serious threat against his life.

> Authorities had received credible reports of threats against JFK, and Tampa authorities had uncovered a plan to assassinate JFK during his long motorcade there. . . . Long-secret Congressional reports confirm that 'the threat on November 18, 1963, was posed by a mobile, unidentified rifleman shooting from a window in a tall building with a high power rifle fitted with a scope.'[65]

So the U.S. Congress and the U.S. Secret Service were both aware of those plots and that has been documented:

> One Secret Service agent told Congressional investigators that 'there was an active threat against the President of which the Secret Service was aware in November 1963 in the period imme-diately prior to JFK's trip to Miami made by 'a group of people.'"[66]

By the way, take note of those words that were above, "a group of people." Guess what, that's the legal definition of a conspiracy, and that's coming to us direct from the United States Secret Service!

The police protection for Kennedy during that Tampa trip was also made aware that there was a serious threat. And *so was President Kennedy himself*:

---

[64] Waldron & Hartmann, *Ultimate Sacrifice*, 145.

[65] Ibid.

[66] Ibid.

The Tampa threat was confirmed to us by Chief of Police (J. P.) Mullins, who also confirmed that it wasn't allowed to be published at the time. However, as with Chicago, JFK knew about the Tampa assassination threat. In the words of a high Florida law-enforcement official at the time, 'JFK had been briefed he was in danger.'[67]

In author Vince Palamara's new book, *Survivor's Guilt*, he examines the Secret Service's protection of JFK:

> Secret Service agents in Tampa were probably subjected to the same pressure for secrecy as those in Chicago. . . . It also explains why, in the mid-1990s, the Secret Service destroyed documents about JFK's motorcades in the weeks before Dallas, rather than turn them over to the Assassinations Records Review Board as the law required.[68]

The issue of threats against the President was mostly kept out of the newspapers:

> While all news of the threat was suppressed at the time, two small articles appeared right after JFK's death, but even then the story was quickly suppressed.[69]

Of course, the Warren Commission—which historian Walt Brown more properly dubbed the "Warren Omission"—neglected to inform the American public about the true and known nature of the previous plots.[70] But that's probably about what you figured, right? Just because they were sworn to serve the public they supposedly represented didn't stop them from following their own pre-formed agenda.

So it was very clear that President Kennedy was being set up. Keep that point in your mind as you read the upcoming entries on the horribly inadequate security precautions in Dallas.

---

[67] Ibid.

[68] Palamara, *Survivor's Guilt*.

[69] Waldron & Hartmann, *Ultimate Sacrifice*, 254.

[70] Walt Brown, Ph.D., *The Warren Omission*.

And the similarities are unnerving. Chicago, then Tampa, then Dallas; they all followed the same M.O. and they were one right after the other:

> The Tampa attempt . . . involved at least two men, one of whom threatened to 'use a gun' and was described by the Secret Service as 'white, male, 20, slender build,'. . . According to Congressional investigators, 'Secret Service memos' say 'the threat on November 18, 1963, was posed by a mobile, unidentified rifleman shooting from a window in a tall building with a high powered rifle fitted with a scope.' That was the same basic scene in Chicago and Dallas.[71]

And even *more* unnerving is the fact that <u>all three plots</u>—Chicago, Tampa, and Dallas—also used the same M.O. to set up their designated "patsy":

> What made the attempts to kill JFK in Chicago and Tampa [and later Dallas] different from all previous threats was the involvement of Cuban suspects—and a possible Cuban agent—in each area. In addition, these multi-person attempts were clearly not the work of the usual lone, mentally ill person, but were clearly the result of coordinated planning.

> In both the Tampa and Dallas attempts, officials sought a young man in his early twenties, white with slender build, who had been in recent contact with a small pro-Castro group called the Fair Play for Cuba Committee (FPCC). In Dallas that was Lee Harvey Oswald, but the Tampa person of interest was Gilberto Policarpo Lopez, who—like Oswald—was a former defector.[72]

Cuban dissidents and a former defector; well *my, my,* doesn't *that* have a familiar ring? That's not just similar, that's downright *eerie.*

In *Ultimate Sacrifice*, Waldron and Hartmann document "eighteen parallels between Dallas suspect Lee Harvey Oswald and Gilberto Policarpo Lopez . . ." (and) here are a few:

---

[71] Waldron & Hartmann, *Ultimate Sacrifice*, cited in: William Kelly, "The Tampa Plot in Retrospect," July 7, 2012: jfkcountercoup.blogspot.com/2012/07/tampa-plot-in-retrospect.html

[72] Ibid.

Like Oswald, Lopez was also of interest to Navy intelligence. Also similar to Oswald, Gilberto Lopez made a mysterious trip to Mexico City in the fall of 1963, attempting to get to Cuba. Lopez even used the same border crossing as Oswald, and government reports say both went one way by car, though neither man owned a car. Like Oswald, Lopez had recently separated from his wife and had gotten into a fistfight in the summer of 1963 over supposedly pro-Castro sympathies. Declassified Warren Commission and CIA documents confirm that Lopez, whose movements parallel Oswald in so many ways in 1963, was on a secret 'mission' for the U.S. involving Cuba, an 'operation' so secret that the CIA felt that protecting it was considered more important than thoroughly investigating the JFK assassination.[73]

So there weren't just previous plots—there were actually previous plots using the *exact same method* of setting up the patsy to take the fall for a very sophisticated assassination scenario.

---

[73] Ibid.

6

Last-Minute Change of
Motorcycle Formation

One of the acts which clearly enabled the assassination of President Kennedy was the removal of the motorcycle police escorts around his limousine for the parade that day in Dallas. Typically—just as there had been on the previous motorcades of President Kennedy—the President is flanked on each side by two motorcycles in what is known as the standard wedge formation. For some reason—and one that I will explain—that standard wedge formation was removed in Dallas, and instead, a wide open formation placing those four motorcycles at the *rear* of the President's car left him completely vulnerable.[74] That's what made President Kennedy a *sitting duck* in Dallas. This is such an important fact that, first off, I want to show you exactly what I'm talking about.

Al Carrier is an expert in dignitary protection, which includes security protocols like protection for presidents in parades. He studied all the photographs from Dallas and other motorcades, including all the films and records. Pay attention to what he noticed:

---

[74] Al Carrier, 2003 "The United States Secret Service: Conspiracy to Assassinate a President," *Dealey Plaza Echo*, Volume 7, Issue 1, March 2003, 36–48: maryferrell.org/mffweb/archive/viewer/showDoc.do?absPageId=389290

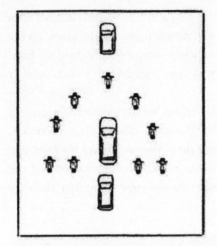 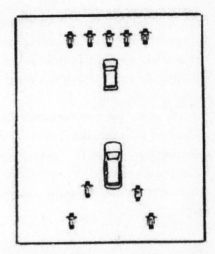

Charts by Al Carrier[75]

The first chart is the Standard Wedge Formation. Note the full protection it provides the President, who is in the middle car.

The second chart is the actual motorcycle formation on November 22, 1963, in Dallas. Notice how needlessly exposed it left the President.

With five of the motorcycle units placed in front of the lead car, they are in a totally ineffective position. With no units at the sides and no Secret Service Follow-Up car tucked in close behind, the President is left wide open to snipers from the front, back, and sides.

When it comes to security, the Standard Wedge Formation is the known and accepted "Gold Standard" for motorcade protocol. It was in use in 1963; in fact, security expert Al Carrier noted that it was "the motorcycle position-ing in the 1962 Berlin Kennedy motorcade and the November 14, 1963, Tampa, Florida, motorcade" which was only a few days prior to the trip to Dallas.[76] Why was it changed in Dallas? Now *that's* a very important question.

So, the government once again had some answering to do on that point. And what did they do? They *blamed the victim*. They came up with the angle that, lo and behold, it was actually President Kennedy himself who ordered the reductions in security because it was basically a campaign trip for publicity and

[75] Carrier, "The United States Secret Service: Conspiracy to Assassinate a President."
[76] Ibid.

he didn't want his protectors interfering with him and his ability to interact with the crowd.[77] How's that for adding insult to injury and placing the blame on the victim who, especially in this case, is completely incapable of defending himself? And on top of that, guess what? It was utter *hogwash*—it was completely invented, totally untrue.

The above point in particular and the Secret Service decisions in general are covered in greater detail than ever before in a new book by Vince Palamara, titled *Survivor's Guilt: The Secret Service and the Failure to Protect the President.* Palamara interviewed dozens of Secret Service agents who remembered the details of protecting Kennedy, and they told him the same thing over and over again:

> President Kennedy was very understanding about his protection and *never ever* interfered with Secret Service protection protocols. That was *their* job and he knew that and let them do it. He *never* told agents how to do their job and *never* ordered changes in motorcade formations or any other protection protocols. *Period.*[78]
>
> _____
> [78] Ibid.

Furthermore, as both the Secret Service and the President of the United States are acutely aware, *no one, not even the President* can overrule the Secret Service on matters related to security. As the Chief of the Secret Service testified to the Warren Commission:

> No President will tell the Secret Service what they can or cannot do.[79]

That's simply how it is. The Secret Service can and has countermanded the orders of the President of the United States.[80] *They* decide when it comes to security. So, especially in this case, blaming JFK for reductions in his protection is blatantly misplaced.

_____

[77] Palamara, *Survivor's Guilt*

[79] Ibid.

[80] Carrier, "The United States Secret Service: Conspiracy to Assassinate a President"; Palamara, *Survivor's Guilt*

So that's one thing that needs to be stated clearly. It was most adamantly <u>not</u> President Kennedy who was responsible for the change in the motorcycle formation. It was the United States Secret Service which was responsible for the change.[81]

Again, the point of note here is that the motorcycle formation was apparently only changed in Dallas. The United States Congress thought the matter was pretty important, too, as an internal memorandum on the matter during the investigation by the House Select Committee on Assassinations revealed the following gem:

> But in comparison with what the SS's [Secret Service's] own documents suggest were the security precautions used in prior motorcades during the same Texas visit, the motorcade alteration in Dallas by the SS may have been a unique occurrence.[82]

So there's a huge smoking gun. Why was it only different in Dallas? Like a true government organization, that House Select Committee on Assassinations played it safe, not making the matter a big public issue. But observe their official conclusion:

> The Secret Service's alteration of the original Dallas Police Department motorcycle deployment plan prevented the use of maximum possible security precautions...Surprisingly, the security measure used in the prior motorcades during the same Texas visit [11/21/63] shows that the deployment of motorcycles in Dallas by the Secret Service may have been uniquely insecure. . .[83]

So, as I said, folks—*There's* your smoking gun.

Let me choose my words very carefully here. I'm not saying that the Secret Service, as an agency, conspired to kill President Kennedy by intentionally reducing his protection that day in Dallas. I have a great deal of respect for the men

---

[81] Ibid.

[82] Vince Palamara, "The Good, The Bad, and the Ugly: A Review of *The Kennedy Detail*, A Compelling but Dangerous Mix of Fact, Faction, and Fiction," *CTKA* (*Citizens for Truth about the Kennedy Assassination*), retrieved 16 April 2013: kennedydetailkennedydetailkennedy.blogspot.com/2012/08/updated-jfk-did-not-order-agents-off.html

[83] Ibid.

and women of the U. S. Secret Service and particularly for the hard work done by the individual agents on the ground. But *I am saying this*: One of the things that enabled the Kennedy assassination was his security reductions that day in Dallas. Those reductions *did not come* from President Kennedy or his staff. Those security reductions are traceable to certain *individuals* in the Secret Service who ordered several things that made President Kennedy a sitting duck as that limo took him through Dealey Plaza, and I am going to tell you *exactly* what they were:

- Changing the standard motorcycle protection from the wedge formation to an insecure formation;
- Ordering Secret Service agents *off* the riding ports of the President's limo, which were designed specifically for them to ride on the back of the car and provide him with cover;
- Changing the already scheduled parade route from its original route to the new path—a path which took the President very slowly through Dealey Plaza and along a dangerous route that was virtually unprotected.

Those last two are so important that they will be covered in the following entries. But if you've read above, you're beginning to get the big picture of what really happened and why these decisions are what enabled the assassination in the first place.

7

Secret Service Agents Ordered Off Limousine

S o, to put it bluntly, President Kennedy was a sitting duck waiting to get shot because he had no protective motorcycle formation around him and no Secret Service agents riding on the back or sides of the car. The agents being ordered off the car is another issue of note.

There's an amazing film on the Internet that you have to see. It was taken at Dallas's Love Field after Air Force One arrived, late on the morning of the fateful day—in fact, less than an hour before President Kennedy is shot and killed. The President and First Lady Jackie Kennedy can be seen in the limousine as it pulls away from the airport . . . and then an amazing thing happens. A Secret Service agent who had positioned himself on the rear riding platform of the slow-moving limousine is ordered *off* the rear of the car by a superior.

The man ordered off the bumper is U.S. Secret Service Agent Don Lawton. SA Lawton then openly questions his superior by gesturing with his open palms up in the air, as if to say "Hey, what's the deal?" He's clearly confused about why he has been ordered off the riding bumper of the car of the President whom he is trying to protect. The order came from Emory Roberts, Shift Leader of the White House Secret Service Detail, which is whom SA Lawton is gesturing toward. It's accessible online: youtube.com/watch?v=lzNS15ssgIk.

But there were not only an absence of agents riding *in* the car; there were not even agents *near* enough to the car. We can see that by the painful crucial seconds that it took Special Agent Clint Hill to finally get to the limo as Jackie Kennedy was reaching in the air on the trunk of the car.

In case you're wondering, the speed of the limousine also has little to do with whether or not agents are placed on the back of the limousine. As one Secret Service agent noted, on a JFK trip to Caracas, Venezuela, he and "Roy Kellerman rode on the back of the limousine all the way to the Presidential palace" at speeds of "50 miles per hour."[84] It's not the traveling speed that determines whether or not the agents ride there, it's the *perceived threat level*. And as we know from the serious threats and previous plots that were learned of just prior to the Texas trip, the perceived threat level in Dallas was very high.

Also bear in mind that, just as you've no doubt seen in film footage, ordinarily Secret Service agents are walking or jogging alongside the President's limousine as it goes through the crowds.[85] The slow crowd speed of the limo makes it easy for agents to keep up. But they weren't there in Dealey Plaza; look at the Zapruder film of the assassination and see how dreadfully long it took any agent to reach the car of the man they were sworn to protect.

Especially from a wider angle view of the assassination, one can clearly note a very disturbing fact: There were no Secret Service agents at the sides—or even near the rear—of the President's car at the time of the shots. In fact, Special Agent Clint Hill, the agent who finally climbed onto the rear running board of the Kennedy limo after it was already far too late, had to run there by jumping off from his position on the riding board of the Secret Service Follow-Up car.

So I respectfully have a very serious question. *Where was the Secret Service?*

---

[84] Palamara, *Survivor's Guilt.*
[85] Ibid.

8

Motorcade Route Changed

hy was the motorcade route changed? Instead of taking the original route planned to the speaking engagement at the Dallas Trade Mart, a new route was ordered that necessitated a long and slow dog-leg turn into the killing zone of Dealey Plaza. That turn was in *blatant violation* of standard Secret Service policy; it was "against the book."[86]

As critics have rightly observed—including other Secret Service agents who have analyzed the security parameters that were not in place—the Secret Service had to have been aware of the fact that the new route was insecure, which was evidenced by the many areas along that route which were completely unprotected by law enforcement officials.[87]

Lynn Meredith of the Secret Service conducted an examination of the security failures in Dallas and these were the conclusions of that study:

I have always believed that the following adverse situations all contributed to the unfortunate and unnecessary death of

---

[86] Ibid.

[87] James H. Fetzer Ph.D., *Murder in Dealey Plaza: What We Know Now that We Didn't Know Then* (Open Court: 2000); Carrier, "The United States Secret Service: Conspiracy to Assassinate a President"; Palamara, *Survivor's Guilt*; James H. Fetzer, Ph.D., 2001, "'Smoking Guns' in the Death of JFK": jfkresearch.com/prologue.htm

President Kennedy. . . . No Secret Service agents riding on the
rear of the limousine…Inadequate security along the entire ten-
mile motorcade route from the airport to downtown Dallas that
day, particularly in the buildings along the route of travel. . . .
The motorcade route published several days in advance. . .[88]

As Professor James Fetzer noted in his study of the security precautions in
Dallas:

Secret Service policies for the protection of the President were
massively violated during the motorcade in Dallas.[89]

And those violations were numerous and serious:

More than a dozen Secret Service policies for the protection of
the President seem to have been violated during the motorcade
in Dallas, including no protective military presence; no coverage
of open windows; motorcycles out of position; agents not riding
on the Presidential limousine; vehicles in improper sequence;
utilization of an improper route, which included a turn of more
than 90 degrees; limousine slowed nearly to a halt at the corner
of Houston and Elm; the limousine came to a halt after bullets
began to be fired; agents were virtually unresponsive; brains and
blood were washed from the limousine at Parkland, even before
the President had been pronounced dead; the limousine was
stripped down and being rebuilt already Monday, the day of the
formal state funeral; a substitute windshield was later produced
as evidence.[90]

Especially when you factor in the point that there was hard evidence that
President Kennedy was being stalked by conspirators for earlier attempts on his
life in Chicago and Florida; especially when you consider that those serious threat
levels were *just prior* to his trip to Texas—it's absolutely incredible to me that
protection for President Kennedy was reduced in Dallas rather than increased!

---

[88] Palamara, *Survivor's Guilt.*
[89] Fetzer, Ph.D., "'Smoking Guns' in the Death of JFK."
[90] Fetzer Ph.D., *Murder in Dealey Plaza.*

Maybe that's why Robert Kennedy, the Attorney General of the United States, had active plans to take over the responsibility for presidential protection from the jurisdiction of the Secret Service and place it under the direct control of his own Attorney General's office.[91] Because he didn't trust the Secret Service either! So let's list this to make it clear.

The main changes that enabled the assassination were the following:

- The re-directed motorcade route;
- Advance publication of the insecure route in Dallas newspapers;
- The change to an inadequate motorcycle formation around the President;
- Agents being ordered off direct protection on the riding platforms of the President's limousine.
- The Vince Palamara study assigns the responsibility for the above changes to the following people[92]:

  o   Emory Roberts, who was the Shift Leader of the White House Secret Service Detail in Dallas;

  o   Winston Lawson, the Special Agent who was in charge of the Advance Detail of the Secret Service in Dallas;

  o   Floyd Boring, who was a higher-ranking Secret Service supervisor in Washington;

  o   George Lumpkin was an Assistant Police Chief in Dallas and also a Colonel in Army intelligence who rode in the pilot car of the motorcade. In addition to being involved in the route change, he was also the man who, right after the assassination, ordered that the Texas Book Depository building be sealed off; and also the man who selected the Russian interpreter for the interrogation of Marina Oswald, the accused assassin's Russian wife;

  o   And Cliff Carter, a top aide to Vice-President Lyndon Johnson, who was involved in many of the plans for the Dallas trip of President Kennedy.

- To that list we should also add Bill Greer, driver of the presidential limousine, via his grossly negligent slowing of the vehicle to look back twice at JFK, thus disobeying the direct order from his superior seated right

---

[91] David Talbot, *Brothers: The Hidden History of the Kennedy Years* (Free Press: 2007).

[92] Palamara, *Survivor's Guilt*

next to him, Agent Roy Kellerman, who had immediately screamed at Greer to "Get us out of line!" after the shooting began—meaning to *floor* it, evasive action to get the target out of the line of fire. Instead, Greer just froze, following human nature instead of his training. As Kellerman later said, "Greer then looked in the back of the car. Maybe he didn't believe me."[93]

I'm not saying that they were part of the conspiracy that killed Kennedy. Maybe their actions were controlled by other people; maybe some just acted ineffectually. I don't know that and I'm being up front with you about it. But I *am* saying that it was the actions of those individuals which altered the protection in Dallas and thereby enabled the assassination of Kennedy to take place. It was their actions which eliminated the necessary protection and left the 35th President of the United States totally exposed to the cross-fire potential that turned Dealey Plaza into an open kill zone.

---

[93] Vince Palamara, email to author, 15 April 2013; Palamara, *Survivor's Guilt.*

9

Too Many Bullets

The Warren Commission said that only three shots were fired at Dealey Plaza. Three shots, huh? Well then how come there is proof of at least two more and likely even three?

Do you remember the name Roy Kellerman? He was the Secret Service agent in charge on the ground in Dallas. He was the guy sitting right in front of President Kennedy; the one who screamed at the driver to get them out of the line of fire. He was the guy who knew what was going on better than anybody; the Special Agent-in-Charge of the White House Secret Service Detail.[94]

The official testimony of Roy Kellerman blew the doors off of the Warren Commission. He basically looked right at 'em and told them that once the limousine had gone into the kill zone of Dealey Plaza that he knew they had driven right into an ambush, taking fire from all over the place, that "a flurry of shells came into the car" and that they were definitely wrong about their gunshot total because "There had to be more than three shots, gentleman."

---

[94] Palamara, *Survivor's Guilt*

As you might imagine, Roy Kellerman was not a real popular guy with members of the Warren Commission. They minimized his testimony as much as they could, even though, quite admirably, Mr. Kellerman refused to buckle under to the obvious pressure and would not conform to the official government version. He told the truth instead.

Mr. Kellerman was, of course, correct. The evidence proves that there were *more than three shots.*

> One shot missed. Even the Warren Commission acknowledged that missed shot. It hit the street, creating sparks and is probably the shot that wounded bystander James Tague. One bullet hit President Kennedy in his back, four inches below the nape of his neck and to the right of his spine. That shot was fired from the rear of the limousine. There's a hole in the back of his clothing that proved it. Then there was the throat shot. It hit President Kennedy in his throat from the front, just as the emergency room doctors in Dallas described it. The doctors observed the wound and described it as a "wound of entry" which they then utilized in order to make their tracheotomy incision. That was probably the same bullet that went through the windshield of the car and was a bullet from the *front.* Some people think that the windshield shot was separate. But let's be very conservative here and say that it was the same one that hit Kennedy in the throat. So that's already three.

There was at least one shot, and in all likelihood two, that hit Governor John Connally. The Governor always held to his testimony that he was *positive* the first bullet that hit him was a separate bullet from the one that struck the President in the throat. After Connally had heard gunfire and turned around from the front seat to look at Kennedy, that's when the governor first got hit . . . which now makes four.

But the extensive wounds that Connally suffered—if you look at the angles and what that bullet would have had to do—make it difficult to think a single shot was all that struck him. It pierced him, came out his nipple, broke his ribs, went through his wrist, and ended up in his left thigh? A "magic bullet" indeed! Here's another very damning reason: A bullet can't grow in size from the time it leaves the rifle and hits the target, can it? But that "magic bullet" could not possibly account for the amount of shrapnel that was found in Connally's body. So if I'm right about this, then that's five so far.

Then there was the head shot. That one hit President Kennedy from the front, entering at his right temple, and causing a massive blowback exit from the right rear of his skull, forcefully driving his head and entire body backward and to his left.[95]

That's six, double the number of shots that Oswald supposedly fired from the sixth-floor window. So you can see why all the Washington lawyers panicked and had to invent a preposterous story about a "magic bullet" that went through Kennedy and then also caused all the wounds in Connally. Because the simple fact of the matter is this: If there were too many bullets, the shooting could not have been done by one "lone assassin," and the whole official government version comes falling down like the house of cards it truly is.

We'll get to the invention of that "magic bullet" in the section on the cover-up. For now, just remember that number. Six probable shots in Dealey Plaza! And some tireless researchers believe there were more than that—as many as nine!

---

[95] Belzer & Wayne, *Dead Wrong*, 106–107, based on work of: Walt Brown, Ph.D., Wim Dankbaar, Robert Groden, Harvard Science Center, Douglas Herman, William Orchard, Craig Roberts.

10

Acoustic Evidence at Dealey Plaza

The acoustic evidence from Dealey Plaza revealed the existence of more than three gunshots, disproving the official government version. And again—that's not my opinion. That was the Congress of the United States. Basically, the government disproved the original government version.

When the U.S. House of Representatives appointed the House Select Committee on Assassinations in 1976, their investigation revealed that there were actually "acoustic fingerprints" of the assassination of President Kennedy. A Dallas police motorcycle that day had a Dictabelt recorder that had been left in the 'on' position and had inadvertently recorded all the audio of the assassination, especially the gunshots. The House Select Committee determined from scientific analysis of that tape that more than three shots were fired and that they came from two different locations; one being the rear of the motorcade and the other being the grassy knoll. This information led to their conclusion that it was a probable conspiracy:

> Scientific acoustical evidence establishes a high probability that two gunmen fired at President Kennedy.[96]

---

[96] United States House of Representatives, "Report of the Select Committee on Assassinations, U.S. House of Representatives, Ninety-fifth Congress, second session" 1979: archives.gov/research/jfk/select-committee-report/

It probably comes as a shock to many people to read that statement above, as most people are unaware that the most recent official conclusion in the JFK assassination is actually that it *was* a conspiracy! Everybody, including most of the people I've known in the government, think that the official version is still the Warren Commission . . . but it's not! That was the United States Congress. Even *they* say it was a conspiracy. Here are their exact words, direct from their own final report:

> The Committee believes, on the basis of the evidence available to it, that President John F. Kennedy was probably assassinated as the result of a conspiracy. The committee was unable to identify the other gunmen or the extent of the conspiracy.[97]
>
> ---
> [97] Ibid.

That's an *official* finding of the United States Government!

That evidence is contested—one later scientific study disputed the original findings.[98] Then yet another scientific study disputed *that* study, re-confirming the original results.[99] Then, further studies included additional findings relative to the acoustics.[100] An excellent examination of all the flip-flopping back and forth on the acoustic forensic evidence is an article by William E. Kelly that's available online, "Dealey Plaza Echo Analysis-Acoustical Forensics 101."[101] The whole thing is best summed up by G. Robert Blakey, who was Chief Counsel to the House Select Committee on Assassinations:

---

[98] Committee on Ballistic Acoustics, National Research Council, "Reexamination of Acoustic Evidence in the Kennedy Assassination," November, 1982: jfk-records.com/NRC_Science/science.htm

[99] Dr. Donald Byron Thomas, *Hear No Evil: Social Constructivism and the Forensic Evidence in the Kennedy Assassination* (Mary Ferrell Foundation Press: 2010): ctka.net/reviews/hay_review.html

[100] Michael T. Griffith, "The HSCA's Acoustical Evidence: Proof of a Second Gunman?," 2013: mtgriffith.com/web_documents/hscaacous.htm and Michael O'Dell, "The Acoustic Evidence in the Kennedy Assassination," retrieved 16 April 2013: mcadams.posc.mu.edu/odell/index.htm

[101] William E. Kelly, "Dealey Plaza Echo Analysis-Acoustical Forensics 101," November 22, 2010: jfkcountercoup.blogspot.com/2010/11/dealey-plaza-echos.html

> They just want this thing to die. They want to cloud it with
> enough uncertainty and questions that it will not continue to be
> a matter that is of concern to people.[102]

And in addition to seeing through all their damn B.S., Chief Counsel Blakey also saw the bigger point:

"There was a conspiracy to kill my president, and yours, and for some reason that entirely escapes me, people don't want to investigate it further."[103]

So there's another example of where our government stands on this case— the authorities refuse to apply highly advanced technologies which are now available, such as the latest enhanced forensic resources at the federal Lawrence Livermore Laboratory.[104] But then they also refuse to release thousands of pertinent JFK documents they still have under lock and key even though they rightfully belong to the American people, so why should that surprise us?

---

[102] Ibid.
[103] Ibid.
[104] Talbot, *Brothers*, 407.

11

Three Rifle Shots in Six Seconds

To get to the bottom of this once and for all, I actually test-fired the exact same rifle that they say was used to kill President Kennedy. I know rifles, I know shooting, and I know combat, as well as being a qualified expert marksman with both pistol and rifle. When I was Governor of Minnesota, I tested and I still qualified expert marksman. In my test-firing of the weapon, I used the same rifle and the same ammunition as the official version. Here's my conclusion in a nutshell: It's a totally unprofessional piece of *junk*, and it's absolutely impossible that all that shooting was done with that rifle. It was such a joke that I posted the video clip of my reenactment on the Internet because I felt like people just had to see it: youtube.com/watch?v=qSWSgcuYqDo.

As you'll hear me say on that clip, "The Mannlicher is so cheap and hard to work, there's *no* way Oswald could get off three shots that fast."[105] Other professional shooters have tested the same rifle and come to the same conclusion that I did—*not* possible.

Back when I was in the United States Military, Carlos Hathcock was a legend—and he *still is* a legend today. He was a combat sniper extraordinaire who,

---

[105] Jesse Ventura, "Jesse Ventura tries to duplicate Oswald's shooting sequence," 2010: youtube. com/watch?v=qSWSgcuYqDo

for many years, held the record for the most confirmed kills. When a shooter thinks about good shooting, they think about Carlos Hathcock. He wasn't just "good"—he was as good as it gets.

So I was very excited when I heard that Carlos was looking into the specifics of the JFK assassination. In fact, he wasn't just looking at it. They set up an exact replica of the specs on the assassination, and then they tried to duplicate the shooting that was attributed to Oswald—with that shooting duplication done by none other than Carlos Hathcock himself. They did that right at Quantico, the Marine Corps base where Carlos was Senior Instructor at U.S. Marine Corps Sniper Instructor School.

> Let me tell you what we did at Quantico. We reconstructed the
> whole thing: the angle, the range, the moving target, the time
> limit, the obstacles, everything. I don't know how many times
> we tried it, but we couldn't duplicate what the Warren Commis-
> sion said Oswald did.[106]

Carlos Hathcock draws a big conclusion from that re-enactment, and it's the *correct* conclusion, too:

> Now if I can't do it, how in the world could a guy who was a
> non-qual on the rifle range and later only qualified 'marksman'
> do it?[107]

So, the point is, one shooter could not have done it. Other researchers have already diagrammed out the exact problems with the alleged shooting from the professional assessment of two military combat snipers:

Logistic	Professional Assessment	Degree of Difficulty
Weapon	A C2766 bolt-action 6.5 mm Mannlicher-Carcano is an extremely unprofessional choice. After the first shot, potential for succeeding fire is severely limited.	Implausible

---

[106] Roberts, *Kill Zone: A Sniper Looks at Dealey Plaza*
[107] Ibid.

Location	The 6th floor window of Book Depository Building is a terrible choice for a professional shooter to set up. The angles are very poor. Sniper's choice would be the Dal-Tex Building.	Highly Implausible
Angle of Engagement	Kill zone is obscured by tree branches. Wall and vertical pipes prevent shooter from positioning properly for shot. Only a professional sniper could correctly gauge/scope the exact high-to-low angle formula necessary for a kill shot.	Virtually Impossible
Shot Choice	Especially if 6.5 Carcano is weapon, shot choice is when target is approaching or beneath window, not when target has trailed off and moving away.	Extremely Implausible
Sequence of Shots	In any realistic shooting scenario, the first shot is the most accurate. In the assassination, it was the least accurate, missing the entire limousine, as well as the target—leading to very logical speculation that first fire was actually a warning shot in an attempt to thwart the assassination.	Extremely Implausible
Timing of Shots	"Re-enactment" could not duplicate shots/hits assigned to Oswald because it never happened that way in reality. If the best combat sniper in U.S history could not accomplish the shooting, it literally could not have been done by Oswald.	Literally Impossible[108]

The point is crystal clear. **Oswald could not have been the shooter.** I, and many others, can attest personally that the Mannlicher-Carcano isn't going to get

---

[108] Belzer & Wayne, *Dead Wrong,* 103–104, citing Carlos Hathcock and Craig Roberts.

off six rounds; I couldn't even get off three. The only way the Mannlicher could do that is if somehow Oswald modified it into a machine gun!

And even if it was logistically possible, think about this: Oswald wasn't even an infantryman, but a Marine radar technician. A pencil pusher! There are those in the Marines too, believe it or not. They go through boot camp, but end up being pencil pushers. So here you had a Carlos Hathcock, specialist sniper infantry who deals in combat, deals in death, who couldn't do it, and on the other hand, this young guy who looks at a radar screen all day or whatever Oswald was supposedly doing at Atsugi, where the U-2 spy planes were based. Come on, who's gonna out-shoot who here? When you go into the military, they give you huge aptitude tests, mental and otherwise. They look at your records and then your shooting scores, tie it all together, and send you where they think you can most effectively use your skills. Oswald looked through a radar screen allegedly, not down the scope of a rifle, which his scores in boot camp prove. There was a reason they didn't send him into 0300 infantry!

12

Shots That Were Too Close Together With a Rifle that Was Not Even "Sighted In"

After reading what an absolute piece of junk that rifle was, and hopefully, watching my video clip which clearly demonstrates that point, I'm sure you can see that—if two of the three gunshots in the official version were close together—then there's *no way in hell* that they could have come from that rifle. And guess what? Two of the shots were actually *very* close together.

I could barely get off three shots in ten seconds. After each shot, I had to struggle with pulling back the bolt of the rifle in order to re-chamber a bullet for the next shot, and then I had to re-sight re-aim. That all takes time, and it was time that one shooter would not have had.

To fire a rifle with a telescopic sight, like the Mannlicher that they say was used in the assassination, you *have* to re-sight the rifle! That's a *huge* point that anyone familiar with weapons will be absolutely astounded by—Oswald's rifle was <u>not</u> properly sighted. And that point was even acknowledged by the Warren Commission! Here's exactly what they said:

> The rifle couldn't be perfectly "sighted-in" using the scope
> (i.e., thereby eliminating the above overshoot completely)

without installing two metal shims (small metal plates),
which were not present when the rifle arrived for testing, and
were never found.[109]

And that's not *me* saying that. That's not some "conspiracy theorist" or anything. That's right out of the freaking official legal hearings!

And even if it *had* been sighted in, the recoil, or backward "kick" of that
rifle, is so hard that it throws the sight off after *every single shot*. So the shooter
has to take the time to re-sight the rifle after every shot.

Walt Brown is a Notre Dame graduate with a doctorate in History who has
studied the JFK assassination for most of his life. From the day the assassination
happened in 1963, Brown has focused his life on that event; devoting countless
hours to cataloging thousands of events related to the assassination as they actually occurred. When it comes to the rifle that was the *alleged* murder weapon,
Walt sums it all up very succinctly:

> It would also have made a difference if the expert rifleman was
> using an expert rifleman's weapon of choice, not a piece of war
> surplus Italian junk whose inadequacies were massively com-
> pounded by the conclusion that the weapon was assembled and
> fired without ever having been sighted in. Ask your friend, the
> hunter. He'll tell you it *can't be done*.[110]

Reliable witnesses have also testified that two of the shots were actually very
close together. That "double bang" that people heard is very important because it
has dramatic implications: two shots close together could *not* have come from the
same weapon, so there had to be more than one shooter.

Tosh Plumlee, a veteran Military intelligence operative, was present
at Dealey Plaza, on the south knoll, opposite the grassy knoll. According to
Plumlee, he was part of a team dispatched to Dallas on an emergency basis, as
a result of intel that was picked up by U.S. intelligence about a possible attempt
to kill the president. Here's how Plumlee described the last shots in a sworn
affidavit:

---

[109] Warren Commission hearings: 3 WCH 440-5.

[110] Walt Brown Ph.D., *The Guns of Texas Are Upon You* (Last Hurrah Press, 2005), emphasis in
original.

Two of those shots were very close together, basically on top of each other—and my partner and I were both aware that it was not the result of an echo-effect, but two clear and distinct rifle reports that were very close together. One of the shots was also from a different direction than the others; one came from the southwest, meaning from the front of the limousine, not the rear. We both knew that with certainty. When my partner and I debriefed each other later that day, we were both sure on that one different-sounding shot. That fact was hard for us to miss because the other shots came from the north and east of us and that one shot from the southwest of us had a totally different sound and came whizzing right over our heads. We were both experienced veterans of gunfire, and very familiar with its sound, and we were both certain that one gunshot came from a westerly direction.[111]

Keep in mind as you look at the other witness testimony that follows that any two shots being close together logistically precludes them having come from the same weapon. Even from a *good* rifle, that would be impossible. And from a piece of junk like the Mannlicher, you'd be lucky if you could even jam back the bolt in a couple of seconds, let alone re-sight, re-aim, and fire.

The evidence is overwhelming that two of the shots were in rapid succession. The following is testimony from qualified witnesses who were *right there* and were sure about what they heard.

> Secret Service Special Agent Roy Kellerman was in the front passenger seat of the limousine, sitting directly in front of President Kennedy. He was considered an expert in gunfire and testified that there was a "double bang" of two shots extremely close together:
> *Let me give you an illustration. . . . You have heard the sound barrier, of a plane breaking the sound barrier, bang, bang? That is it. It was like a double bang—bang, bang.*

---

[111] Belzer & Wayne, *Dead Wrong*, "Affidavit of William R. Plumlee," 111–115.

Secret Service Special Agent William Greer, who was driving the limousine, testified that:

. . . the last two shots seemed to be just simultaneously, one behind the other.

Secret Service Special Agent George Hickey testified that:

At the moment he was almost sitting erect I heard two reports, which I thought were shots and that appeared to me completely different in sound than the first report and were in such rapid succession that there seemed to be practically no time element between them.

Secret Service Special Agent Clint Hill testified that the second noise he heard was different from the first shot:

. . . like the sound of shooting a revolver into something hard . . . almost a double sound.

Secret Service Special Agent William A. McIntyre:

The Presidential vehicle was approximately 200 feet from the underpass when the first shot was fired, followed in quick succession by two more.

Dallas Officer Seymour Weitzman:

First one, then the second two seemed to be simultaneous.

Ladybird Johnson, the wife of the Vice-President, was riding behind the President and said that after the first shot, there was a pause and then two rapid shots:

Then a moment and then two more shots in rapid succession.

Dallas Mayor Earle Cabell described the same thing:

They were in rather rapid succession.

An eyewitness, S. M. Holland, who watched the motorcade from the railroad overpass, testified that he heard four shots with the third and fourth sounding like a "double shot" and these did not sound at all alike:

Well it would be like you're firing a .38 pistol right beside a shotgun, or a .45 right beside a shotgun . . . the third shot was not so loud.[112]

---

[112] John S. Craig, *The Guns of Dealey Plaza*, retrieved 24 April 2013: acorn.net/jfkplace/09/fp.back_issues/11th_issue/guns_dp.html

So if that's not shots from two different guns, then all of those people were wrong.

13

Oswald Couldn't Have Carried in the Murder Weapon

Oswald is accused of carrying the murder weapon that morning on his way to work at the Depository, but lied by saying it was actually curtain rods. Well, most likely he was telling the truth! The way the Mannlicher-Carcano Italian weapon is made, when you disassemble it, the rifle has an unusually long wooden stock. In other words, the metal barrel only sticks out a little ways from the end of the wooden stock. I could never cup it in my hand and get it up under my armpit, and I'm 6-foot-4! Oswald was 5-foot-11 or shorter, depending on when he got measured. So how was he carrying a rifle under his armpit, according to a fellow who supposedly went to work with him that day? No way! It's a physical impossibility. The stock of that Mannlicher is not a breakdown weapon, but the actual barrel only sticks out five or six inches from the end of the long stock. Curtain rods would fit, the Mannlicher wouldn't.

14

No Eyewitnesses

Not a single witness *ever* placed Oswald at the actual crime scene. Even the Dallas Chief of Police acknowledged that the case against Oswald was entirely circumstantial:

> We don't have any proof that Oswald fired the rifle, and never did. Nobody's yet been able to put him in that building with a gun in his hand.[113]

That was the Chief of Police who said that, for goodness sake! Jesse Curry was Chief at the time of the assassination and is telling us *flat out* that there's no proof Oswald even fired a shot!

That's a matter of huge importance in a trial. A person has to have had the means to have committed the crime.

There are so many reasons why that rifle could not have done all the shooting, it's almost mind-boggling:

> Ammunition for the rifle was known to be faulty and rarely shot straight. Gun experts that testified in front of the Warren

---

[113] Jim Marrs, *Crossfire: The Plot that Killed Kennedy* (Carroll & Graf: 1989), citing *Dallas Morning News*, Nov. 6, 1969.

Commission characterized the Carcano as a cheap, old weapon that was poorly constructed; a rifle that could be purchased for three dollars each in lots of twenty-five. On the day the rifle was found, the firing pin was found to be defective or worn-out, the telescopic sight was not accurately sighted, and no ammunition clip was officially reported. The lack of an ammunition clip would require a shooter to hand-load cartridges. Without an ammunition clip, rapid fire would be impossible.

No reference was ever made to the clip in the original inventories of evidence. Only when the Warren Report was released was there any report that an ammunition clip was found.[114]

Ballistics and firearms expert, Howard Donahue, examined the case and documented eight specific points of evidence indicating that Oswald could not have done the shooting:

1. The official trajectories given for the alleged rear entrance wound on JFK's head are incompatible with a shot from the sixth-floor window.
2. The bullet that mortally wounded Kennedy in the head behaved like a high-velocity, frangible missile, whereas Oswald is said to have used medium-velocity, non-frangible ammunition.
3. The reported width of the rear entrance wound in the head, 6.0 mm, is incompatible with the diameter of a 6.5 mm Carcano bullet. (Dr. James Humes, the chief autopsist, said he measured the rear entrance wound on the head and that it was 6 mm wide, which means it could not have been caused by a 6.5 mm missile.)
4. The windshield damage was too high to have been caused by a bullet coming down into the car from the alleged sniper's nest. (Even the HSCA's trajectory expert admitted that this seemed to be the case.)
5. Several witnesses said two of the shots came in very rapid succession, nearly simultaneously, too quickly to have been fired from the bolt-action Mannlicher-Carcano rifle.
6. Secret Service Agent Roy Kellerman heard Kennedy cry out that he had been hit well before the Governor was wounded.

---

[114] John S. Craig, *The Guns of Dealey Plaza*, retrieved 24 April 2013: acorn.net/jfkplace/09/fp.back_issues/11th_issue/guns_dp.html

7. There do not appear to be any traces of human tissue on the fragments that were found in the limousine, yet the WC said these fragments came from the bullet that hit Kennedy in the head. If these fragments had in fact passed through JFK's skull, they would have had traces of brain tissue, blood, and fluid on them. Donahue went to the National Archives, and with the aid of a 30-power jeweler's loupe, studied the fragments from the head shot—or at least what he was told were the fragments from the head shot—and to his surprise, found no traces of blood or tissue on them, not even in their grooves.

8. The 6.5 mm fragment that was deposited on the outer table of Kennedy's skull in the back of his head could not have come from the kind of ammunition that Oswald allegedly used. Forensic science knows of no case where a fully metal-jacketed (FMJ) bullet has ever deposited a sizable fragment on the outer table of the skull upon entering the skull. Such behavior by FMJ bullets is simply unheard of.[115]

The same point keeps coming up over and over again and from every angle that you look at it: One shooter simply could *not* have done all the shooting.

> If Oswald were the only shooter there would have to be at least 2.3 seconds between shots, assuming he used the telescopic sight found on the Mannlicher Carcano. The three shots that the Warren Commission claimed were fired from Oswald's rifle could not have been shot faster than 6.9 seconds. Secret Service Agent Roy Kellerman described the shots as a "flurry." Two of the shots were often described by witnesses as so closely spaced that they seemed "simultaneous" and had "practically no time element between them." Additionally, there is a substantial amount of testimony, presented in this article, that describes the later shots as sounding different from the first shot. Governor Connally's initial reaction to the gunfire was "that there were either two or three people involved or more in this or someone was shooting with an automatic rifle."[116]

---

[115] Michael T. Griffith, "Faulty Evidence: Problems with the Case Against Lee Harvey Oswald," 2001, Third Edition, citing Bonar Menninger, *Mortal Error: The Shot That Killed JFK, A ballistics expert's astonishing discovery of the fatal bullet that Oswald did not fire* (St. Martin' Press: 1992): michaelgriffith1.tripod.com/faulty.htm

[116] Craig, *The Guns of Dealey Plaza.*

15

Logistically Impossible That Oswald Fired Shot

Acouple of minutes after President Kennedy had been shot, a clerical supervisor was returning to her office on the second floor of the lunch room in the Texas School Book Depository building. Her statement said that on the way to her office, she saw an employee whom she knew, Lee Harvey Oswald; that he had a Coca-Cola bottle in his hand and seemed very calm. Her exact words were, "I had no thoughts or anything of him having any connection with it all because he was very calm."[117]

She had no reason to lie. She was just saying what she saw. That was all she could recall about him at that time, as there was a lot going on. But those were the two things about seeing Oswald on the second floor that afternoon that she clearly remembered. That he was very calm and had a Coca-Cola bottle in his hand. Remember that. If you've studied this like I have, you're now a "juror for history"; and those are two things that you'll need to remember later.

Motive, means, and opportunity. Those are the things you have to prove to convict a defendant in a murder trial. People often get confused on the opportunity aspect. What that means is that it has to have been possible for the defendant to have committed the crime. If they had a solid alibi, for example, that they were

---

[117] Anthony Summers, *The Kennedy Conspiracy?* (Sphere Books: 2007), 64.

in a different location at that exact time then—since they could not have been in two places at once—their attorneys can prove that they lacked *opportunity.*

It is logistically impossible that Oswald was the one who fired from the sixth floor of that building and even a half-decent defense attorney could have proven that to a jury's satisfaction.

In addition to the fact that "no one could put him in that window"—i.e. at the scene of the crime, which comes direct from the Dallas Police Chief, no less—it has been conclusively established that Oswald was already elsewhere and that he, therefore, did not possess opportunity. Let me explain.

Solid eyewitness testimony confirms that Oswald was in the lunchroom on the second floor *fifteen minutes* before the shooting of the President. As veteran investigative researcher Anthony Summers noted:

> The bald fact is that Oswald cannot be placed on the sixth floor either at the time of the shooting or during the half hour before it. The last time he was reliably seen before the assassination was by Mrs. Arnold—in the second floor lunchroom. The next time Oswald was firmly identified was immediately after the assassination—again in the second floor lunchroom.[118]

Those are strong indications that Oswald was exactly where he told the police he was—eating lunch in the first floor domino room and then going up to the second floor lunchroom and buying a Coca-Cola from the vending machine. Oswald correctly described two employees who walked by him while he ate lunch—researchers have verified the individuals as well as the timing—so he was either right where he said he was, or possessed psychic powers.[119]

It gets even better. One witness—a man named Howard Brennan—stated that, from outside Oswald's building, he saw two men in the sixth floor window and one of them had a rifle. As any jury would note—and any defense attorney would absolutely love—even though Mr. Brennan had seen Oswald's picture on television before going to the police lineup, he *failed to make a positive identification* of Oswald as one of the men whom he saw in the sixth floor window.

But an employee named Bonnie Ray Williams was eating lunch on the sixth floor until at least 12:15 p.m. and testified that Oswald was *not* there.[120] Williams

---

[118] Summers, *Kennedy Conspiracy,* 62.

[119] Ibid, 59.

[120] Ibid, 59.

was right, because as witness Carolyn Arnold substantiated, at 12:15, Oswald was *still in the lunchroom*. She's certain she saw him there "about 12:15. It may have been slightly later." The time that Arnold Rowland saw the rifle in the window was pinpointed by events correlating to the police log: it was between 12:15 and 12:16.[121] So the timing actually proves that whoever Rowland saw in that window, it was not Lee Harvey Oswald. Sightings of Oswald downstairs by four eyewitnesses—both before and after Rowland saw the man on the sixth floor with a rifle—make it impossible that Oswald was the man he saw.[122]

But that didn't stop the government. They made the case that Oswald finished his lunch, raced upstairs to the "sniper's nest" that was set up behind some boxes at the sixth floor window, fired three shots at the President, killing him and wounding the Governor of Texas, then—since the elevator was not used—raced down the stairs, *back* to the second floor lunchroom, where he was seen by Dallas Police Officer Marion Baker and building supervisor Roy Truly. Wouldn't Oswald have been more than a little out of breath, instead of the calmly collected guy that other witnesses saw?

So, the problem quickly became one of *timing*.

Keep in mind that the shooter had to also take the time to hide that rifle:

> The rifle was found tightly wedged within a stack of books,
> a task that would seem to require more than a few seconds. It
> was so deeply hidden in the boxes that one of the Dallas sheriffs
> claimed that searchers could have walked right by it and not
> noticed it.[123]

So the would-be investigators from the Warren Commission quickly sent Dallas police officers scurrying up and down the stairs of the Book Depository and timed them with a stopwatch. But the problem was that there wasn't really enough time after the assassination for Oswald to have stashed the rifle, run down the stairs from the sixth to the second floor, bought a Coca-Cola at the vending machine, and actually *been there* at the time the Dallas cop saw him there.

So what did they do? They tried to correct this impossibility by shaving off the time that it took to buy the Coca-Cola from the vending machine! Then the

[121]   Ibid, 61.

[122]   Gil Jesus, "Evidence Oswald was on the 1st floor at the time of the shooting," retrieved 18 April 2013: giljesus.com/jfk/alibi.htm

[123]   John S. Craig, *The Guns of Dealey Plaza*, retrieved 24 April 2013: acorn.net/jfkplace/09/ fp.back_issues/11th_issue/guns_dp.html

timing was better. While acknowledging that it was close, they said that they had proved that it was physically *possible*.

Independent researchers tried it and reached quite a different conclusion:

> Alternative, independent calculations say that, if Oswald had
> really been a gunman, he could not have reached the lunchroom
> in time for the meeting with the policeman.[124]

Numerous studies have substantiated that, by any realistic standard, Oswald could have not have done it and even if he had, certainly would not have been so calm, cool, and collected when seen right after the assassination.[125] It's quite logical to assume that any person would exhibit *some* sense of anxiousness after just having killed the President of the United States and wounding the Governor. Especially after racing down the stairs afterwards, sweating would be expected, rapid breathing would be expected, and excitement would be expected. But none of the aforementioned were present in the calm and composed Lee Harvey Oswald.

Add to that the highly significant point that President Kennedy's motorcade was *late*. Had it been on time—the *published* time that any assassin would have had to plan for—then the motorcade actually would have passed Oswald's building at 12:25 p.m., raising a huge timing problem on the front side of the issue as well, because credible witness testimony placed Oswald in the lunch room at 12:15. So he's calmly eating lunch at 12:15 on the *second* floor, raising the following huge red flag:

> A killer who had planned the assassination would hardly have
> been sitting around downstairs after 12:15 p.m., as the evidence
> about Oswald suggests, if he expected to open fire as early as
> 12:25.[126]

It got even worse for the government. To prove that it was even possible time-wise for Oswald to have made it downstairs in two minutes after doing the shooting, they had to eliminate the purchase of the Coca-Cola from the vending machine. In fact, if you look at the official statement of Dallas Police Officer

---

[124] Summers, *Kennedy Conspiracy*, 63.

[125] William Kelly, "Physics Proves Oswald Innocent," 7 Feb. 2010: educationforum.ipbhost.
com/index.php?showtopic=15429 Richard Belzer, "Defaming History or, Who Didn't Kill
JFK," August 13, 2007, *Huff Post*. huffingtonpost.com/richard-belzer/defaming-history-or-
who-d_b_60188.html

[126] Summers, *Kennedy Conspiracy*, 63.

Marion Baker, the words "drinking a coke" are crossed out with his initials above. He and Roy Truly, the building supervisor, also specifically noted in their Warren Commission testimony that Oswald did not have a Coca-Cola!

Well, *nice try*, fellas! Now remember back if you will, fellow juror, to the two points I made at the beginning of this entry.

A witness with no reason to lie.

Two minutes after the assassination.

Two things she remembered about Oswald.

He was very calm; and he had a Coca-Cola in his hand.

If the case went to trial and you were Oswald's attorney, you'd have a pretty tough time keeping a grin off of your face at that exact point of evidence. But don't you love it when these sleazebags get caught by their own lies?

And as Anthony Summers and others have pointed out, if there *wasn't* a Coca-Cola in his hands, then why on earth was everyone referring to it?

> Baker himself initially wrote in his statement that he "saw a man standing in the lunchroom drinking a Coke." One of the details announced by Police Chief Curry was that Oswald was seen by Baker and the building superintendent Roy Truly, carrying a Coke. If that were not so, it is hard to see how such a precise detail arose in the first place. Yet Baker and Truly ended up saying Oswald had nothing in his hand when they met him.[127]

So the infamous Coca-Cola in Lee Harvey Oswald's hand *officially disappeared*. It had to disappear, because if Oswald had taken all that time after the assassination—coming down all those stairs from the sixth floor to the second, going to the vending machine and buying a Coke—then he could not have been standing there calmly in the lunchroom as Officer Baker officially discovered him.

> The question is important to the issue of whether Oswald could have got down from the sixth floor to encounter Baker and Truly when he did. Without obtaining a Coke, it would have been a close shave. If Oswald had purchased and started drinking a Coke by the time of the encounter with the policeman, the known time frame is stretched to the bursting point—some would say beyond.

---

[127] Summers, *Kennedy Conspiracy*, 403.

[Oswald himself, incidentally, told the Chief of Homicide he was "drinking a Coca-Cola when the officer came in."] In this author's opinion, the balance of the evidence suggests he was.[128]

The matter can be put even more bluntly than the manner expressed above by Mr. Summers with his British politeness:

(Officer) Baker was asked by the FBI to give an affidavit regarding his encounter with Oswald in the lunchroom, Commission Exhibit 3076, Baker makes no mention of seeing someone moving through the glass in the doorway and states that he "saw a man standing in the lunchroom drinking a coke."

The phrase "drinking a coke" is crossed out and initialed by Baker, but that deleted phrase, by its spontaneous mention, corroborates Oswald's story that he had already purchased a Coke when stopped by Baker and makes a liar out of both Baker and Roy Truly.[129]

So the facts are pretty clear and would play that way to a jury. Oswald bought a Coca-Cola, just like he said he did, and just like the witness who had no reason to lie swore that they saw him standing there after the assassination with a bottle of Coke in his hand. That, in itself, proves he could not have had time to fire three shots from the "sniper's nest" on the sixth floor, stash the rifle, come down to the second floor via the long stairway (which was also slow to traverse because the configuration had a gap between floors, meaning that you had come down one flight of stairs and then had to walk over to the area where the stairs continued down again), go to the vending machine, purchase a drink, and then be in the lunchroom two minutes after the assassination of the President. With the landings between staircases, it actually made it eight flights of stairs that Oswald would have had to run down to get to the lunchroom from the sixth floor.[130] The fact that he was already in that lunchroom, and was even *calm and unshaken*—as several eyewitnesses confirmed—speaks loudly that he was not the shooter on the sixth floor a mere two minutes prior to that time.

---

[128] Summers, *Kennedy Conspiracy*, 403.

[129] Gil Jesus, "The Lunchroom Encounter," retrieved 18 April 2013: giljesus.com/jfk/lunchroom_encounter.htm

[130] Belzer, "Defaming History or, Who Didn't Kill JFK"

16

Mauser Rifle Was Found

There's a *huge* problem with the Mannlicher rifle that was supposedly found on the sixth floor and was used to connect Oswald to the assassination. When the rifle was first found, it was *not* identified that way. It was identified instead as a 7.65 millimeter Mauser rifle. That identification was made—and made quite clearly—by law enforcement officials themselves who were right at the scene. It was even made by law enforcement officials at the scene who were closely familiar with rifles!

Deputy Sheriff Eugene Boone discovered the rifle and then wrote the following words in his official statement:

> I was assisting in the search of the 6th floor of the Dallas County
> Book Depository at Elm St. and Houston St. proceeding from
> the east side of the building. Officer Weitzman DPD and I were
> together as we approached the Northwest corner of the building.
> I saw the rifle partially hidden behind a row of books with two
> (2) other boxes of books against the rifle. The rifle appeared to
> be a 7.65mm Mauser with a telescope sight on the rifle.[131]

---

131 Savage, Gary, JFK: *First Day Evidence* (The Shoppe Press: 1993), 158.

That Officer Weitzman of the Dallas Police Department, whom Deputy
Boone refers to above, not only *agreed* with Boone on the rifle, but, now get a load
of this: Weitzman was a "gun buff" who had even "had a sporting goods store at
one time" and was hence, an expert on rifles.

In Deputy Boone's second report, he again made the point of describing the
rifle they found on the 6th floor as a 7.65 Mauser:

> In the northwest corner of the building approximately three
> (3) feet from the east wall of the stairwell and behind a row of
> cases of books, I saw the rifle, what appeared to be a 7.65mm
> Mauser with a telescopic site. The rifle had what appeared to be
> a brownish, black stock and blue steel, metal parts.[132]

Deputy Sheriff Boone also told the Warren Commission that Captain Will
Fritz himself—the Chief of the Homicide Detail—also described the rifle as a
7.65mm Mauser. Notice though, that when covering such a delicate matter in the
official transcript, they sort of hedge the issue:

MR. BALL: Who referred to it as a Mauser that day?

DEPUTY BOONE: I believe Captain Fritz. He had knelt down
there to look at it, and before he removed
it, not knowing what it was, he said that is
what it looks like. This is when Lieutenant
Day, I believe his name is, the ID man was
getting ready to photograph it. We were
just discussing it back and forth. And he
said it looks like a 7.65 Mauser.[133]

But, according to Deputy Sheriff Roger Craig, Officer Weitzman and the
others were not just "discussing it back and forth"[134]—they had positively identified that rifle as a Mauser 7.65:

> I believe Day [Lieutenant Carl Day who was in charge of the
> Dallas Police Crime Lab] pulled the rifle out and handed it to

---

[132] Ibid.
[133] Savage, *JFK: First Day Evidence*, 159.
[134] Ibid.

Captain Fritz, who held it up by the strap . . . and asked if anyone knew what kind of rifle it was. By that time, Deputy Con-
stable Seymour Weitzman had joined us. Weitzman was a gun
buff. He had a sporting goods store at one time and he was very
good with weapons and he said it looks like a Mauser. And he
walked over to Fritz and Captain Fritz was holding the rifle up
in the air and I was standing next to Weitzman who was standing next to Fritz. And we were no more than 6 to 8 inches from
the rifle and stamped right on the barrel of the rifle was "7.65
Mauser". And that's when Weitzman said, "It *is* a Mauser," and
pointed to the 7.65 Mauser stamp on the barrel.[135]

That sounds pretty damn clear to me. The rifle they found was a Mauser.
That would even make sense. A Mauser 7.65 is a darn good rifle. An assas-
sin could actually do some shooting with a weapon like that; as opposed to the
Mannlicher which, we've already established, is a total piece of junk.

So, just to further complicate matters that are already ridiculously complicated regarding that rifle, the entire provenance of the rifle is also highly suspect; there's no way to be sure that the Mannlicher rifle they *say* was used in
the shooting—actually was or was not used in the shooting. There are even
a lot of reasons to doubt that the Mannlicher rifle was the rifle that was actually found! And that's not because of me or because of some "conspiracy theorist"—that's because of the direct testimony from the Dallas Police Department
and the Dallas County Sheriff's Department! The record proves one thing very
clearly—at first they said the rifle that they found was a Mauser rifle, *not a
Mannlicher.*

Keep in mind, please, the *context* of the situation. This is the "Crime of
the Century"; the President of the United States has just been assassinated in
broad daylight. They find the rifle. They hold it up. The head of Homicide
is there. The head of the crime lab is there. A cop who's a gun expert is there.
Doesn't it defy credulity to say that they all got it wrong on such a simple point
at an extremely important time? It sure in hell does to me. They said it was even
stamped on the rifle, for Pete's sake. If these guys knew how to read, then it was
a Mauser.

---

[135] Savage, *JFK: First Day Evidence*, 162.

I don't know why they changed the official version to read that a Mannlicher was used in the assassination, but I do say that the rifle they found on the 6th floor was a Mauser, not a Mannlicher. In fact, I don't even have to say that. The Dallas authorities are clearly on record as having said that themselves.

Various news reports, including Walter Cronkite on CBS News, also verified that the rifle was a Mauser.[136] The CIA also described the rifle as a Mauser.[137]

And if you listen to Sheriff Craig describe the discovery of the rifle in a clip that is available right on the Internet,[138] it sure in hell sounds like they found a Mauser.

There are also other serious discrepancies regarding the search and discovery of the rifles—that's right, plural—that were found that day.

Frank Ellsworth was an ATF agent (Department of Alcohol, Tobacco, and Firearms) and was in his office not far from the Depository when he was told of the shooting. He ran to the Depository and entered the building with Captain Will Fritz. Ellsworth said that he found the so-called "sniper's nest" on the sixth floor, but was sure that the "gun was not found on the same floor as the cartridges, but on a lower floor by a couple of city detectives . . . I think the rifle was found on the *fourth floor.*"[139]

Agent Ellsworth said he then participated in a second search of the Depository after 1:30 p.m. on November 22, 1963. The gun that was found during that later search was the Italian Mannlicher-Carcano and it was hidden behind boxes near the "stairwell back in the northwest corner."[140]

Numerous other reports distinctly named a completely different rifle being found during one of the searches of the building—not a Mannlicher-Carcano *or* a Mauser. NBC reported that police found a British Enfield .303 rifle—and they sounded sure about it.

Gary Mack, the archivist for the Sixth Floor Museum in Dallas, noted that this was even in the NBC book *There Was A President*. Tom Whalen was a

---

[136] Wim Dankbaar, "A 7.65 Mauser," retrieved 19 April 2013: youtube.com/watch?v=-RGZPa8FdbA

[137] *The JFK History Forum*, "The Mauser Explained," retrieved 19 April 2013: jfkhistory.com/forum/index.php?topic=736.0

[138] Wim Dankbaar, "A 7.65 Mauser,": youtube.com/watch?v=-RGZPa8FdbA

[139] Dick Russell, *The Man Who Knew Too Much: Hired to Kill Oswald and Prevent the Assassination of JFK* (Carroll & Graf: 2003), 568.

[140] Ibid, 569.

reporter for the NBC affiliate in Dallas-Fort Worth, WBAP-TV. And there is even a news videotape that shows Whalen being given the following announcement from the WBAP studio in Fort Worth:

Reporter Tom Whalen, at 2:13 p.m. CST, said, "The weapon which was used to kill the president, and which wounded Gov. Connally, has been found in the Texas School Book Depository on the sixth floor—a British .303 rifle with a telescopic sight. Three empty cartridge cases were found beside the weapon. It appeared that whoever had occupied this sniper's nest had been here for some time."[141]

So I'm not sure what exactly was going on with all of that musical rifles game, but I can tell you this—our government sure in hell isn't giving us the straight story on that.

---

[141] Gary Mack, 16 July 1999, "NBC Announces Enfield .303 Rifle Found on TSBD 6th," citing NBC, *There was a President: 70 Hours & 30 Minutes-The Weekend No One Will Ever Forget* (Random House: 1966): educationforum.ipbhost.com/index.php?s=feb030e01b96e1d3b8680 ac5fece9439&showtopic=19810&st=15

17

No Fingerprints

A partial fingerprint was reportedly lifted by Dallas Police from the left side of the trigger housing of the Mannlicher-Carcano rifle. Examination of the print and comparison to Oswald's only matched in 3 points of identity. Legal jurisdictions vary cross-country, requiring from a 6-point to 12-point certain match verification for conviction parameters.[142] Therefore, only a 3-point match is incredibly weak and dramatically insufficient for a professional determination of a match. So much for the fingerprint evidence.

As for the rest of the print evidence supposedly against Oswald, a partial palm print was found on the rifle, but it's also a convoluted piece of evidence. First off, the palm print wasn't on the outside portion of the rifle where a shooter, or anyone else, would actually touch it. It was only found after taking the rifle apart and was a partial print of someone's palm, which—they say—matched Oswald's palm.[143] However, there was also a very disturbing "interrupted chain of evidence" concerning the entire matter. The FBI could not match the palm print to Oswald. Then, according to funeral home director Paul Groody, some very serious government agents came to the funeral home while Oswald's body was there and insisted on being alone with the corpse; after which the director

---

[142] Gary Savage, *JFK: First Day Evidence* (The Shoppe Press: 1993), 105, 116.

[143] Savage, *JFK: First Day Evidence*, 105.

of the funeral home testified that he found a lot of ink on the deceased Oswald's hands that hadn't been there previously.[144] Then, the Dallas Police Department said they had taken a palm print and that it was a match to Oswald. Plus, the Dallas police admitted to also taking Oswald's prints *after* he was dead.[145] Let's put it this way—you wouldn't have to be a famous TV lawyer like Perry Mason to keep Oswald from getting convicted on the fingerprint evidence. As one thorough summary of all the print evidence concluded:

> The inability of the FBI examiners to detect anything other than faint fingerprints on the rifle; the failure of the Dallas police to supply the FBI with contemporaneous photographs of the palm print; and the lack of any official announcements about an incriminating palm print, make it not unreasonable to suppose that the palm print on the rifle was manufactured after the event, and that there is consequently no evidence that Oswald had handled the rifle at all.[146]

Oswald paraffin tested negative for nitrates on his right cheek, which is an indication that he probably hadn't fired a rifle recently. He tested positive for nitrates on his hand, which is an indication that he *may* have been in contact with a firearm—or been in contact with urine, *or* with the ink used for fingerprinting, or any number of other things which are known to corrupt the results of paraffin testing. And we already know he was in contact with a handgun because he was found carrying one. But that certainly does not equate with having fired a rifle.

Taken in totality, the crime scene "evidence" against Oswald is so thoroughly convoluted that any decent criminal defense attorney could have totally demolished it in a courtroom. That's why they had to make sure that Oswald didn't get to a courtroom. As we shall soon see, there were some very good reasons that Oswald had to be eliminated before he could talk.

---

[144] Michael T. Griffith, "Was Oswald's Palm Print Planted On The Alleged Murder Weapon?: Some Questions About The Latent Palm Print," 2012: mtgriffith.com/web_documents/ palmprint.htm Also see *Oswald's Palm Prints*, retrieved 11 April 2013: garvandwane.com/ conspiracy/oswalds_palm_prints.html

[145] Savage, *JFK: First Day Evidence*, 111.

[146] *22 November 1963: An Introduction to the JFK Assassination*, citing Sylvia Meagher, *Accessories After The Fact: The Warren Commission, The Authorities & The Report* (Random House: 1988), retrieved 11 April 2013: 22november1963.org.uk/oswald-fingerprint-palmprint-evidence

18

Oswald was a U.S. Intelligence Operative

Lee Harvey Oswald was an operative for U.S. intelligence. It's been estab-lished that his public "defection" to the Soviet Union was actually part of a False Defector Program that was being run by the CIA and ONI (Office of Naval Intelligence) out of a facility in Nags Head, North Carolina, in the 1950s. That fact has also been cross-corroborated by two CIA special operations people who were very familiar with that terrain.

William Robert "Tosh" Plumlee is a U.S. intelligence veteran with a career in covert operations spanning over fifty years. He was one of the whistle-blowers who alerted the U.S. Congress to the illegal activities during the first Bush Administration that wound up being known as the Iran-Contra scan-dal. Plumlee's intelligence "bonafides" can be accessed on the Internet.[147] Of particular note is a letter from then-U.S. Senator Gary Hart to Senator John Kerry regarding the importance of Plumlee's help in the investigation.[148] Read

---

[147] "FBI/DEA/CIA files on William Robert 'Tosh' Plumlee," retrieved 23 April 2013: toshplumlee.info/

[148] Senator Gary Hart, "Letter to The Honorable John Kerry, Chairman, Subcommittee on Terrorism, Narcotics and International Communications," February 14, 1991: toshplumlee. info/pdf/sengaryhart.PDF

it yourself so you can see how "for real" this guy is: toshplumlee.info/pdf/sengaryhart.PDF

Plumlee's early intelligence training coincided with the training that Lee Harvey Oswald received. Aware of the significance of the fact that Oswald was present during the course of government-sponsored intelligence training, Mr. Plumlee agreed to document those circumstances in a sworn affidavit. In that affidavit, he clearly documents the context of Oswald's intelligence training:

> I first met Oswald at Illusionary Warfare training [propaganda,
> language instruction, false identities, maintenance of cover sto
> ries, etc.] at Nag's Head, North Carolina in 1957. Oswald was
> taking language courses at the same complex where I was tak
> ing Illusionary Warfare training classes. These courses, at the
> time, were referred to as 'Spook School' and were preparatory
> to 'going covert in international operations.' Everybody who was
> there was CIA or Military intelligence, or at least they were in
> some form of government training for their particular covert
> mission.[149]

Plumlee saw Oswald again, as the marine was shipping out from Hawaii, and more importantly, also encountered the fellow operationally in Dallas:

> Several years later, in 1962, I accidentally ran into Oswald again
> in Dallas at a Cuban 'safe house'—an apartment house behind
> the house where he had rented a room on North Beckley Street
> in Oak Cliff. I thought it strange that he was present in the
> course of a government-sanctioned gunrunning operation in
> which I was a participant.[150]

Plumlee checked with his military superiors and they verified Oswald's intelligence "bonafides":

> When I asked about this strange encounter or coincidence, I was
> told that Oswald was somehow associated with ONI intelligence.
> It was also confirmed to me by my associates that Oswald was

---

[149] Belzer & Wayne, *Dead Wrong*, "Affidavit of William R. Plumlee," 111–115.
[150] Ibid.

connected in some format as an operative of sorts. At that early
date, that was as far as it went. This limited information was
passed to me through my liaison with Captain Edward G. Sei-
well of the Fourth Army Reserve, Dallas, Love Field, and Captain Gilbert C. Cook of a special unit from the 49th Armored
Division, 156th Tank Battalion, connected to the 112th MIG
(Military Intelligence Group), Dallas, Texas and San Marcos,
Texas. I was informed by them that Oswald was somehow attached to ONI and was or had been, active at two known ONI
facilities in the Dallas area; Hensley Field in Grand Prairie,
Texas and a facility at Bachman's Lake, near Dallas' Love Field.
They were confident in their statements, regarding Oswald's
affiliation with ONI.[151]

Plumlee was involved in government-sanctioned gunrunning operations to
Cuba and realized that Oswald's presence in those same circles was related to
operational activity:

Oswald also had access to another safe house for a very short time
on Elsbeth Street, a few blocks from the Beckley street address
where a Cuban, whom I knew by the name of Fernandez, had
a room. These individuals were known by me to be functioning operationally at that time with the Alpha 66 anti-Castro
group out of Miami, Florida. My operational understanding and
assumption was that Oswald was working some form of military
operations associated with the Dallas gunrunning operations of
the time.[152]

So Plumlee puts it point-blank:

Oswald was Military intelligence. He was operational in military
ops. I know that from both direct experience and from liaison
with my superior intelligence officers. That's not an allegation—
that's a fact. Oswald was Military intelligence.[153]

---

[151] Ibid.

[152] Ibid.

[153] William Robert Plumlee, interview with author, 12 June 2006.

That information was cross-confirmed by longtime CIA officer, Victor Marchetti. Marchetti corroborated the False Defector Program being run out of the facility at Nags Head, North Carolina, during the same time frame:

> One of these activities was an ONI (Office of Naval Intelligence) program which involved three dozen, maybe forty, young men who were made to appear disenchanted, poor, American youths who had become turned off and wanted to see what communism was all about. Some of these people lasted only a few weeks. They were sent into the Soviet Union, or into Eastern Europe, with the specific intention the Soviets would pick them up and 'double' them if they suspected them of being US agents, or recruit them as KGB agents. They were trained at various naval installations both here and abroad, but the operation was being run out of Nags Head, North Carolina.[154]

And the CIA's Marchetti *also* confirmed that that's exactly what was going on with Oswald:

> Interviewed from his Northern Virginia home, Marchetti confirmed the existence of the ONI base to me privately, saying the plan was to send young men to the Soviet Union as defectors, but who in actuality were hoping to be picked up as agents by the KGB. This process is known as 'doubling,' as the young men would then in effect be double agents for both American and Soviet intelligence. Once placing an agent in the KGB, American intelligence could then begin funneling in disinformation. According to Marchetti, this was the plan for Oswald.[155]

These guys obviously knew what they were talking about.

That was also confirmed by U.S. Senator Richard Schweiker, who was Co-Chairman of a U.S. Senate Subcommittee to investigate the JFK assassination in 1975. Senator Schweiker substantiated that Oswald's phony defection to

---

[154] Anthony Summers, "Interview of Victor Marchetti," in John Simkin, "Lee Harvey Oswald: Biography," *Spartacus Educational*, retrieved 22 April 2013: spartacus.schoolnet.co.uk/JFKoswald.htm

[155] Dr. Grover B. Proctor, Jr., "The Raleigh Call," 17 July 1980 and 24 July 1980, *Spectator Magazine*: groverproctor.us/jfk/jfk80.html

the Soviet Union in 1959 was actually part of an intelligence operation, the False Defector Program:

> The accused assassin was the product of a fake defector pro-
> gram run by the CIA.[156]

Think about it. It makes *total* sense. *How* else could a guy like Oswald have gotten in and out of Russia so easily, right at the height of the Cold War? It was all *spy games* and both sides knew it.

If you saw the show I did on the JFK assassination on *Conspiracy Theory with Jesse Ventura* in 2010 then you know that Marina Oswald, wife of the accused, also strongly believed that her husband was working for U.S. intelligence.[157] I posted that episode online because it's got very important information and we need to keep the truth available: youtube.com/watch?v=sfDASCapA9Q.

David Atlee Phillips was a very high-ranking officer at the CIA, rising all the way to Director of Western Hemisphere Operations. It's a little-known fact and you probably won't hear it on television unless it's coming from my mouth, but it's true nonetheless: Phillips admitted CIA involvement in the assassination. Here's what he said near the end of his life:

> My final take on the assassination is there was a conspiracy,
> likely including American intelligence officers.[158]

Phillips also left behind this remarkable comment in an unpublished manu-script, which mirrors what many thought was his exact role and how he knew exactly what he knew:

> I was one of the two case officers who handled Lee Harvey
> Oswald. After working to establish his Marxist bona fides, we
> gave him the mission of killing Fidel Castro in Cuba . . . I don't
> know why he killed Kennedy. But I do know he used precisely
> the plan we had devised against Castro.[159]

[156] Talbot, *Brothers*, 381.

[157] Jesse Ventura, *Conspiracy Theory with Jesse Ventura*, 2010, truTV.

[158] Larry Hancock, *Someone Would Have Talked: The Assassination of President John F. Kennedy and The Conspiracy to Mislead History* (JFK Lancer: 2006).

[159] Jefferson Morley & Michael Scott, *Our Man in Mexico: Winston Scott and the Hidden History of the CIA* (University Press of Kansas: 2008).

There are a lot of things in Oswald's background that make it pretty freaking obvious that he was involved in covert operations:

A military doctor noted that on his medical record that Oswald should not be reprimanded for venereal disease because it was contracted "in the line of duty." Oswald was associated with prostitutes at a posh nightclub in Tokyo who were suspected by U.S. intelligence of passing secrets to the Communists;[160]

Oswald failed a Russian proficiency test on February 25, 1959. Only six months later, he was totally fluent, as witnessed by two native speakers (his wife and George de Mohrenschildt). Russian is an extremely difficult language, so either he was given intensive language training by U.S. intelligence or it was his intelligence "double" (see point 19) who was actually the Russian speaker;[161]

Even though the CIA lied and said that Oswald was not debriefed when he returned to the United States from the Soviet Union, it has been established that he actually was debriefed. A CIA officer confirmed his viewing of the CIA debriefing report of Oswald;[162]

While still in the Marines in Japan, he was involved in the defection-targeting of Soviet Colonel Nikolai Eroshkin;[163]

A spy camera was found in his belongings;[164]

Oswald's notebook not only contained references to guns and microdots (the "method of microscopic photographic reproduction favored by spies"), but also utilized a cryptogram system employed by spies to disguise the information and phone numbers, including the unlisted phone number of Jack Ruby.[165]

---

[160] Robert J. Groden, *The Search for Lee Harvey Oswald: A Comprehensive Photographic Record* (Penguin: 1995).

[161] John Armstrong, *Harvey and Lee: How the CIA Framed Oswald* (Quasar: 2003).

[162] *Who Was Lee Harvey Oswald?* November 20, 2003, Frontline, PBS; pbs.org/wgbh/pages/frontline/shows/oswald/etc/script.html

[163] Russell, *The Man Who Knew Too Much,* 72–73.

[164] Judyth Vary Baker, "Oswald Framed: Convenient Lies and Cover-Ups," June 29, 2011: oswald-framed.blogspot.com/2011_06_01_archive.html

[165] Hoke May, "Simple Enciphering System Used To Encode Oswald Notebook—DA," *New Orleans States-Item*, 13 May 1967: docs.google.com/viewer?a=v&q=cache:P60YWB3eL g8J:jfk.hood.edu/Collection/White%2520Materials/Garrison%2520News%2520Clippin gs/1967/67-05/Item%2520043.pdf+Simple+Enciphering+System+Used+To+Encode+Oswa ld+Notebook%E2%80%94DA,%E2%80%9D+New+Orleans+States-Item&hl=en&gl=us&p id=bl&srcid=ADGEESg-5KJlzwgoflVgEwgAdj4vF2unjPgRehk2ZO07UivJd5Kut6BFbW isyi4GACc5CB5pTNG4DPoaT7Lt1MLRHcrWbK64PGA1v6YgHiXk62z5Ndun7POCli2 ZvwO4TSJJ5DGUysLm&sig=AHIEtbTMJg-KSH-GDP1dApxLWySp1nzHTA

Colonel L. Fletcher Prouty was the key liaison between the U.S. Air Force and CIA for covert operations. This was a guy who knew his way around the National Security Council and the Joint Chiefs of Staff. He studied the assassination for years and concluded that Oswald's links to the intelligence community were what made him the perfect "patsy": the perfect guy to set up to take the blame for the assassination because they'd have to slam the door shut on any investigation. And true to form, Colonel Prouty put it bluntly:

Oswald was a patsy. There's no question about it.[166]

Colonel C. William Bishop was another guy who really knew what he was talking about. Colonel Bishop was the highest-ranking military intelligence officer attached to the CIA's elite assassination squad called Executive Action. Wanna hear what he had to say about Oswald?

Oswald was a decoy. There's no way in hell he could have fired
three shots in that space of time, with that accuracy, with that
weapon . . . I'll tell you one damn thing. Whoever set up that
poor little son of a bitch did a first-class job.[167]

So Colonel Bishop agreed with Colonel Prouty all the way. And all I can say is this—when guys like that are all agreeing, we'd better perk up our ears and pay close attention.

---

[166] Colonel L. Fletcher Prouty, "The Col. L. Fletcher Prouty Reference Site," retrieved 23 April 2013: prouty.org/
[167] Russell, *The Man Who Knew Too Much,* 330.

19

Oswald Had A Look-Alike
Intelligence Double

Either Oswald knew how to clone himself or he had what's called an "intelligence double." One of those two things is true because—on several occasions—it's been established that Oswald was in two places at the same time.

If you read the evidence, especially the long study of the matter by researcher and author, John Armstrong, you'll see that there had to be two Oswalds.

Those mysterious anomalies in the history of Lee Harvey Oswald have made some researchers conclude that the only explanation that's viable is that U.S. intelligence had been "running" two Oswalds as part of an operation. This theory is not as wild as it may at first seem; in fact, quite to the contrary. When it comes to spies and covert operations, the employment of a double is a very useful technique.

In the context of intelligence work, those multiple uses of identity are very common; even sometimes involving the utilization of identical twins. Multiple citings of Lee Harvey Oswald at locations inconsistent with one identity are a telltale sign of the employment of this intelligence tactic. There are also well-substantiated height differentiations in the "two different Oswalds." Differentiations in Oswald's height and other physical characteristics, as well as multiple citings of Oswald in separate locations at the same time, lead to a conclusion of identity manipulation *in an intelligence context.*

I know that probably sounds pretty wild, but keep reading and you'll understand what I'm talking about.

Consider the following facts. Upon his return from the Soviet Union, changes in Oswald became apparent to family members.

> Back in Fort Worth, Lee's family noticed radical changes in his appearance, such as a great loss and thinning of his hair, adding to the mysteries surrounding Lee's identity since he was a teenager. A comparison of his height on his Defense Department ID card (5'11") with his height at the time of his arrest (5'9") supports his family's claims. Oswald's apparent pro-communist activism also fragmented into seemingly conflicting camps.[168]

That height discrepancy was even more obvious when the "two Oswalds" were younger. The Lee Harvey Oswald who was seen by a doctor named Milton Kurian compared to the Lee Harvey Oswald enrolled at the same time in school in New York City—who was supposedly the same person—revealed dramatic height differential.

> Dr. Kurian says Oswald was in the Youth House prior to that time, yet the Warren Commission says Oswald was only confined to Youth House once—a month after speaking to Kurian. Dr. Kurian says Oswald was 4'6" tall, yet New York school records list his height only a month later as 5'4".

> These discrepancies suggest there were two different people— both apparently named Lee Harvey Oswald—in New York in the spring of 1953. This would explain the testimony of Oswald's half-brother John Pic when the Warren Commission showed him a series of photographs from the February 21, 1964, issue of *Life* magazine of Lee Oswald as a youth. Pic identified photographs of Oswald from ages two through twelve.

---

[168] Ken Biggs, "Famous Texans: Lee Harvey Oswald," 2006: famoustexans.com/leeharveyoswald.htm

But when Warren Commission attorney Albert Jenner showed Pic a photograph of a thirteen-year-old Oswald standing in front of the Bronx Zoo and asked, "Do you recognize that photo?" John Pic replied, "Sir, from that picture, I could not recognize that that is Lee Harvey Oswald." Attorney Jenner prompted him: ". . . [T]hat young fellow is shown here, he doesn't look like you recall Lee looked in 1952 and 1953 when you saw him in New York City?" John Pic replied, "No, sir." This is the only known photograph taken during Oswald's year-and-a-half stay in New York. Robert Oswald testified that the boy in the picture was Lee Harvey Oswald, and he himself had taken the picture. John Pic, who testified months later, said he would never have known it was Lee Harvey Oswald.

Lee Oswald, the 5'4" southern boy, moved to New York in 1952 and was teased by his classmates for his southern accent and for wearing blue jeans. "Harvey," who already lived in New York, was the 4'6" kid interviewed by Dr. Kurian, photographed at the Bronx Zoo, and unrecognized by John Pic.[169]

If you think about it, that all makes perfect sense. As historian John Armstrong—a man who has written for decades on this particular subject— puts it, "If the KGB recruited young boys, can there be any doubt that our intelligence agencies ran similar operations?"[170]

There are a lot of indications of stark differences in the past of Lee Harvey Oswald that imply they were actually two different individuals:

Mortician Paul Groody was asked twice if he noted a mastoid scar on the left side of Oswald's neck or scars near his left elbow. In 1945, Oswald had a mastoidectomy operation at Harris Hospital in Fort Worth. A three-inch mastoid scar was noted on his Marine medical records. In 1957, Lee shot himself in the arm with a .22 Derringer. Yet neither the three-inch mastoid scar nor scars from the bullet wounds were observed by Groody

---

[169] John Armstrong, "November In Dallas 1997" Presentation on *Harvey & Lee*, Transcribed by Jerry Robertson: acorn.net/jfkplace/03/JA/JR-JA.html
[170] Ibid.

or noted on his 1963 report. Jack Ruby shot Oswald, who had no
such scars.[171]

In January of 1957, military records show "Lee Harvey Oswald" was treated
for tonsillitis. He was treated again for tonsillitis in 1958 and given injections
of penicillin. But according to an FBI report, Dr. Philben, of Dallas, Texas had
removed Oswald's tonsils twelve years earlier—in January of 1945.[172]

I want to point out here that *these are not theories*, but rather documented
facts. You can examine the documentation in the actual records which are
reproduced online: mindserpent.com/American_History/books/Armstrong/
Tonsillectomy/Tonsils.htm.

> Oswald's Marine medical records indicate the following: "Mas-
> toid operation 1945; Hospitalized 2 weeks, Ft. Worth, Texas."
> But despite a careful examination of his body for scars as small
> as a quarter of an inch in size, Oswald's autopsist recorded none
> remotely near the mastoidectomy. The mortician who prepared
> Oswald's body for burial couldn't find scars that should have
> been there either. The scar from a self-inflicted gunshot wound
> in the left elbow from Oswald's Marine years also appeared to
> have disappeared after his death.
>
> In October of 1957, Lee shot himself in the left arm with a .22
> derringer. The entrance wound was closed with stitches and
> the bullet left in his arm. Later an incision was made on the
> back side of his arm and the bullet removed. Two incisions—
> two scars. After Oswald was shot and killed by Jack Ruby an
> autopsy was performed. Photographs were taken of Oswald's
> arms. There are no scars from a bullet wound, nor are any
> scars noted on the autopsy report. Oswald was prepared for
> burial and embalmed by Mortician Paul Groody. Groody was
> twice asked about scars on Oswald's arms. Groody said he had
> not seen any scars on Oswald's arms.[173]

---

171 DiEugenio, James & Pease, Lisa, *The Assassinations: Probe Magazine on JFK, MLK, RFK &*
Malcolm X (Feral House: 2003), 131.

172 Armstrong, "November In Dallas 1997"

173 John Armstrong, *Harvey and Lee:* "Magic Tonsillectomy, Vanishing Scars": mindserpent.
com/American_History/books/Armstrong/Tonsillectomy/Tonsils.htm

Scars simply do *not* disappear like that!

> Years earlier, when Lee Oswald was six years old, he had a mas-
> toidectomy operation behind his left ear. In 1956 Lee's Marine
> medical examination report lists a 3" mastoid scar behind
> his left ear. When Harvey was killed by Jack Ruby, Dr. Earl
> Rose performed the autopsy. Dr. Rose noted many scars in his
> autopsy report, some were as small as 1/16." Dr. Rose also took
> twenty-seven color slides of Oswald's body which are now in the
> National Archives. There is no 3" mastoidectomy scar on the
> autopsy report nor can such a scar be seen in any of the color
> slides. It was Lee Oswald who had the 3" mastoidectomy scar—
> not Harvey. Harvey had no such scar.

> These mysteries have long puzzled JFK researchers, but the
> solution is simple enough. One Lee Harvey Oswald had a tonsil-
> lectomy and a mastoidectomy in 1945 and shot himself in the
> left elbow in 1957. The other Oswald did not.[174]

But there's an even bigger "whopper" from a forensics standpoint, and
here it is:

> Oswald's body was ordered exhumed in 1981 after author
> Michael Eddowes brought suit in Texas to determine who was
> actually buried in Oswald's grave. The pathologists assigned to
> the case officially identified the body as Oswald's. However, the
> funeral director who originally buried the body insisted it could
> not be the same since the one he buried clearly showed a crani-
> otomy, which had been done during autopsy, and the exhumed
> skull showed no craniotomy. Also, the pathologists used dental
> records to identify the corpse, but ignored the fact that Oswald
> had lost a front tooth in a fight in high school (there is a photo
> of him in class with a gap-tooth smile, and many classmates
> remember the fight and the missing tooth). The exhumed skull
> had a full set of natural front teeth.[175]

---

[174] Ibid.
[175] Biggs, "Famous Texans: Lee Harvey Oswald"

Oswald's "legend"—which is a term in covert intelligence to describe a manufactured personal history—also gives an indication of the existence of a sophisticated intelligence operation.

> Accounts of co-workers, other eyewitnesses, and records from schools, employment and the military began to conflict greatly on such details as his appearance, whereabouts and abilities in such areas as driving and foreign languages. From the time he was a young teen it was as if his identity was being used by several people at once. While no specific official program or operation has been publicly documented involving the requisition of identities, similar activities have long been common in spy tradecraft. Certainly by 1963, one or more persons was actively impersonating Oswald in ways that helped incriminate him in the Kennedy assassination.[176]

As a result, many in the assassination research community began to look at the possibilities.

> It was suspected by several assassination researchers that, early on in Oswald's Marine career, someone started to impersonate him. The man, or men, used the names Lee Harvey Oswald, Harvey Lee Oswald and Alek James Hidell. These researchers believe that Hidell or one of the others took over the identity of Lee Harvey Oswald as a US or Soviet intelligence agent for the rest of his life. One might then believe that the real Oswald was given another identity—as in the Witness Protection Program . . .[177]

The evidence for two Oswalds is dramatic:

- By June of 1960, J. Edgar Hoover was aware of an Oswald in the states and an Oswald in Russia. He sent a memo to his field offices warning them that an imposter may be using Oswald's birth certificate. FBI files contain many reports of Lee Oswald in the States while Harvey is in Russia, but you won't find them in the Warren Commission volumes.

---

[176] Ibid.

[177] Groden, *The Search for Lee Harvey Oswald*

- In early 1964, Warren Commission member and Georgia Senator Richard Russell was very troubled and asked Army Intelligence Colonel Phillip Corso to quietly conduct an investigation into the "Oswald matter." Corso soon reported to Senator Russell that there had been two United States Passports issued to Lee Harvey Oswald, which had been used by two different men. He obtained this information from the head of the U.S. Passport office, Francis Knight. He also reported to Senator Russell there were two birth certificates in the name of Lee Harvey Oswald and they too had been used by two different people. He obtained this information from William Sullivan, head of the FBI's Domestic Intelligence Division. Corso said he and Senator Russell concluded the assassination had been a conspiracy.

- James A. Wilcott, a former CIA finance officer, told the House Select Committee on Assassinations that Lee Oswald had been recruited from the military by the CIA 'with the express purpose of a double agent assignment in the USSR.' His testimony was ignored.[178]

Here's how Oswald's *own brother* knew that something was up:

> After Harvey quit high school, he worked briefly for
> J. R. Michels, and then left New Orleans for California.
> We know about his residing in California thanks to Texas
> Employment Commission employee Laurel Kittrell. She
> interviewed the two Oswalds in 1963 in Dallas. She remem-
> bered they looked remarkably similar.

> Russian-speaking "Harvey" replaced Lee at El Toro and took
> a Russian language exam in February, 1959. Lee Oswald's
> brother, John Pic, wasn't fooled by the switch. When shown a
> photograph of 'Lee Harvey Oswald' wearing a Marine helmet,
> Pic told the Warren Commission, "I would never guess that that
> would be Lee." Pic knew this person was not his brother. So did
> Robert Oswald.

> When Lee Oswald's older brother, John Pic, saw 'Harvey' Oswald
> after his return from Russia, Pic told the Warren Commission

---

[178] Armstrong, "November In Dallas 1997" Presentation on *Harvey & Lee*

'the Lee Harvey Oswald I met in November of 1962 was not the
same Lee Oswald I had known ten years previous.'

When Attorney Jenner asked Pic how he looked physically 'as
compared with when you had last seen him,' Pic replied, 'I
would never have recognized him, sir.' You noticed a material
change in his appearance? Pic replied, 'much thinner, didn't
have as much hair, different facial features, eyes set back, his
face was rounder, and he no longer had a bull neck.'

The Oswald that Pic saw on Thanksgiving Day in 1962 wrote
his name in Pic's address book as 'Harvey.'[179]

In an eerie event, Oswald's Russian wife provided the most interesting revelation of all:

She insisted on seeing Oswald's body during his autopsy. Marina
entered the room, stood next to the body of Lee Harvey Oswald
and did a most curious thing. She raised his eyelids and looked
at his eyes. Four months later she told a French journalist, 'I had
two husbands: Lee, the father of my children, an affectionate
and kind man; and Harvey Oswald, the assassin of President
Kennedy.'[180]

Therefore, the comparative evidence strongly suggests that:
- There was at least one other individual actively impersonating Lee
  Harvey Oswald, either as part of a sophisticated intelligence operation,
  or as part of a hijacked intelligence operation.
- There were at least "two Oswalds" as a component of that operation.
  Two separate individuals who formed the composite identity and legend
  of "Lee Harvey Oswald" for U.S. intelligence.
- As a component of the False Defector Program of U.S. Intelligence,
  it was the operational design for "Harvey" Oswald (who spoke fluent
  Russian) to step into the "Lee Harvey Oswald legend" prior to "defection" to Russia.

---

[179] Armstrong, "November In Dallas 1997" Presentation on *Harvey & Lee*
[180] Ibid.

- According to Armstrong's research, the "real" or original Lee Harvey Oswald was not the man who was shot by Jack Ruby, nor the corpse that was buried in Oswald's grave.

Note the striking and *substantiated* differences between the two Oswalds:

- One spoke fluent Russian; the other did not.
- One was 5 feet, 9 inches tall; the other was 5 feet, 11 inches.
- One had a tattoo of a dagger with a snake on his left forearm; the other did not.
- One had a mastoidectomy scar on the left side of his neck; the other did not.
- One had two scars on his left forearm; the other did not.
- One still had all his permanent teeth; the other did not.
- One still had his tonsils; the other did not.
- One is buried in the grave of Lee Harvey Oswald; the other is not.[181]

Richard Helms was a major player at the CIA. He was the head of covert operations for many years and eventually rose to CIA Director. Some researchers think he may have been involved in the assassination. Whether he was involved in its planning or not, it seemed he knew more than he was telling. For example, he made a very odd comment once which seemed very hard for people to put into context. Pay close attention to the strange words chosen by former CIA Director Helms:

> In 1978, former CIA Director Richard Helms exited from his executive-session testimony before the House Select Committee on Assassinations. He paused to talk with the press. *Washington Post* reporter George Lardner, Jr. described the encounter in his paper's August 10 edition:

> Helms told reporters during a break that no one would ever know who or what Lee Harvey Oswald, named by the Warren Commission as Kennedy's assassin, represented. Asked whether the CIA knew of any ties Oswald had with either the KGB or the CIA, Helms paused and with a laugh said, "I don't remem-

---

[181] Armstrong, *Harvey and Lee*

ber." Pressed on the point, he told a reporter, "Your questions
are almost as dumb as the Committee's."[182]

"No one will ever know who or what Lee Harvey Oswald represented."
What a bizarre thing to say. But if what researchers like John Armstrong seem to
have figured out about there being two Oswalds is actually true, then that cryptic
comment by Helms above suddenly makes a helluva lot of sense.

After the assassination, U.S. intelligence apparently created a new and false
legend for Lee Harvey Oswald. The new legend was actually a composite of
Lee Oswald and Harvey Oswald and explains why the two legends at times
overlap; i.e. one Oswald was sighted (or even interviewed) in the United States
at a time when we know Oswald was supposed to be in Russia, etc. The purpose of the final legend was to distance themselves from the assassination of
President Kennedy and to manufacture and sustain believability for the "lone
gunman theory." Most of that research is available online: acorn.net/jfkplace/03/
JA/DR/.04-sources.html

New Orleans District Attorney Jim Garrison investigated Oswald's background more tenaciously and with much more factual thoroughness than did the
Warren Commission.

> In 1967, Jim Garrison and his staff recognized the discrepancies
> in Oswald's background. Investigator Alberto Fowler told Car-
> los Bringuier that Garrison had information that an identical
> double of Lee Harvey Oswald existed and this individual was a
> 'double agent' of the FBI.[183]

As a result of their investigation into the inconsistencies in Oswald's background, New Orleans District Attorney Garrison wrote the following in a memorandum to one of his associates:

> If you really want to know what I think, it is that Robert Os-
> wald knew this returning defector was not really Lee [his broth-
> er] and this is what Robert's problem was the night of the assas-
> sination when he found it necessary to take such a long drive to

---

[182] Philip H. Melanson, *Spy Saga: Lee Harvey Oswald and U.S. Intelligence* (Prager
Publishers: 1990): democraticunderground.com/discuss/duboard.php?az=view_
all&address=104x756522

[183] Armstrong, "November In Dallas 1997" Presentation on *Harvey & Lee*

think things out. He knew things were far more complicated than they appeared on the surface.[184]

There were some very cogent reasons why Garrison reached that conclusion.

Lee Oswald remained in the U.S. while Harvey went to Russia. When Harvey Oswald met Marina, she thought he was a native Russian with a Baltic accent. When she learned he was a foreigner, she asked which of his parents was Russian. His March 1961 medical records from Minsk list his name as 'Harvey Alik Oswald.' A State Department Security Office memo of March 2, 1961, refers to 'Harvey' Oswald. A letter written to Oswald in May 3, 1961, is addressed to Esteemed Citizen 'Harvey Oswald.' A CIA memo of November 25, 1963, explained the Agency's interest in the 'Harvey' story. The merging of Harvey Oswald with Lee Oswald's background had been successful. Russian speaking Harvey was in Russia and Lee was working with CIA operatives in New Orleans, Texas, and Florida. People who look similar, like Harvey and Lee, are often used by the intelligence community. Castro's top agents were identical twin brothers— Patricio and Antonio De La Guardia. Lee and Harvey were not identical in appearance, but they looked similar enough to confuse, deceive, and fool those who saw or knew them. This is the smoke and mirrors Jim Garrison spoke of—trademarks of the intelligence community."[185]

This all relates to one particular thing that Oswald said while in custody that I always thought was more important than it first looked. After he was arrested Oswald made that eerie statement: "Now everyone will know who I am."[186]

Worldwide attention centered on Harvey Oswald after his arrest. Former FBI Agent Gayton Carver said Oswald was being paid by the FBI as a 'potential security informant.' When he [Oswald] said 'now everyone will know who I am,' he knew his work as

---

[184] Ibid.

[185] Ibid.

[186] "The Last Words of Lee Harvey Oswald: Compiled by Mae Brussell"

an undercover informant was finished. Harvey Oswald, sitting in the Dallas jail, now had both the CIA and the FBI desperately trying to distance themselves from him, link him with Castro and/or Cuba, frame him for the assassination, hide his true identity, and create a legend that portrayed him as a 'lone nut.'[187]

Robert K. Tanenbaum was a heroic Deputy Counsel of the House Select Committee on Assassinations who resigned because he realized that Congress was preventing him from conducting a real investigation.[188] He has stated for the historical record that his staff located a film showing Oswald and David Ferrie at an anti-Castro training camp near New Orleans in the summer of 1963.

Tanenbaum's book describes this film as containing Lee Harvey Oswald, David Ferrie, Guy Banister, Antonio Veciana, and David Atlee Phillips—all in the presence of one another—and an Oswald look-alike just barely discernible from the real thing.

Author and long-time assassination researcher James DiEugenio asked Tanenbaum:

> "Was it really as you described in the book, with all the people in that film?"

> Robert Tanenbaum replied: "Oh yeah. Absolutely! They're all in the film. They're all there."[189]

> Tanenbaum also affirmed the aforementioned fact in his testimony before the Assassination Records Review Board.[190]

Charles E. O'Hara is the author of an important textbook in the practice of criminology entitled *Fundamentals of Criminal Investigation*. A preface was added to the second edition of the book which reads as a procedural indictment on the framing of Lee Harvey Oswald; a classic book points out their classic mistake.

---

[187] DiEugenio & Pease, The Assassinations, 133.

[188] Gaeton Fonzi, *The Last Investigation* (The Mary Ferrell Foundation: 2008)

[189] James DiEugenio, "The Probe Interview: Bob Tanenbaum," *Probe Magazine*, July–August 1996, Vol. 3 No.5: ctka.net/pr796-bti.html

[190] *Assassination Records Review Board*, Testimony of Robert Tanenbaum, September 17, 1996, Los Angeles, California.

On review, however, it would appear that insufficient attention
had been given to the role of the investigator in establishing
the innocence of persons falsely accused. It was thought that
this aspect of investigation was too obvious to stress; that the
continued insistence on objectivity and professionalism in the
investigator's conduct should meet this requirement. After all,
the process of establishing innocence is hardly separable from
the task of detecting the guilty. One does not, that is to say,
prove guilt by the method of exhaustion.[191]

One would think that especially true in a purported democracy. Yet that
"method of exhaustion" is clearly the process in which Lee Harvey Oswald has
been wrongly convicted in a public relations trial that was void of the sufficient
actual evidence.

The evidence for "Two Oswalds" is overwhelming and now merits serious
attention.

As a number of researchers have observed, the most logical scenario is that
Oswald went to the Texas Theater after the assassination for a prearranged ren-
dezvous with his intelligence handler; otherwise he certainly chose one of the
oddest moments in history for the sudden urge to take in a film. The fact that
Oswald moved from seat to seat, as though he was in search of something, is further indication of such an attempted liaison. Movie theaters are a typical locale
for intelligence liaison.

I'd also like to point out a little thing here called *common sense*. Look at
Oswald's arrest in the movie theater. The only thing they knew at that exact
point in time was that someone hadn't bought a ticket. So just imagine the *real*
context of the thing for a minute: It's an hour after the murder of the President
of the United States, plus in close proximity to the murder of Officer Tippit, and
you're a police dispatcher and you get a phone call at least a mile away from one
of the crimes and multiple miles away from the other crime—and the only thing
you hear is somebody didn't a buy a 60-cent ticket before they went in to see the
Audie Murphy movie that was playing that afternoon over at the theater in the
Oak Cliff section of Dallas. Why would you send ten squad cars, two dozen cops,
and the news media to arrest a guy who didn't buy a ticket going into the theater?
Wouldn't you kind of say we have more important fish to fry here? We have a

---

[191] Charles E. O'Hara, *Fundamentals of Criminal Investigation* (Thomas Books: 1970)

dead cop and a dead President, and you're telling me to send police out to a theater because someone didn't buy a ticket, went in behind the booth, and you happened to notice it? Common sense—why would there be that type of reaction?

They had no description of Oswald, except that one that went out on him, because that one witness was looking from the street at a window—how the heck would they know his height?! Looking from the street up to the 6th floor window, you'd have no clue how tall anyone was, especially if he's in a shooter's position. The point is, they would have no description of Oswald and if they do that's fraudulent—and this guy who doesn't have a ticket fits him perfect so that they send ten squad cars, the news media, and twenty-four cops down there to make the arrest?

Well, when I was a kid, we used to sneak into the theater every now and then. If they caught you, it wasn't done like that at all. The trick we used to do was that somebody would buy a ticket, go down, and sit in the dark theater, then when it was right you'd go over to the exit door, prop it open, and your friends would sneak in and sit in the seats. But start at the front of the theater and work their way back in unison, turn the lights on in the theater? No, they'd come in, find the guy, quietly escort him out of the theater, and give him a kick in the pants. They wouldn't even charge him with a crime, you know?

How would they have the police wherewithal and the conviction to say, hey, this guy who snuck in the theater fits the description of the killer of the President? Why would the killer of the president go to a movie? Oswald probably went there to meet a contact, but let's not go that far. You've just killed the President. You go to the movies? I think you'd be on the first thing out of town, you'd want to get as far from the scene, quietly, as you possibly could. Or go somewhere and get in the basement for a week, and not show your face.

So you shoot the President and you decide to take in the afternoon movie? You decide *that*, right? You say "Hey, I just shot the President of the United States and a cop, but hey, I think I'll go to the matinee." I mean, *come on*!

20

Oswald Had No Motive for Murder

Now I'm going to tell you a fact that's often overlooked, but is very important. In addition to not having the *means* to commit the crime, Oswald did not possess a sufficient *motive*. Neither the Warren Commission nor the House Select Committee on Assassinations was ever able to establish any motive for Oswald to have committed the crime. That's a big red flag to any real investigator. Why did he do it? It's your Basic Crime Scene 101. They couldn't even come up with a good reason so that's why they always just described him as some kind of a "lone nut."

Since when does such a high-profile crime not need a motive?

> Why did Oswald do it? To this most important and most mysterious question the commission had no certain answer. It suggested that Oswald had no rational purpose, no motive adequate if "judged by the standards of reasonable men."[192]

---

[192] Anthony Lewis, "Warren Commission Finds Oswald Guilty and Says Assassin and Ruby Acted Alone; Rebukes Secret Service, Asks Revamping," 27 September 1964, *The New York Times*, Page One: nytimes.com/learning/general/onthisday/big/0927.html

But in addition to not having any motive, just the opposite appears to be the real story here. Oswald—and not many people know this—is *on record* as having admired President Kennedy.

> After his arrest, he told the police that "My wife and I like the President's family. They are interesting people."

> He said, "I am not a malcontent; nothing irritated me about the President."[193]

Well, it sounds to me like they should have thrown their whole "lone nut" theory right out the frigging window. He didn't sound like a nut at all! In fact, he sounded like just what he said he was—a "patsy."

Any way you look at it, Oswald's actions were not consistent with those of a murderer. His actions and comments at the time of his arrest and afterwards are not indicative of his being one of the first political assassins in history to emphatically deny involvement in the murder. In fact, quite to the contrary, Oswald's comments are indicative of a man concerned with much smaller issues.

The following compilation appeared in the 1978 edition of *The People's Almanac*. They undertook that project for a very good reason, and they state that reason very clearly:

> Almost everyone, it seems, has been heard from on the Kennedy assassination and on Lee Harvey Oswald's guilt or innocence, except one person—Lee Harvey Oswald himself. From the time of Oswald's arrest to his own assassination at the hands of Jack Ruby, no formal transcript or record was kept of statements made by the alleged killer. It was said that no tape recordings were made of Oswald's remarks, and many notes taken of his statements were destroyed.

> Determined to learn Oswald's last words, his only testimony, *The People's Almanac* assigned one of the leading authorities on the Kennedy assassination, Mae Brussell, to compile every

---

[193] Ibid.

known statement or remark made by Oswald between his arrest
and death.[194]

And Ms. Brussell's conclusion bears noting:

> After fourteen years of research on the JFK assassination, I am
> of the opinion that Lee Harvey Oswald was telling the truth
> about his role in the assassination during these interrogations.[195]

Consider this. During questioning on the afternoon of his arrest, Oswald
recognized FBI agent James Hosty, whom he had previously met, and Oswald
told Agent Hosty the following:

> You have been at my home two or three times talking to my
> wife. I don't appreciate your coming out there when I was not
> there . . . Mr. Hosty, you have been accosting my wife. You mis-
> treated her on two different occasions when you talked with her
> . . . I know you. Well, he threatened her. He practically told her
> she would have to go back to Russia.[196]

Now ask yourself the following question: If you had just been involved in the
assassination of the President of the United States *and* had just murdered a police
officer in cold blood only a few hours before, would the matter of an FBI agent
questioning your spouse without your permission be the focus of your attention
and a priority about which you would be visibly concerned? The facts of the
matter are that Oswald *was* concerned with points like that, nothing larger. His
statements revealed that he was merely worried he was in trouble for having been
caught with a revolver.

At the time of his arrest, Oswald's comments in fact showed a man who was
completely uncertain about the actual circumstances of his situation:

- I don't know why you are treating me like this. The only thing I have
  done is carry a pistol into a movie.
- I don't see why you handcuffed me.

[194] David Wallechinsky & Irving Wallace, *People's Almanac #2;* (Bantam Books: 1978) 47–52;
"The Last Words of Lee Harvey Oswald: Compiled by Mae Brussell"
[195] Ibid.
[196] Ibid.

- Why should I hide my face? I haven't done anything to be ashamed of.
- I want a lawyer.
- I am not resisting arrest.
- I didn't kill anybody . . . I haven't shot anybody.
- I protest this police brutality.
- I fought back there, but I know I wasn't supposed to be carrying a gun.
- What is this all about?[197]

The same was true of his comments in the police car on the way to the police station and then at the station after his arrest:

- What is this all about?
- I know my rights.
- All I did was carry a gun.
- Nothing irritated me about the President.
- John Kennedy had a nice family.
- I had nothing personal against John Kennedy.
- I really don't know what the situation is about. Nobody has told me anything except that I am accused of murdering a policeman. I know nothing more than that, and I do request someone to come forward to give me legal assistance.
- When asked, "Did you kill the President?" Oswald replied:
  - o No. I have not been charged with that. In fact, nobody has said that to me yet. The first thing I heard about it was when the newspaper reporters in the hall asked me that question . . . I did not do it. I did not do it . . . I did not shoot anyone.
- I didn't even know Governor John Connally had been shot.
- Well, I really don't know what this is all about, that I have been kept incarcerated and kept incommunicado.[198]

It's quite an oddity that the man suspected of killing the President was actually very fond of the man, as investigative authors Anthony Summers and Robbyn Swan noted:

> It is clear from a dozen witnesses that Oswald repeatedly spoke about John F. Kennedy in terms of admiration. He "showed

---

[197] Ibid.
[198] Ibid.

in his manner of speaking that he liked the president," said
a policeman who talked with him in August of 1963. In a
conversation about civil rights a month before the assassination,
Oswald said he thought Kennedy was doing "a real fine job, a
real good job."[199]

Oswald displayed confidence—even *bragged*—that his innocence would be
revealed by the evidence, rather than fearing it for the sake of incrimination:

- What are you trying to prove with this paraffin test, that I fired a gun?
- You are wasting your time. I don't know anything about what you are
  accusing me.
- The FBI has thoroughly interrogated me at various other times...They
  have used their hard and soft approach to me, and they use the buddy
  system . . . I am familiar with all types of questioning and have no inten-
  tion of making any statements.
- When arrested, Oswald had FBI Agent James Hosty's home phone and
  office phone numbers and car license number in his possession.[200]

Oswald's actions were interpreted by experienced police officers as being
somehow above and beyond his actual situation. Here's how Dallas Police Officer
B. J. Dale described him:

When Oswald would come out of the office and down the hall,
what I observed was that he seemed to be toying with everybody. He was way ahead of everybody else. He knew what he
was doing and seemed very confident. He acted like he was in
charge and, as it turned out, he probably was.[201]

Oswald's confidence—or, more accurately, outright cockiness—may have
been the result of his conviction that he was protected by his relationship to U.S.
intelligence. He made numerous references which could be construed as such in
the brief period between his arrest on Friday afternoon and his murder on the
following Sunday morning:

---

[199] Anthony Summers & Robbyn Swann, *The Arrogance of Power* (Penguin Books: 2001).

[200] "The Last Words of Lee Harvey Oswald: Compiled by Mae Brussell."

[201] Joe Nick Patoski, "The Witnesses: What They Saw Then, Who They Are Now," *Texas Monthly*, November, 1998.

- Call the FBI. Tell them you have Lee Oswald in custody. (Spoken to Lieutenant Frank Martello, the interviewing officer at the time of his arrest in New Orleans.)[202]
- Everyone will know who I am now. (This statement was made in a somber manner, as though now his cover was blown; not as though seeking fame, but in fact, quite the opposite.)[203]
- I refuse to take a polygraph. It has always been my practice not to agree to take a polygraph.[204]
- I am waiting for someone to come forward to give me legal assistance.[205]
- (To Marina, his wife): It's a mistake. I'm not guilty. There are people who will help me.
- Everything is going to be all right. If they ask you anything, you have a right not to answer. You have a right to refuse. Do you understand? You are not to worry. You have friends. They'll help you.[206]
- (To his brother, Robert:) Don't believe all the so-called evidence.[207]
- (When Robert stared into Lee's eyes for a clue, Lee told him:) Brother, you won't find anything there.[208]
- My friends will take care of Marina and the two children.[209]

Even in the minutes before his own murder, Oswald displayed a self-evident confidence. The following testimony is from the Dallas police officer who was handcuffed to him when Oswald was gunned down and killed in the Dallas jail:

OFFICER LEAVELLE: I was a homicide detective.

QUESTION: He was handcuffed to your left wrist?

OFFICER LEAVELLE: Right.

QUESTION: On his right wrist?

---

[202] Joan Mellen, *A Farewell to Justice: Jim Garrison, JFK's Assassination, And the Case That Should Have Changed History* (Potomac Books: 2007).

[203] "The Last Words of Lee Harvey Oswald: Compiled by Mae Brussell."

[204] Ibid.

[205] Ibid.

[206] Ibid.

[207] Ibid.

[208] Ibid.

[209] Ibid.

OFFICER LEAVELLE: Correct.

QUESTION: Anything said as you enter the basement?

OFFICER LEAVELLE: Well, I said this several times, but anyway, I did tell him on the way down,
I said, 'Lee, if anybody shoots at you,
I hope they're as good a shot as you
are.' Meaning they'd hit him and not
me. And he kind of laughed and he
said, 'Ah, you're being melodramatic.'
Or something like that. 'Nobody's
going to shoot me.' I said, 'Well, if
they do start, you know what to do,
don't you?' He said, 'Well, Captain
Fritz told me to follow you, and I'll do
whatever you do.'[210]

I don't know about you but—after all the years of what our Government
and our media have been telling us; *fifty frigging years* of it—that conversation
noted above that took place right before Oswald got shot is sure a surprise to me.
After all the malarkey we've had force-fed to us for decades, you just wouldn't
expect that he'd be kidding around with the people taking him around the jail
and subservient like that—even *respectful*—to the officer escorting him and in
the reference to Captain Fritz, the Chief of Homicide.

Oswald consistently denied committing any crime other than a scuffle during his arrest at the Texas Theater:

- I didn't shoot John Kennedy.
- I did not kill President Kennedy or Officer Tippit (this was later in the
  questioning of Oswald, and he now knows the name of the officer, which
  he did not previously). If you want me to cop out to hitting or pleading
  guilty to hitting a cop in the mouth when I was arrested, yeah, I plead
  guilty to that. But I do deny shooting both the President and Tippit.
- If you ask me about the shooting of Tippit, I don't know what you are
  talking about. . . . The only thing I am here for is because I popped a

---

[210] Patoski, "The Witnesses: What They Saw Then, Who They Are Now"

policeman in the nose in the theater on Jefferson Avenue, which I readily admit I did, because I was protecting myself.
- I didn't shoot anyone . . . I never killed anybody.[211]

Oswald's confidence in his innocence was such that it even allowed him to
focus attention on the defense of other's rights:

- In the past three weeks the FBI has talked to my wife. They were abu-
  sive and impolite. They frightened my wife, and I consider their activities obnoxious.
- Sheriff Roger Craig saw Oswald enter a white station wagon fifteen
  minutes after the assassination. Oswald confirmed this in Captain
  Fritz's office. Oswald then responded:

  o   That station wagon belongs to Mrs. Ruth Paine. Don't try to tie her
      into this. She had nothing to do with it.[212]

Oswald constantly and confidently defended his rights while in custody.

U.S. Secret Service Inspector Thomas J. Kelley approached Oswald, out of
the hearing of others, except perhaps Captain Fritz's men, and said that as a
Secret Service agent, he was anxious to talk with him as soon as he secured
counsel, as Oswald was charged with the assassination of the President but had
denied it. Oswald said:

> I will be glad to discuss this proposition with my attorney, and
> after I talk with one, we could either discuss it with him or dis-
> cuss it with my attorney, if the attorney thinks it is a wise thing
> to do, but at the present time I have nothing more to say to you.

> It isn't right to put me in line with these teenagers. . . . You
> know what you are doing, and you are trying to railroad me . . .
>   I want my lawyer.

> You are doing me an injustice by putting me out there dressed
> different than these other men . . . I am out there, the only one
> with a bruise on his head . . . I don t believe the lineup is fair,
> and I desire to put on a jacket similar to those worn by some of

---

[211] "The Last Words of Lee Harvey Oswald: Compiled by Mae Brussell."
[212] Ibid.

the other individuals in the lineup. . . . All of you have a shirt on, and I have a t-shirt on. I want a shirt or something. . . . This t-shirt is unfair.

Why are you treating me this way?

I am not being handled right . . . I demand my rights.

Can I get an attorney?

I have not been given the opportunity to have counsel.

As I said, the Fair Play for Cuba Committee has definitely been investigated, that is very true. . . . The results of that investigation were zero.

I insist upon my constitutional rights. . . . The way you are treating me, I might as well be in Russia . . . I was not granted my request to put on a jacket similar to those worn by other individuals in some previous lineups.

I have been dressed differently than the other three. . . . Don't you know the difference?

I still have on the same clothes I was arrested in. The other two were prisoners, already in jail.

Seth Kantor, reporter, heard Oswald yell, "I am only a patsy."

I refuse to answer questions. I have my t-shirt on, the other men are dressed differently. . . . Everybody's got a shirt and everything, and I've got a t-shirt on. . . . This is unfair.[213]

So the bulk of the evidence, as far as what transpired while Oswald was in custody, indicates that Lee Harvey Oswald was precisely what he said he was: A patsy set up to take the fall for the actions of others.

---

[213] Ibid.

21

Paper Trail on the Rifle Was Intentional

If you were going to shoot at the President of the United States, would you leave a paper trail that led directly to you? Neither would I.

The paper trail was ridiculously intentional and there was no effort to disguise it. If anything, it has the appearance of someone trying to *establish* a paper trail; to lead a clear trail to the person the conspirators were planning to set up which, in this case, was Lee Harvey Oswald.

But you have to ask yourself that one burning question: If you're planning to murder the President of the United States, would you really order a junk rifle through the mail and leave an obvious paper trail showing that you did exactly that? The only scenario I can see where a person might do that would be if, after the shooting, they were just going to throw up their hands and say, "Yeah, I did it."

But that's *not* what Oswald did. In fact, if you look at what he *did* do, it makes no sense at all for an assassin to have done this:

> In 1963, a gun could be purchased in the state of Texas without a permit or any record of the purchase. However, the rifle

the Warren Commission claimed was the murder weapon was purchased by A. J. Hidell and shipped to a post office box owned by Lee H. Oswald. When apprehended by Dallas police on November 22, 1963, Oswald carried a fake Selective Service card with the name of A. J. Hidell and an expired U.S. Department of Defense card. Though he could have purchased a rifle without any paper trail, we are led to believe the following:

1. Oswald purchased a mail order rifle under an alias of A. J. Hidell.
2. Oswald's alias was used on a fake Selective Service card that he kept in his wallet.
3. The Mannlicher-Carcano he purchased by mail order was sent to a post office box that was linked to his real name.
4. When he was questioned by the Dallas police, he claimed he didn't own a rifle.[214]

Lord almighty, folks. So if you could walk into any gun store in Texas back then and buy a rifle with no record of the purchase, then why would a criminal buy one by mail-order instead that left a paper trail right to their own doorstep? Let me answer that one for you: they wouldn't!

So why *would* somebody do that? You'd only do that if you were trying to set somebody up. That's why Oswald—as has been proven—was actually at work when they say he was buying the money order that paid for that rifle.[215]

The rifle purchase and everything about it are very peculiar and not directly linkable to Oswald.[216] All this leads to a very interesting chain of evidence.

We already know about Oswald's many established links to the CIA. But in addition to that, there's also a lot of evidence that he was working as an informant with the FBI, and part of that work seemed to be Oswald's participation in a federal government "sting" operation aimed at mail-order rifle purchases.

In January of 1963, Senator Thomas Dodd held committee hearings on the unrestricted delivery of weapons through the U.S.

---

[214] John S. Craig, *The Guns of Dealey Plaza*, retrieved 24 April 2013: acorn.net/jfkplace/09/fp.back_issues/11th_issue/guns_dp.html

[215] Anthony Summers, *Conspiracy* (Paragon House: 1989), 213.

[216] Michael T. Griffith, "Faulty Evidence: Problems with the Case Against Lee Harvey Oswald," 2001, Third Edition: michaelgriffith1.tripod.com/faulty.htm

mail. Dodd was interested in the unregulated traffic of Italian Mannlicher-Carcanos as well as the company that Oswald supposedly purchased his rifle from Klein's of Chicago.[217]

Senator Dodd of Connecticut was a powerful influence in Congress and conducted investigations on how traffic in mail-order weapons was harming business for domestic gun manufacturers.

> In 1963, as head of the Senate's Juvenile Delinquency Subcommittee, Senator Thomas Dodd of Connecticut was experimenting with ordering arms from mail order houses in an attempt to gather information allowing Congress to stem unregulated traffic. Senator Dodd instituted the program on behalf of Colt and other small firearms producers in Connecticut who complained of foreign imports.

> Oswald might have participated in this program. Dodd, a former FBI agent and long-time J. Edgar Hoover loyalist, was also a leading member of the Cuba Lobby [which grew out of the right-wing, red-hunting, China Lobby] through which he was in touch with some of the same Cuban-exile mercenaries as Oswald. He was also investigating the Fair Play for Cuba Committee [FPCC] in which Oswald may have been an infiltrator.[218]

Author George Michael Evica, one of the first investigators of the JFK assassination, focused on that linkage between Oswald and the Congressional gun investigation and found that the same type of rifle used to kill Kennedy was ordered during that Senate investigation, under the name of Oswald or the known alias, A. J. Hiddel, which was used by Oswald:

> I have learned that according to two unimpeachable sources, Senator Thomas Dodd indeed caused at least one Mannlicher Carcano to be ordered in the name of Lee Harvey Oswald (or in the name of 'A. J. Hiddel') sometime in 1963.[219]

---

[217] Craig, "Guns of Dealey Plaza."

[218] Walter F. Graf & Richard R. Bartholomew, "The Gun That Didn't Smoke," 1994, 1997: assassinationresearch.com/v1n2/gtds_3.html

[219] Ibid.

The above points are some very strong links between Oswald and that government gun investigation.

> Two of the gun mail-order houses that Dodd's subcommittee
> was investigating were the ones from which Oswald allegedly
> ordered his Smith and Wesson .38 revolver [Seaport Traders
> of Los Angeles] and his Mannlicher-Carcano rifle [Klein's of
> Chicago]. Oswald ordered his pistol two days before Dodd's sub-
> committee began hearings on the matter on January 29, 1963.
> The subcommittee's sample statistics later showed a purchase
> in Texas made from Seaport Traders. One of the groups being
> investigated for firearm purchases had a listing by Oswald in his
> address book, the American Nazi Party. One of the investigators
> looking into interstate firearms sales at this time was Manuel
> Pena, the Los Angeles police lieutenant who was later one of the
> pivotal officers investigating Robert Kennedy's assassination. It
> was Pena who traced Oswald's telescopic sight to a California
> gun shop. And one of the primary culprits, robbing domestic
> manufacturers of profits, was the Mannlicher-Carcano.[220]

Senator Dodd was also involved in the formation of the immediate associations of Oswald being a communist and, specifically in information linking Oswald to communist Cuba.

> In the summer of 1963, Dodd had presided over a Senate Inter-
> nal Security subcommittee investigation of the Fair Play for Cuba
> Committee. Oswald was the only member of the New Orleans
> branch. In 1963, Dodd called the Fair Play for Cuba Committee
> a chief public relations instrument for Castro.[221]

So Senator Dodd was apparently a key player in everything from making sure the public perception of Oswald was as a Cuba-loving commie to expanding American military action in Cuba and the Vietnam War:

> After the assassination, Dodd, using CIA sources, helped the Sen-
> ate Internal Security Subcommittee publish a story that Oswald
> had been trained at a KGB assassination school in Minsk. At the

---

[220] Ibid.

[221] Craig, "Guns of Dealey Plaza."

time, Dodd was on the payroll of the American Security Council, "the leading public group campaigning to use U.S. military force to oust Castro from Cuba, and to escalate the war in Vietnam."[222]

As Dick Russell established in the book *The Man Who Knew Too Much*, ATF Agent Frank Ellsworth, whom we discussed in the earlier entry about finding the rifle, was also involved in some of the gun investigations happening at that time in Dallas. A local undercover informant had set up an illegal weapons purchase that Agent Ellsworth was running as part of his operation. Ellsworth would never divulge the name of the informant but some surmised it was Oswald or "one of the Oswalds" that was operational in Dallas at the time. There was an Oswald "look-alike" who was a local gunsmith in Dallas and may have been the one who set up the illegal sale of the full automatic weapons to a Dallas group of anti-Castro Cubans, who was the focus of Ellsworth's investigation.[223]

On the day of the assassination, Agent Ellsworth was asked by the Dallas Police Department to come and interview the suspect that he had released the day before. So Ellsworth assumed they were talking about Oswald, but it was actually in reference to John Thomas Masen, who was a dead ringer for Lee Harvey Oswald. The whole thing seemed way too coincidental to Agent Ellsworth, who certainly knew his way around the Dallas gun-running subculture very well. Masen also was closely connected to the extreme right-wing Minutemen group and oil millionaire H. L. Hunt.[224]

And in that same book, military intelligence operative Richard Case Nagell, whose specific intelligence mission was to investigate how Oswald was being set up and why, also shows us that H. L. Hunt was possibly connected to Oswald and to the activities that set the stage for the JFK assassination.[225]

Now add to all of that gun purchase drama, the point that I made earlier, that another military intelligence operative, Tosh Plumlee, in his sworn affidavit, states that when he came across Oswald in Dallas, he was acting operationally in an undercover role as part of a government-sanctioned gunrunning operation involving an anti-Castro Cuban group in Dallas.[226]

---

[222] Graf & Bartholomew, "The Gun That Didn't Smoke."

[223] Russell, *The Man Who Knew Too Much,* 357–358.

[224] Ibid.

[225] Ibid, x, xxxii–xxxiii, 110–111, 143, 173, 189, 200, 203–204, 206, 252–254, 358–359, 374–376, 378, 519, 555, 588.

[226] Belzer & Wayne, *Dead Wrong,* "Affidavit of William R. Plumlee," 111–115.

All of a sudden, connecting the dots, it sure looks like that's what was actually happening with Oswald in Dallas.

So we've looked at Oswald's intelligence connections and already know that he was a "false defector" to the Soviet Union as part of an intelligence operation. Looking now at all this gun evidence, it sure as hell looks like he was *also* working undercover for the Feds in the above-described sting operation.

By the way, Oswald even wrote a letter to a "Mr. Hunt" asking for "clarification," and handwriting experts have substantiated that it was in Oswald's writing.[227] You've probably never heard that before, but it's true. Some have speculated the Mr. Hunt was E. Howard Hunt Jr., the future Watergate burglar who was an agent specializing in Cuba for the CIA. But an even more likely suspect, if you ask me, was H. L. Hunt. Oswald's letter was written on November 8, 1963, just a couple weeks before the assassination took place. Here's the contents of that letter, *verbatim*:

> Nov. 8, 1963
> Dear Mr. Hunt,
> I would like information concerning my position.
> I am asking only for information
> I am suggesting that we discuss the matter fully before any steps are taken by me or anyone else
> Thank You,
> (signed) Lee Harvey Oswald[228]
>
> ───────────
> [228] news.google.com/newspapers?nid=1891&dat=19770403&id=56QfAAAAIBAJ&sjid =PdYEAAAAIBAJ&pg=3049,190328

Speechless? You should be! But you should also be asking yourself why it is that the government has never shown the slightest interest in that letter, since it first surfaced back in 1975. Lord Almighty, it's been *fifty years* of this! Can't they just give all the evidence to the public, once and for all?

I've said it before and I'll say it again, folks:

We Can Handle The Truth!

───────────

[227] Michael T. Griffith, "Just The Facts: Established Facts About the JFK Assassination That Point to Conspiracy," March 5, 2002: michaelgriffith1.tripod.com/justthefacts.htm

22

The "Backyard Photo" Of Oswald Was Deemed a Forgery

The Warren Commission said that Oswald was linked to the rifle that killed JFK because two photographs were found of Oswald posing with what they said was the exact same rifle. The photographs were taken in the yard of someone's house and have since come to be known as the "backyard photos."

Even though they were not found in the first police searches of Oswald's belongings—which one would think were fairly thorough considering the fact that they were already saying that he had just killed the President of the United States—the Dallas police said they found two photographs of Oswald holding a rifle. Since the rest of the evidence was so weak, those two photos were used to spotlight his link to the murder weapon. The photo of Oswald with that rifle was plastered right onto the front cover of *Life Magazine*. Everybody saw that and it basically convicted Oswald in the court of public opinion.

Both of those photos show Oswald's figure in a different pose but in the same location.

However, there are a number of anomalies regarding the photographs, as well as a number of irregularities concerning the circumstances surrounding the discovery of the photographs.

Photographic expert Major John Pickard was a former commander of the photographic department of the Canadian Defense Department. He professionally examined the photographs and declared them to be fakes.

Another photographic expert, Detective Superintendent Malcolm Thompson (retired), was a past president of the Institute of Incorporated Photographers in England. Detective Thompson analyzed the photographs in question and came to the same professional conclusion as Major Pickard—they were faked.

Yet another photographic expert, Jack White, has spent more than two decades on the case and also concluded that the photos were faked. Many of White's professional determinations are explained in a video study that's available online. If that study gets removed, just Google "Fake: The Forged Photograph That Framed Lee Harvey Oswald": youtube.com/watch?v=UJemmagl0tI.

That photograph of Oswald with the rifle was actually shown to Oswald at the police station while he was in custody after the shooting. Quite obviously, Oswald knew something about that photograph of himself standing with a rifle. Oswald seemed to be playing it cagey, holding his cards close to his vest. Here's how he responded to the police when shown the photograph—and note the implied knowledge in Oswald's response:

> In time I will be able to show you that this is not my picture, but
> I don't want to answer any more questions . . . I will not discuss
> this photograph without advice of an attorney. . . . That picture
> is not mine, but the face is mine. The picture has been made by
> superimposing my face. The other part of the picture is not me
> at all, and I have never seen this picture before. I understand
> photography real well, and that, in time, I will be able to show
> you that is not my picture and that it has been made by someone
> else. . . . The small picture was reduced from the larger one,
> made by some persons unknown to me.[229]

Photographic experts think they have figured out what Oswald was talking about in that cagey remark.

There are indications of fraud in the backyard photos that are obvious even to the layman. For example, the shadow of Oswald's

---

[229] "The Last Words of Lee Harvey Oswald: Compiled by Mae Brussell."

nose falls in one direction while the shadow of his body falls in
another direction. And the shadow under Oswald's nose remains
the same in all three photos even when his head is tilted.[230]

Another photo was also discovered later, making that three, as the above
quote references.

Then, in 1977, a much clearer version of 133-A was found
among the possessions of George de Mohrenschildt, a wealthy
member of the Dallas Russian community who had intelligence
connections and who was a friend of Oswald's. The de Mohrenschildt family has stated they believe the photo was planted in
their father's belongings to further incriminate Oswald in the
public mind.[231]

Another indication that they were artificially produced is the sameness of
everything in the background. It's a strong indication that the things in the fore-
ground were manipulated, because background just can't be exactly the same in
every different photograph.

Another indication of fakery in the photos is the fact that the
HSCA's photographic panel could find only minute ("very
small") differences in the distances between objects in the backgrounds. This virtual sameness of backgrounds is a virtual
impossibility given the manner in which the pictures were supposedly taken. In order to achieve this effect, Marina would have
had to hold the camera in almost the exact same position, to
within a tiny fraction of an inch each time, for each of the three
photos, an extremely unlikely scenario, particularly in light of the
fact that Oswald allegedly took the camera from her in between
pictures to advance the film.

Furthermore, graphics expert Jack White has shown that the
backgrounds in the photos are actually identical, and that the
small differences in distance were artificially produced by a
technique known as key stoning.[232]

---

[230] Griffith, "Faulty Evidence: Problems with the Case Against Lee Harvey Oswald,":
michaelgriffith1.tripod.com/faulty.htm

[231] Ibid.

[232] Ibid.

There are a lot of strange things about those photos.

- The shadows are all wrong and photographic experts agreed on that point;[233]
- The totally identical backgrounds are not photographically possible under actual circumstances;[234]
- The background shadows were never duplicated. It was claimed that photographer Lawrence Schiller managed to duplicate them, but upon examination, that was clearly not the case;[235]
- As investigative author Anthony Summers observed, another major oddity in the backyard photos is that in one of them, the Oswald figure is wearing a ring on a finger of his left hand, but in another photo, the ring is not visible. That is definitely "a curious difference, if, as Marina testified, she took one picture after another in the space of a few moments";[236]
- The shirt and watch worn that appear to be on the Oswald figure in the photographs could not be located anywhere in Oswald's possessions;[237]
- The shirt on the Oswald figure in the photos was a pullover style shirt and was not the type of shirt that Oswald wore;[238]
- Oswald's wife, Marina Oswald, is the one who supposedly took those photos, according to the United States Government. But get a load of this. Marina is *on-camera* saying that she never took them. When she was shown those photographs, her exact words were, "These aren't the pictures I took."[239]

Then there's what I would call the Common Sense Factor.
Note that *all of these* photographs were found after:

- Oswald told the police that some of his belongings were in the garage of the house of some friends named the Paines;

---

[233] Griffith, "Faulty Evidence."

[234] Ibid.

[235] Ibid.

[236] Summers, *Conspiracy.*

[237] Griffith, "Faulty Evidence."

[238] Ibid.

[239] Harrison Edward Livingstone, *High Treason 2*, (Carroll & Graf: 1992).

- Oswald told police where the Paines' house was;
- The house was thoroughly searched on several occasions by "various waves" of FBI agents and Dallas and Irvine police search teams;
- Then and *only* then, were the two incriminating photos of Oswald with the rifle supposedly discovered;
- The third photograph in the "matching set" was not found until fourteen years later in 1977 at an entirely different location, and the family who lived there believed that it was planted there.[240]

So think this out for a second: You're being grilled by the police, but even under intense questioning, you completely maintain your innocence. You even *tell* the police precisely where they can locate some of your belongings. Now ask yourself this one: Would a guy who left incredibly incriminating photos really direct the cops right to their specific location? Do you really think Oswald thought those photos were there? And if he did, why would he send the police there? In fact, if he knew those photos were there, why wouldn't he have destroyed them before committing the planned out "murder of the century"? I don't think so.

But hey, don't take my word for it. It doesn't matter what I think. Below are some excerpts from the transcript of testimony by a well-acknowledged forensic photographic expert. For twenty-five years, Detective Superintendent Malcolm Thompson was head of a Police Forensic Science Laboratory Identification Bureau. And it *does* matter what he thinks.

QUESTION: Mr. Thompson, would these photographs be acceptable as evidence in a British court of law?

DETECTIVE

THOMPSON: No. I have examined these photographs and have established without doubt that there is retouching on them...

QUESTION: So you think that those shadows have actually been touched in?

---

[240] Griffith, "Faulty Evidence."

DETECTIVE
THOMPSON: They have been touched in. Again, there is something peculiar about this hand. The entire hand and arm is very, very unnatural. It possibly could have been stuck in afterward; but I can't relate physiologically the position of that arm to the body.

The butt of the rifle I think is the telltale in this picture here where we see very, very little of the butt actually protruding beyond the trouser line and yet down here having been painted in is a very, very large butt. I say very large in relation to the length of the shadow and we can measure the length of that shadow in relation to the height of the person and measure off the butt of the gun as against the shadow of the butt and that is to me unnatural.

The head itself, I have seen photographs of Oswald and his chin is not square. He has a rounded chin. Having said that, the subject in this picture has a square chin but again it doesn't take any stretch of the imagination to appreciate that from the upper lip to the top of the head is Oswald and one can only conclude that Oswald's head has been stuck on to a chin, not being Oswald's chin.

Then to cover up the montage, retouching has been done both to the right, that is Oswald's right and Oswald's left and when we consider this area of retouching here—compare it with what we see in photograph A [where] we have a shadow cast by this wooden pillar. I have measured those and even allowing for the difference and degree of enlargement between photograph A and photograph B the area we see in shadow here is far in excess of what it should be and of course that is the area to which I referred

earlier on where the pillar coming down does not continue in a straight line but has this bulge in it.

QUESTION: Are there other things about the face itself which would
make you suspicious?

DETECTIVE
THOMPSON: Yes, again we have a shadow underneath the nose. In
photographs A and B you see Oswald's face in a different posture and yet the shadow under the nose hasn't
moved or if it has moved it is only fractional compared
with the actual movement we see in the face and one
comes to the conclusion that it is the same picture used
for both faces, possibly in this face here he has got a
scowl on his face and there has been retouching done
in the chin area which is what one would expect if my
conclusion is correct, that this face has been added on
to the chin.

He has a very, very thick lower lip here which is
not consistent with Oswald's lip and again the shadow
underneath the lip is a horizontal shadow, that is consistent in both, even allowing for the fact that we have
a slight tilt in the head of photograph B as against that
in photograph A.

QUESTION: How easy is it to make a photo montage like this, how
would people go about it?

DETECTIVE
THOMPSON: It's not difficult. If one has a background scene, the
subject [is] photographed against a white background
making it simpler to cut out the subject from the back.

QUESTION: Do you believe that those photographs are a fake?

DETECTIVE
THOMPSON: I think they are false and possibly the shadow detail
and its relation to the static scene and the body are the
giveaway, plus the fact there is retouching in sufficient
salient places to make one appreciate that something

peculiar has gone on in relation to the head and the body and the areas surrounding it.

QUESTION: Was your method to look for discrepancies?

DETECTIVE

THOMPSON: Exactly, that has been my life's work looking for the unusual and comparing one thing with another to see similarities or dissimilarities.

QUESTION: And what in general has been your conclusion in looking at those two photographs?

DETECTIVE

THOMPSON: In general I have come to the conclusion that we have a montage of three pictures to make one end product as we see it here today.

QUESTION: So does it strike you as strange that in their search, after all connected with the assassination of a president, that they should find such damning evidence the next day?

DETECTIVE

THOMPSON: It does, it does seem unusual. One would think that the officers involved would be highly experienced officers, would know and have been trained to carry out the search of premises.

QUESTION: Is there any possibility in your mind that those two photographs are genuine?

DETECTIVE

THOMPSON: I don't think there is any possibility; having examined them for a considerable time it is my considered opinion that they are not genuine.[241]

---

[241] Griffith, "Faulty Evidence."

23

Oswald Denied Shooting the President and Modern Voice Technologies Determined He Was Telling the Truth

If you haven't heard the clip where Oswald proclaims his innocence, you should really listen closely to it. It's right on the Internet; just search "Lee Harvey Oswald declares 'I'm just a patsy'" or go straight to: youtube.com/watch?v=T9F-szqv_RIv.

What you see and hear on that clip is a man who seems genuinely confused about the circumstances of his arrest, yet stringently maintains his innocence. He asks for legal representation which, as he says, has been denied. He acknowledges he was in that Book Depository building but points out that he works there, so of course he was there. He denies shooting anyone and says that he was "a patsy"; that he was set up. It's pretty powerful stuff.

Well, it occurred to some very savvy researchers, that technologies even by the mid-1970s had improved a great deal since 1963 and they had yet to be applied to the case of the Kennedy assassination. So they took the clearly recorded voice of Oswald saying those things and subjected it to the latest voice technologies.

Psychological Stress Evaluation (PSE) is a scientific method of measuring voice stress. It measures and registers the stress level of the person as they say each word. PSE testing was actually developed by experts in the intelligence community.[242]

> The PSE was invented in 1970 by a group of intelligence experts
> who sought to improve upon the traditional polygraph. Two of
> the PSE's inventors, Allan D. Bell Jr. and Charles H. McGuiston,
> both retired lieutenant colonels from army intelligence, discovered
> that the frequencies composing the human voice shift from eight
> to fourteen times every second. But when the speaker is under
> stress, this frequency modulation disappears. What remains are
> the pure component frequencies of the voice—and a strong indi-
> cation that the speaker is lying…[243]

George O'Toole, the former head of the CIA's Problem Analysis Branch,[244] wrote the book on PSE—literally—and explains the function:

> Stress is a necessary, but not sufficient, condition of lying; it
> must be interpreted, and therein lies the margin of error. But
> the absence of stress is a sufficient condition of truthfulness. If
> someone is talking about a matter of real importance to him-
> self and shows absolutely no stress, then he must be telling the
> truth.[245]

It's acknowledged legally, and in fact—unlike the lie detector test, the poly-graph—Voice Stress Analysis evidence *is* admissible evidence in a court of law. As historian Michael Griffith notes:

> The PSE has been shown to be reliable in several tests. It is used
> by hundreds of U.S. law enforcement agencies, and it is accepted
> as evidence in more than a dozen states.[246]

---

[242] Penthouse News Release, "Lee Harvey Oswald apparently was telling the truth when he said he did not kill President John F. Kennedy, a new-type lie detector that examines the human voice for stress reveals," 10 March 1975: jfk.hood.edu/Collection/Weisberg%20Subject%20Index%20Files/O%20Disk/O'Toole%20George%203-10-75/Item%2001.pdf

[243] Ibid.

[244] Ibid.

[245] George O'Toole, *The Assassination Tapes: An electronic probe into the Murder of John F. Kennedy and the Dallas Cover-up* (Penthouse Press, 1975).

[246] Michael T. Griffith, "Hasty Judgment: A Reply to Gerald Posner-Why the JFK Case is Not Closed," 8 April 1998: karws.gso.uri.edu/jfk/the_critics/griffith/Hasty_Judgment.html

That scientific voice analysis and evaluation of Oswald's recorded voice overwhelmingly indicated that Oswald was being truthful about his innocence. Here are the results of those tests on Oswald's recorded statements, direct from and in the words of Lloyd H. Hitchcock, the man who conducted the testing. Hitchcock was not only a member of the American Polygraph Association; he actually wrote the manuals on polygraph training and was also a former Army intelligence officer:[247]

- Oswald denied shooting anybody—the president, the policeman, anybody. The psychological stress evaluator said he was telling the truth.[248]
- There is no other plausible interpretation of the Oswald PSE charts than the explanation that Oswald was simply telling the truth.[249]
- My PSE analysis of these recordings indicates very clearly that Oswald believed he was telling the truth when he denied killing the president.[250]

The plain fact of the matter is that Oswald didn't act *anything like* an assassin. And now we know that he didn't sound like one either!

---

[247] Penthouse News Release, "Lee Harvey Oswald apparently was telling the truth."

[248] O'Toole, *The Assassination Tapes.*

[249] O'Toole, *The Assassination Tapes.*

[250] Ibid.

24

"Umbrella Man" and "Radio Man" in Dealey Plaza Appeared To Be Acting Operationally

"Umbrella Man" and "Radio Man" were two individuals in Dealey Plaza who appeared to be operational in some sort of signaling capacity that enabled the assassination. The crossfire on JFK initiated right after the opening of the umbrella and the device the other man was carrying is identifiable as a radio transmitter. The reactions of the two men also differed from those of everyone else in the plaza. While people were frantically running around, they behaved quite differently. They were calmly sitting down right next to each other on the curb, and then parting in opposite directions without saying a word. Efforts to explain their odd actions have been notably inadequate.

Still photography and film footage taken at the time of the assassination confirmed that the actions of the two men were in stark contrast with what would be expected from having just witnessed the murder of the President at close range and with the actions of others who were also eyewitnesses to that event.

The existence of the "umbrella man" and the dark-complexion[ed] man is fact. Their activities after the assassination

> especially bear study. While virtually everyone in Dealey Plaza
> was moved to action by the assassination—either falling to the
> ground for cover or moving toward The Grassy Knoll—these
> two men sat down beside each other on the north sidewalk of
> Elm Street.[251]

The two men were both standing very close to President Kennedy's car when the shots rang out. One of the men held an umbrella—even though it was a sunny day and was not raining—which he thrust up in the air just as the President went by him and pumped the umbrella open and closed. The other man stood right at the curb as the President passed by and held his arms up, swinging them in the air, and then made a fist with one of his upheld arms high in the air.

You can see a good photograph of that, too. If it *was* a signal to shooters or to a com team (communications coordinators), it was a pretty clear one. Right at the curb, just as the President's car passes through the most open area of that kill zone, you've got a white man in dark clothes holding an open umbrella; and even closer—in fact, on the street itself—you've got a dark-complexioned man in a white shirt holding his tight fist as high as he could in the air. It sure *looks* like a signal, because it would have been hard to miss. Check it out for yourself; the photo at the top of Russ Baker's article[252] is pretty clear: whowhatwhy. com/2011/11/28/ny-times%E2%80%99-umbrella-man-exposed/.

Then, when the flurry of gunshots had finally stopped, the photographic evidence also established that the two men reacted very differently than everyone around them. Almost every eyewitness reacted in one of two ways: either they hit the ground, shielding their loved ones from gunfire, or they joined the few dozen other people who raced up the grassy knoll area because it had seemed to many like that area was the source of the gunfire.

But instead, as the footage reveals, the two men casually sat down upon the curb. One man pulled out what clearly appeared to be a two-way radio and

---

[251] Marrs, *Crossfire: The Plot that Killed Kennedy*, 29–32; Jim Fetzer, "JFK, the CIA and the New York Times," 29 November 2011: veteranstoday.com/2011/11/29/jfk-the-cia-and-the-new-york-times-2/

[252] Russ Baker, "New York Times' Umbrella Man Exposed," 28 November 2011: whowhatwhy.com/2011/11/28/ny-times%E2%80%99-umbrella-man-exposed/

spoke into it. Then the two men—without seeming to talk to each other even though they had been sitting right next to each other—stood up from the curb and walked calmly away in the exactly *opposite* directions. And as the man who spoke on the radio walked away, he could be seen hiding the radio.

There are a number of photographs in existence of the two men and it's an accurate description to say that their actions are disturbingly unusual. They can be seen online, too; for a good compilation of them, just Google: JFK Umbrella Man & Dark-Complexioned Man or go to: youtube.com/watch?feature=player_detailpage&v=NB-TLTWAh6s.

Since those actions took place just as the gunfire opened up on the motorcade, researchers noted that they may have been a signal of some sort to the shooters, possibly of noting that the target—the President—was not yet down. Whether or not it was a signal, the head shot that killed President Kennedy took place immediately after. Since the man with the umbrella had not been identified, he was referred to as the "Umbrella Man." No one knew who the man with the radio was either so, since he had a dark complexion, researchers called him the "Dark-Complexioned Man."

Here's the way author Jim Marrs described the eerie event:

About the time that Kennedy was first hit by a bullet, two men standing near each other on the north sidewalk of Elm Street acted most strangely—one began pumping a black umbrella while the other waved his right arm high in the air.

As Kennedy's limousine began the gentle descent into Dealey Plaza, a man can be seen standing near the street-side edge of the Stemmons Freeway sign holding an open umbrella. He holds the umbrella in a normal fashion and the top of the umbrella almost reaches the bottom of the sign.

In photos taken minutes before Kennedy's arrival, the umbrella is closed and, immediately after the shooting, pictures show the umbrella was closed again. The man's umbrella was only open during the shooting sequence. Furthermore, as seen in the Zapruder film, once Kennedy is exactly opposite the man with the umbrella, it was pumped almost two feet into the air and then lowered.

At the same time, the second man—in photos he appears to be
of a dark complexion, perhaps a black man or Hispanic—raised
his right hand into the air possibly making a fist. This man was
located on the outer edge of the Elm Street sidewalk opposite
the umbrella man, who was on the inner edge.

The man with the open umbrella was the only person in Dealey
Plaza with an open umbrella. Under the warm Texas sun, there
was no reason to carry an open umbrella at that time.[253]

By the time of the Congressional hearings by the House Select Committee
on Assassinations, researchers drew public attention to "Umbrella Man" and
"Radio Man" and asked Congress to investigate them.

Well, coincidentally—or quite suspiciously, depending on your point of
view—someone then came forward. A man who had been a Dallas insurance
salesman in 1963 announced, during the hearings of the Committee, that he had
been the man with the umbrella. His name was Louie Steven Witt.

Mr. Witt sounded pretty strange from the start. He contacted two authors
and they agreed to meet with him. Here's the way one of those authors described
their meeting and his impression of Mr. Witt:

I felt the man had been coached. He would answer no questions
and pointedly invited us to leave. His only positive statement,
which seemed to come very quickly, was that he was willing to
appear before the House Select Committee on Assassinations in
Washington.[254]

He got his wish, though. Witt was called to testify at the Congressional hearing. It was some very interesting testimony, too.

Witt told the Committee that on the spur of the moment, he
grabbed a large black umbrella and went to Dealey Plaza to
heckle Kennedy. He claimed that someone had told him that
an open umbrella would rile Kennedy. While Witt offered

---

[253] Marrs, *Crossfire: The Plot that Killed Kennedy*, 29–32; Jim Fetzer, "JFK, the CIA and the
New York Times," 29 November 2011: veteranstoday.com/2011/11/29/jfk-the-cia-and-the-
new-york-times-2/

[254] Marrs, *Crossfire: The Plot that Killed Kennedy*, 32.

no further explanation of how his umbrella could heckle the
president, Committee members—not Witt—theorized that the
umbrella in some way referred to the pro-German sympathies
of Kennedy's father while serving as U.S. ambassador to Britain
just prior to World War II. They said the umbrella may have
symbolized the appeasement policies of Britain's Prime Minister
Neville Chamberlain, who always carried an umbrella.[255]

Well, as much as I hate to correct my former colleagues in the government (and yes, I'm smiling when I write that), it is historically inaccurate that
an umbrella symbolizes Chamberlain's appeasement policies to the Nazis; and
neither Chamberlain *nor* Joe Kennedy were ever pro-Germany; they were just
anti-war, as many people were at the time.[256] But that was supposedly why
Mr. Witt did what Mr. Witt did; which doesn't make any sense, and we'll get
to that in a minute.

As far as what he actually did, Mr. Witt went into precise detail about his
actions of that afternoon; where he was, when he opened up the umbrella, what
he saw and what he did not see, and when he saw it. Well, there's one big problem here, folks:

> Based on the available photographs made that day, none of
> Witt's statements were an accurate account of the actions of
> the "umbrella man" who stood waiting for the motorcade with
> his umbrella in the normal over-the-head position and then
> pumped it in the air as Kennedy passed.

> Witt's bizarre story—unsubstantiated and totally at variance with
> the actions of the man in the photographs—resulted in few, if any,
> researchers accepting Louie Steven Witt as the "umbrella man."[257]

---

[255] Marrs, *Crossfire: The Plot that Killed Kennedy*, 29–32; Jim Fetzer, "JFK, the CIA and the New York Times," 29 November 2011: veteranstoday.com/2011/11/29/jfk-the-cia-and-the-new-york-times-2/

[256] Russ Baker, "JFK Umbrella Man – More Doubts," 6 December 2011: lewrockwell.com/orig11/baker-r8.1.1.html

[257] Marrs, *Crossfire: The Plot that Killed Kennedy*, 29–32; Jim Fetzer, "JFK, the CIA and the New York Times," 29 November 2011: veteranstoday.com/2011/11/29/jfk-the-cia-and-the-new-york-times-2/

His account of his entire day doesn't add up either. Here are some of the incongruities in his testimony that research veteran Jim DiEugenio noticed:

1. He never planned on doing what he did until that morning.
2. He did not know the exact parade route.
3. He just happened to wander around for a walk and guessed where it would be.
4. He did what he did with no relation to JFK's policies, only Joseph Kennedy Sr.
5. What did the Cuban-looking guy say? Words to the effect of "They shot those people." (Oh really, Louie?)
6. Admits he sat there for up to three minutes and that he never even looked behind him at the picket fence! (Truly surprising.)
7. He never did anything like this before or since, and he was not a member of any conservative group or organization.
8. He placed the umbrella on the sidewalk and then picked it up. He wavers on whether this is definitely the umbrella he had that day.
9. He often uses the conditional, like I think that is me, or that may be the guy I sat next to.[258]

So his testimony just didn't add up at all, but also—and way too conveniently in many observers' opinions—it explained away an uncomfortable aspect of the evidence that researchers had forced Congress to take a look at even though they hadn't really wanted to look there. In other words, *next case, please.*

> It seemed far more likely that, by pumping his umbrella, Witt
> was signaling to the assassins that JFK was still alive, which
> makes sense, rather than an obscure historical allusion that no
> one, including Jack Kennedy, would have grasped.[259]

On top of all that, Witt testified under oath that he had no recollection of a dark-complexioned man who, in photographs, appeared to possibly be Cuban. Witt said that a "Negro man" sat down near him and kept repeating, "They done shot them folks."[260]

---

[258] Jim DiEugenio, "Tink's Performance in The New York Times," 25 November 2011, *The Education Forum*: educationforum.ipbhost.com/index.php?showtopic=18412&page=6

[259] Jim Fetzer, "JFK, the CIA and the New York Times," 29 November 2011: veteranstoday. com/2011/11/29/jfk-the-cia-and-the-new-york-times-2/

[260] Marrs, *Crossfire: The Plot that Killed Kennedy*, 29–32.

I'd like to point out here that—whether it made any sense or not—Mr. Witt's dubious and even evidence-contradicting testimony was, as you might have guessed, welcomed and highlighted by all the illustrious Warren Commission supporters in the press with headlines like "'Umbrella man' not sinister after all"; and in a way that strongly implied that at least another wacko conspiracy theory had fortunately now been debunked.[261] They embraced that false conclusion immediately, and very publicly, too. But I guess that's just another coincidence, right? That must be just another delusion from another paranoid kook who sees conspiracies everywhere.

But, if any of those delightful "debunkers" of conspiracy theories were to actually examine the *testimony* of that witness, they may be surprised to see that—depending on your generosity—it's not in accordance with the evidence, preposterous or ludicrous. And that's not *me*, mind you; that's the way that serious researchers have referred to it.[262]

His account of his activities that day don't track with what
Umbrella Man actually did, raising questions as to whether this
man who volunteered to testify to the assassination inquiry is
even the real umbrella-bearer, or someone whose purpose was to
end inquiries into the matter.[263]

And on top of all those reasons, how 'bout this one? *It didn't make any sense!* The witness would have been a little kid when Chamberlain had his umbrella, so how would he have understood all the subtleties and political significance of that? That's even if the umbrella reference *was* historically correct, which it wasn't![264] Plus, President Kennedy riding by thousands of people in his motorcade that day would probably never have noticed one guy with an umbrella. Even if he *had* noticed, what exactly is this guy's story here? If Kennedy saw one guy (out of thousands) holding an umbrella, he then is automatically supposed to think "Oh, an umbrella—That *must* be in reference to Prime Minister Neville

---

[261] Margaret Gentry, "'Umbrella man' not sinister after all," September 26, 1978, *Associated Press*: news.google.com/newspapers?nid=1298&dat=19780926&id=6wFOAAAAIBAJ&sjid=HowDAAAAIBAJ&pg=4995,3669986

[262] Russ Baker, "New York Times' Umbrella Man Exposed," 28 November 2011: whowhatwhy.com/2011/11/28/ny-times%E2%80%99-umbrella-man-exposed/

[263] Ibid.

[264] Russ Baker, "JFK Umbrella Man – More Doubts," 6 December 2011: lewrockwell.com/orig11/baker-r8.1.1.html

Chamberlain, and thereby, Joseph Kennedy's appeasement policies during World War II when my Dad was Ambassador to Great Britain!" *Are you kidding me?*

Isn't that the most insane explanation of something you've ever heard in your life? And they call conspiracy theorists *nuts?* I don't know about you, but I'd say that "delightful weirdness" is an extremely generous description of the above explanation!

Of course, that didn't stop *The New York Times* from pushing a piece that they liked on how an explanation of such "delightful weirdness" with such a "non-sinister" reality just simply *had* to be true.

That was in an *Op-Doc* for *The New York Times* a couple years ago in a splashy piece they did for the anniversary of Kennedy's assassination. Watch it online and see the sly, sneaky ways that they twist the truth with their media spin. Just Google: Op Doc Umbrella Man or go right to: dailymotion.com/video/xmmhck_the-umbrella-man-errol-morris-for-the-new-york-times_shortfilms.

This is from that little film clip that *The New York Times* spoke so lovingly of. Without even questioning the total absence of logic in the witnesses' story of what happened, they somehow manage to reach the following conclusion which is *every bit* as illogical as that man's testimony:

> What it means is, if you have any fact which you think is really sinister—*Forget it*, man. Because you can never, on your own, think up all the *non*-sinister, perfectly valid explanations for that fact. A cautionary tale![265]

Well that'd be nice, and even comforting (like it's apparently meant to be), except for the fact that it *simply isn't true.* So I guess it'd be cute, even "delightful," if it wasn't for the point that it was completely wrong regarding an occurrence that quite probably had something to do with how the brains of the 35th President of the United States got splattered all over a Texas street in broad daylight one Friday afternoon. And in broad *sunlight* it should be noted too, in regard to "Umbrella Man," whoever that individual actually was.

---

[265] "The Umbrella Man - Errol Morris for The New York Times," *Op-Doc for The New York Times*, November 22, 2011: dailymotion.com/video/xmmhck_the-umbrella-man-errol-morris-for-the-new-york-times_shortfilms

25

The "Three Tramps" Photographed in Dealey Plaza After the Assassination Were Not Actually Tramps

Another issue that stirred controversy was that several photographs were taken of three men who were arrested shortly after the assassination. In point of fact, they never *were* arrested, but they *appear* to be in custody and look to be led down the street by officers.

But there are a lot of weird things that researchers noticed about those photographs. The men were reportedly "three tramps" who police had found inside the boxcar of a freight train near the spot where Kennedy was killed. But they didn't actually *look* like tramps. For example, they had very good shoes. If you look closely at the photos, the cops who are with them seem very relaxed; *too* relaxed, in some observers' opinions. If you look online by searching "JFK three tramps," you'll see what I mean.

The FBI said that the three men in the photos were just tramps; that they were arrested, checked out, and then released. They even released their names: Gus Abrams, Harold Doyle, and John F. Gedney. Researchers checked it out, and sure enough, the specific three individuals whom the FBI had conveniently identified, actually *were* arrested and were apparently homeless. But notably absent was any proof that they were actually the same three men who had appeared in those photos. So everybody sort of wrote that one off; even Oliver Stone, director of the film *JFK*, apparently said that "he'd be happy to concede that one mystery had been resolved" on the condition that he'd still like to see photos of the men matched with the photos of the tramps.[266]

But further controversy has ensued over the years because other researchers have attributed "photographic matches" to various individuals. You may have heard or seen it written that CIA agent E. Howard Hunt was "one of the three tramps in Dealey Plaza." Part of the confusion resulted from sorting out the arrest records of men who were taken in by police after the assassination. Other researchers "identified" people they thought were likely conspirators—such as Sturgis and Hunt—and became convinced by the photographic similarities that it was actually them in the photos.

But it's easy to compare photographs and be "taken in"; convinced of a match in identities that turns out to have been incorrect. That's why police departments only trust forensic artists to make scientific matches using proven methods in the practice of criminology.

Forensic expert Lois Gibson is known as The World's Most Successful Forensic Artist. She is the world record holder for the most forensic success stories; over a thousand criminals have been caught by her forensic methods.[267] So Lois Gibson was the perfect person to examine the evidence and make the precise photographic comparisons between the photographs taken of the three men and those whom various people allege they may have actually been. Her work was successful in that regard.

She knows what she's doing and you can see that for yourself. Lois Gibson's "Slide Presentation of The Three Tramps" is online at: jfkmurdersolved.com/lois1.htm.

Analysis by Lois Gibson positively identified the three men—via an extensive and professional match process that she documents very specifically in that study—as Chauncey Holt, Charles Rogers, and Charles Harrelson.[268]

---

[266] John Aloysious Farrell, "'JFK' director, in capital, discusses files," March 5, 1992, *Boston Globe*: pqasb.pqarchiver.com/boston/access/61720029.html?FMT=ABS&FMTS=ABS:FT&type=current&date=Mar+05%2C+1992&author=John+Aloysius+Farrell%2C+Globe+Staff&pub=Boston+Globe+(pre-1997+Fulltext)&desc=%60JFK'+director%2C+in+capital%2C+discusses+files&pqatl=google

[267] LoisGibson.com, "Bio of Lois Gibson," retrieved 3 May 2013: loisgibson.com/biography.asp

[268] Wim Dankbaar, "The Three Tramps," retrieved 3 May 2013: jfkmurdersolved.com/lois1.htm

Who are they?

Well, Chauncey Holt was an expert forger and career criminal with mobsters and also did work for the CIA; Charles Harrelson and Charles Rogers [also known as Richard Montoya] were convicted killers.

What's their story?

Rogers was a cold-blooded killer—*literally*, in his case. He's known as "The Icebox Killer" because in 1965 they found the pieces of his parents' chopped up bodies inside the freezer at Rogers' home. But Rogers disappeared; he took off on a private plane just as police came looking for him, and is still a wanted fugitive. Rogers was also known to do "work" for the CIA.[269] So *his* only comment on being one of the three tramps was *Adios.*

Harrelson was a professional hit man who was convicted for the assassination of a federal judge, John Wood, in Texas in 1979, and then died in prison of heart disease in 2007. He was also the estranged father of actor Woody Harrelson. During a six-hour standoff with police before his arrest, he confessed to killing both the federal judge and John F. Kennedy. But authorities wrote that off to the fact that he was "high on cocaine."[270] An attorney in Texas testified in court that Harrelson had told him that he killed President Kennedy and even drew the attorney a map of where he hid after the assassination.[271] But the FBI "discounted any involvement by Harrelson in the Kennedy assassination" and the information all went to a quiet resting place somewhere far from public scrutiny.[272] There's a chilling prison interview with Charles Harrelson in which he mockingly refers to the absurd naiveté of believing for one second that lone gunman Lee Harvey Oswald pulled off the

---

[269] John R. Craig & Phillip A. Rogers, *The Man on the Grassy Knoll* (Avon Books: 1992).

[270] Marrs, *Crossfire: The Plot That Killed Kennedy*, 333–335.

[271] Jay Jorden, "Kennedy controversy still goes on," *Associated Press*, November 22, 1982: news.google.com/newspapers?id=neBNAAAAIBAJ&sjid=H4sDAAAAIBAJ&pg=6841% 2C3312974

[272] Ibid.

assassination all by himself. Below is what he says, but I also suggest that you watch it for yourself at: youtube.com/watch?v=RpVlqh14WHY.

> Well, do you believe Lee Harvey Oswald killed President Kennedy. *Alone?* We'll get back to that. Without any aid from a rogue agency of the U.S. government, or at least a portion of that agency? I believe you're very naïve if you do.[273]

So Harrelson did or didn't really have a lot to say, depending on how you look at it.

Chauncey Holt was a completely different story though. He not only talked about it, he confessed to it, wrote about it, and even did a film about it. In fact, Chauncey Holt is *still* speaking about it, even from the grave! He died in 1997, but has his autobiography coming out later this year![274] So you probably won't see that in mainstream media anytime soon, but it's out there, believe me.

Holt was a career criminal who was a very colorful character. He was an expert in weaponry, ammunition loads, forgery, and accounting practices.[275] Holt describes the whole boxcar incident in detail in his book, as well as the details that preceded it.

The statements of Chauncey Holt *also* explain how the real "three tramps" were never traced. It's because they were never actually arrested.[276] There was no record of them in Dallas. They told police they were undercover agents with the ATF, showed their forged IDs, and said they were working on an operation involving stolen weapons. According to Holt, since that matched up with the weapons that were in the boxcar where the men were found, police let them go.[277] Veteran FBI Special Agent Zack Shelton has thoroughly verified the *bona fides* of Chauncey Marvin Holt.

Holt's criminal expertise dated back to working with Meyer Lansky, a criminal genius often credited with masterminding the Mob's entry into legitimate businesses as well as with organizing the intricacies of money laundering. Holt was a gifted artist who used those skills to become an expert forger. He was

---

[273] Charles Harrelson, "Hitman Charles Harrelson on the assassination of JFK," retrieved 3 May 2013: youtube.com/watch?v=RpVlqh14WHY

[274] Chauncey Holt, *Self-Portrait of a Scoundrel* (TrineDay: 2013).

[275] Ibid.

[276] Ibid.

[277] Ibid.

working out of a company called the Los Angeles Stamp & Stationery Company (LASCO). That company was what's known as a proprietary, a "CIA front" that was established with the help of William Harvey, the Agency's point man on assassinations as head of its program named ZR/Rifle. Most of LASCO's business was legitimate, but they also performed special work for "The Company" such as forged identifications of various types.

Holt began producing fake IDs that were used in Dallas for the assassination. Here it is summarized briefly, from the work substantiated by FBI veteran Zack Shelton:

> Chauncey Holt, an expert forger affiliated with both the Mafia and CIA, began producing IDs for Lee Harvey Oswald, including all of his aliases, around April, 1963. In June, Holt delivered the IDs to Guy Bannister in New Orleans, at which time Holt was photographed by news reporters in the same photo with Oswald. In or around October, Holt was instructed by his handler to prepare Secret Service Identification Pins for the President's trip to Dallas. On November 16, Holt received a letter from mobster Peter Licavoli stating that Chuck Nicoletti was at the Grace Ranch in Arizona and for Holt to come and drive Nicoletti to Dallas. On November 21, Holt drove Nicoletti to Dallas. On November 22, Holt delivered the Secret Service Pins; he drove into the railroad yard in a white 1959 Oldsmobile Station Wagon. This was corroborated by the testimony of [Lee] Bowers. When the shots rang out, he reported to the boxcar of the freight train, as he had been instructed, and met up there with Charles Harrelson and Charles Rogers (known to Holt as Richard Montoya). All three of these individuals were detained by the Dallas Police Department and later released. Several photographs were taken of these three men and they are known as the three tramps. Lois Gibson, respected forensic artist, verified the three as Holt and Charles Harrelson and Charles Rogers, two violent criminals.[278]

---

[278] Wim Dankbaar, *Files on JFK* (TrineDay: 2008) and Zack Shelton, *The Shelton Report*, in Belzer & Wayne, *Dead Wrong*, 132–135.

So the "three tramps," in addition to *not* being tramps, were actually three very experienced criminals who were apparently involved operationally in the JFK assassination. They may not have fired the actual shots (although in the case of Harrelson and Rogers, we do not know where they were at the time of the shots and they *were* both highly professional killers), but they seem to have all three been involved, at least in some type of support capacity.

26

Oswald Could Not Have Murdered Officer Tippit

In the exact same way that Oswald could not have shot President Kennedy, it has also been shown that he could not have shot Officer J. D. Tippit. He did not possess motive, means, or the opportunity. And if you can prove to a jury that you were not even present when a crime was committed, then that jury would find you not guilty of that crime. About forty minutes after President Kennedy was assassinated in Dealey Plaza, Dallas Police Officer J. D. Tippit was shot and killed by an unknown suspect in the Oak Cliff section of Dallas, a few miles away from Dealey Plaza. The official government version states that it was Lee Harvey Oswald who committed that crime, after which he sought shelter from police in a nearby movie theater and was arrested by an army of Dallas police officers shortly thereafter. To which I say, Bullshit!

Let's start with the official government version:

Dallas Police Officer J. D. Tippit saw a man who fit the description of the man wanted for President Kennedy's murder and attempted to arrest him, but the man—Lee Harvey Oswald—drew a weapon and gunned down Officer Tippit. As I believe I may have already emphatically stated, Bullshit!

In the [Warren] commission's account, J. D. Tippit, who was a
"fine, dedicated officer," was driving his patrol car when he saw
a man who fit the general description of the suspect wanted in
the murder of President Kennedy. This "fine, dedicated officer,"
who had the chance to make the arrest of a lifetime, did not try
to arrest this dangerous suspect, nor did he draw his gun [accord-
ing to the wanted description broadcast over the police radio, the
suspect was carrying a 30.06 rifle]. Instead, he called the man
over to his car and began having a casual conversation.[279]

Would you like to know the actual police description that really went over
the radio right before Tippit was killed? Here it is, *verbatim*:

Attention, all squads, the suspect is believed to be a white male,
age 30, 5 feet 10 inches, slender build, 165 pounds, armed with
what is thought to be a 30-30 rifle. No further description or
information at this time.

Thus the broadcast description was for a suspect that was neither short nor tall, a man that was neither large nor small, and
neither young nor old. It was a description for the average white
guy, while Oswald, a slight young man at 24 years of age and
only 131 pounds, was not a good fit for the description.[280]

So that didn't really fit Oswald's description even though it did fit the
description of thousands of other men in Dallas; not to even mention the huge
point that Oswald obviously was not carrying a rifle! So how the hell could that
explain stopping Oswald?

Then there's the bizarre fact of what actually happened when Tippit pulled
this pedestrian, whoever he was, over by the sidewalk after the officer curbed his
car. Tippit didn't even get out of his police car, let alone draw his weapon or tell
this guy to "assume the position." He just talked to him through the passenger
side of the police car. According to several eyewitnesses, they were conversing

---

[279] Michael L. Kurtz, *Crime of the Century: The Kennedy Assassination from a Historian's
Perspective* (University of Tennessee Press: 1993).

[280] Donald Byron Thomas, *Hear No Evil: Social Constructivism and the Forensic Evidence in the
Kennedy Assassination* (Mary Ferrell Foundation Press: 2010) 493. maryferrell.org/ mffweb/
archive/viewer/showDoc.do?docId=145592&relPageId=519

"amiably"; it was a *friendly* conversation. That's why all the witnesses were surprised when Tippit got shot by the guy. Because it hadn't seemed like anything sinister at all. But that *proves* that Tippit didn't think that guy was the killer, or else he obviously would've acted very differently. Everybody thought Tippit even *knew* the guy. And maybe he did.

First of all, it's a simple matter of timing. The official scenario is *not logistically plausible*. Oswald's exact whereabouts are clearly established at an *exact* time.

Oswald's whereabouts at 1:04 p.m. were pinpointed by his landlady, who looked out of the window and saw Oswald standing at the bus stop at that time.[281] At 1:06 p.m., only two minutes later, Officer Tippit, by some reports, had already been shot and lay dead on the ground. District Attorney Jim Garrison figured out that it wasn't logistically possible. He put the time of the shooting at 1:06 p.m. Garrison knew that *there wasn't time* for Oswald to have made it to that crime scene. Here's the way that a District Attorney figured the math on that one:

> First of all, given what was known about Oswald's movements, it was highly improbable that he could have been physically present at the time of Tippit's murder. According to several eyewitnesses at the scene, Tippit was shot anywhere from 1:06 p.m. to 1:10 p.m. Deputy Sheriff Roger Craig, who was at the Book Depository at the time, confirmed this. When he heard the report of Tippit's death on the radio, he looked at his watch; it was 1:06 p.m.

> And yet Oswald, it was generally acknowledged, had returned to his rooming house at around 1:00 p.m. He left quickly and Earline Roberts, the housekeeper, observed him standing by the northbound Beckley Avenue bus stop at 1:04. The area where Tippit was killed was in the opposite direction, a mile to the south. Using the broadest interpretation of the time element, even if Oswald had changed his mind about the bus and run southward, it was virtually impossible for him to have arrived at the scene before the shooting of the police officer.[282]

---

[281] Jim Garrison, *On the Trail of the Assassins: My Investigation and Prosecution of the Murder of President Kennedy* (Sheridan Square: 1988), cited at *Lee Harvey Oswald's "Murder" of Policeman JD Tippit*: scribblguy.50megs.com/tippit.htm

[282] Ibid.

Case closed, to borrow the term. That's a qualified District Attorney telling you that a suspect could not have even *been* at that crime scene!

So the Lone Nut Brigade was stuck and they apparently knew it. But try as they may:

> The Commission could not locate even one witness who saw
> Oswald walking or running between his rooming house and the
> scene of the Tippit slaying.[283]

So what did those wondrous protectors of justice known as the Warren Commission do about that point? I'll tell you what they did: they *moved the time*. That's right, Ladies and Gents, they just moved up the time of Tippit's murder to make it late enough for Oswald to have made it there. I kid you not.

> The Warren Commission officially placed the time of Tippit's
> death at 1:16 p.m., solving the aforementioned timing problem
> that was apparent after it became known that Oswald was wait-
> ing at the bus stop at 1:04 p.m.[284]

Then there's the problem with the eyewitnesses to the shooting. Big problem there, too. For openers, most of the eyewitnesses described the shooter as looking nothing at all like Lee Harvey Oswald.

> Acquilla Clemons lived on the north side of Tenth Street in Dal-
> las. On November 22, 1963, Clemons was sitting on the porch of
> her house when she saw Officer J. D. Tippit killed. Afterwards
> she claimed that there were two men involved in the attack on
> Tippit. She later testified that the gunman was a "short guy and
> kind of heavy" . . . The Dallas police warned her not to repeat
> this story to others or "she might get hurt." Clemons was not
> called to give evidence to the Warren Commission.[285]

You'll begin to notice a pattern in the witness testimony *and* in the way that testimony was "received" by law enforcement authorities in this case:

---

[283] Marrs, *Crossfire: The Plot that Killed Kennedy*, cited at:
spot.acorn.net/jfkplace/03/JDT/brundage.tippit
[284] Belzer & Wayne, *Hit List*, 8.
[285] John Simkin, "Acquilla Clemons: Biography," *Spartacus Educational*, accessed 30 Sept 2012:
spartacus.schoolnet.co.uk/JFKclemons.htm

Domingo Benevides, a dark, slim auto mechanic, was a witness to the murder of Officer Tippit who testified that he "really got a good view" of the slayer. He was not asked to see the police lineup in which Oswald appeared. Although he later said the killer resembled newspaper pictures of Oswald, he described the man differently: "I remember the back of his head seemed like his hairline sort of went square instead of tapered off...it kind of went down and squared off and made his head look flat in back." Domingo reports that he has been repeatedly threatened by police, and advised not to talk about what he saw.[286]

And here's one more, just to make sure that you notice the pattern:

Warren Reynolds did not see the shooting but saw the gunman running from the scene of the crime. He claimed that the man was not Oswald. After he survived an attempt to kill him, he changed his mind and identified Oswald as the man he had seen.[287]

Well, doesn't that speak highly of the legal system that was supposed to be investigating the assassination of the President and an officer of the Dallas Police Department? Instead of *following* the evidence, they *manipulated* it. And unfortunately, that's a pattern we see throughout this case by the various "Powers that Be" who were involved.

Then there was also the problem with the guns. It was reported that Officer Tippit was shot with an automatic weapon, yet Oswald was carrying a revolver. That's a huge difference.

Two witnesses at the scene of the shooting who were very familiar with firearms—a police Sergeant and a combat-experienced former Marine—said that the crime scene gun was an automatic.[288]

---

[286] David Welsh, "In the Shadow of Dallas: The Legacy of Penn Jones, Jr.," *Ramparts Magazine*, November 1966, pp 39–50: unz.org/Pub/Ramparts-1966nov-00039

[287] John Simkin, "Primary Sources: Murder of J. D. Tippit," *The Education Forum*, accessed 3 May 2013: spartacus.schoolnet.co.uk/JFKStippet.htm

[288] Michael T. Griffith, "Did Oswald Shoot Tippit?: A Review of Dale Myers' Book *With Malice: Lee Harvey Oswald and the Murder of Officer J.D. Tippit*," 2002: kenrahn.com/jfk/the_critics/griffith/With_Malice.html

District Attorney Garrison was keenly aware of that important point as well:

> As I continued my research, I discovered that beyond the eye-
> witnesses there was other evidence gathered and altered by
> the Dallas homicide unit showing that Lee Oswald had been
> framed in the Tippit murder. For instance, I read transcripts
> of the messages sent over the Dallas police radio shortly after
> the murder. These were recorded automatically on a log. Just
> minutes after a citizen first reported the murder on Tippit's
> radio, Patrolman H. W. Summers in Dallas police unit number
> 221 [the designation for the squad car] reported that an "eyeball
> witness to the getaway man" had been located. The suspect was
> described as having black wavy hair, wearing an Eisenhower
> jacket of light color, with dark trousers and a white shirt. He
> was "apparently armed with a .32, dark finish, automatic pistol,"
> which he had in his right hand. Moments later, Sergeant G. Hill
> reported that "the shell at the scene indicates that the suspect is
> armed with an automatic .38 rather than a pistol."[289]

It's pretty clear that if the crime scene gun was an automatic, then Oswald could not have shot Tippit.

Garrison arrived at that same conclusion:

> It seemed clear to me from this that the hand gun used to shoot
> Tippit was an automatic. But the gun allegedly taken from Lee
> Oswald when Dallas police later arrested him at the Texas The-
> atre was a revolver. Unless Oswald had stopped and changed
> guns, which no one had ever suggested, this fact alone put a severe
> hole in the government's case.[290]

People said a lot of things about Oswald, but having had an automatic was never one of 'em.

Then, on top of all of that, as I already showed in #19, the whole movie theater scenario was utterly ridiculous. All Oswald was accused of at that particular

[289] Jim Garrison, *On the Trail of the Assassins: My Investigation and Prosecution of the Murder
of President Kennedy* (Sheridan Square: 1988), cited at *Lee Harvey Oswald's "Murder" of
Policeman JD Tippit*: scribblguy.50megs.com/tippit.htm
[290] Ibid.

time—by anyone on this planet—was going into a movie theater without having paid for the 60-cent ticket. That's the *only* law he'd broken. No one accused him of anything else.

So, in summary, just a quick question here for you, dear reader. What would be the first thing you did after shooting the President of the United States? You've just shot the President . . . what now? You have a Coke and a smile, just like the TV ad, right? Wouldn't your hands be trembling to the point that you couldn't even get your hands in the frigging vending machine? You just killed the President and possibly the Governor, too! So you grab yourself a Coke and then—hey, why not, it's still early—you head off to a matinee. Yeah, *right—sure ya do*. Oswald was not that type of cold-blooded assassin.

There *are* some things that still aren't clear about the murder of Officer J. D. Tippit, but one of the things that *is* clear is that Oswald didn't do it.

So, like I said, when it comes to the whole "Oswald shot a cop" business, one word sums it up real well, and now you know what that word is, so remember it when people tell you about Oswald and that cop: Bullshit!

27

The Murder of Oswald Was
Obvious Witness-Silencing

If you weren't around in 1963, it's almost impossible to convey how crazy it was when Oswald was gunned down, right in the middle of a damn police station on live television.

People were outraged, and rightfully so. It was an unforgettable shock. Something clearly stunk about the whole thing and everyone sensed it. It was like an obvious aberration of justice.

> In the most obvious case of witness elimination in history, the accused assassin—there was never a trial or eyewitnesses—of President Kennedy was gunned down in broad daylight, even though he was surrounded by a bevy of law enforcement officers, as the prisoner was being transferred to another jail. A stunned nation watched in silent disbelief because the event had been televised and everyone had wanted to get a look at the accused killer. We all got much more than a look. We got a taste of incredulity because people literally could not believe the obviousness of a crucial witness being eliminated before their eyes.[291]

---

[291] Belzer & Wayne, *Hit List*, 27.

A popular national columnist named Dorothy Kilgallen was pretty darned shocked by it all, too. She was also obviously disgusted at the blatant dismissive manner by which the government handled the whole case. This is from her column, full of righteous indignation, right after Oswald got shot:

> The case is closed is it? Well I'd like to know how in a big smart town like Dallas, a man like Jack Ruby—operator of a striptease honky tonk—could stroll in and out of police headquarters as if it were a health club at a time when a small army of law enforcers was keeping a "tight security guard" on Oswald.
>
> Security! What a word for it.
>
> I wouldn't try to speak for Dallas, but around here, the people I talk to really believe that a man has the right to be tried in court.
>
> When that right is taken away from any man by the incredible combination of Jack Ruby and insufficient security, we feel chilled.[292]

If Oswald would have been eliminated at his original location—as was presumably the conspirators' plan—there would have been little to question as far as the crime.

Think about that for a second. If Oswald *had* been killed by police (or anyone else) while he was still in that building, the whole thing would have turned out *very* differently. We all would have gone to bed that night, *horrified* by the assassination, yes; but also secretly relieved that the President's killer had been eliminated.

Well, the guy that they had set-up to "take the fall" actually *was* eliminated. It just took a little bit longer than they'd originally planned.

But Oswald must have smelled a rat and he ducked out of that book depository building and for some reason—which may have been to meet his intelligence handler at a pre-set safe point, because it's the only thing that actually makes sense—he headed straight for the one spot that no one has been able to explain. You guessed right: a movie theater.

---

[292] Dorothy Kilgallen, 29 November 1963, *New York Journal American*.

So that was probably the conspirators plan: snuff out Oswald at the spot and *presto*, case closed. The President's dead, but at least we got the guy who did it. People would've swallowed that right down with no problem at all. You know it's true. It's just human nature. Then, instead of a nation in shock, we would have been a nation in shock that could come to closure about it.

That's why a lot of people figured that Oswald then *had* to be killed to keep him from ever telling his story in a courtroom. And guess what? That's not only exactly what happened, it's also just what some people close to some of the probable conspirators have said was *exactly* the motivation behind killing Oswald. They didn't *want* to kill Oswald; they *had* to kill Oswald.

Johnny Roselli was a mobster who was part of the CIA's efforts to try and assassinate Fidel Castro. I should point out here that it's against the law to attempt to assassinate foreign heads of state; and U.S. presidents have historically respected that.[293] The reasons are obvious. It's impossible to have successful diplomatic relations with most countries if it's known that you have no respect for the sanctioned leaders of foreign states. Formal U.S. policy forbids assassinations and forbids them very clearly. Executive Order 12333 is still in effect and specifically bans U.S. intelligence agencies from taking part in assassinations.[294] Yet, in defiance of that policy, the CIA has an established record of using assassination to remove its political enemies. Here's an example:

> The CIA's Secret Assassination Manual . . . a 19-page CIA document that was prepared as part of a coup against the Guatemalan government in 1954 and declassified in 1997. Maybe they should change the name to the CIA's 'secret-first degree murder manual.' How is it that we are allowed to kill other people if we're not in a declared war with them? Clearly this is a premeditated conspiracy involving more than one person. My big question is, who makes the call on this? To arbitrarily go out in the world and kill someone without their being charged with a crime![295]

---

[293] *Title 18, United States Code, 1116*, "Murder or manslaughter of foreign officials, official guests, or internationally protected persons": law.cornell.edu/uscode/text/18/1116

[294] *Executive Order 12333: United States Intelligence Activities*: fas.org/irp/offdocs/eo/eo-12333-2008.pdf

[295] Jesse Ventura & Dick Russell, *63 Documents the Government Doesn't Want You to Read* (Skyhorse Publishing: 2011), 16.

President Kennedy respected that policy and was genuinely shocked when he learned that the CIA had assisted in the "fatal removal" of President Diem in Vietnam.[296] But that longstanding policy, of course, didn't stop the CIA in 1963, a few weeks before Kennedy was himself killed.

Roselli was a key component of that whole anti-Cuban nexus from which the plan to assassinate JFK was hatched; and himself had to be eliminated, as we'll see in a later entry.

A nationally syndicated columnist named Jack Anderson got to know Johnny Roselli and developed him as a source. Here's how Roselli explained the killing to Anderson. Anderson published this *after* Roselli had been killed in 1976:

> **When Oswald was picked up, Roselli suggested, the under-world conspirators feared he would crack and disclose information that might lead to them. This almost certainly would have brought a massive US crackdown on the Mafia. So Jack Ruby was ordered to eliminate Oswald, making it appear as an act of reprisal against the President's killer.[297]**

Other information indicated the same thing. Frank Sheeran was a well-connected mobster who summarized the whole sordid story pretty well in a book that was basically his "deathbed statement." Sheeran referred to the rumors among mobsters that Jack Ruby's role in the conspiracy had been to silence Oswald by arranging to have the President's alleged assassin conveniently killed by the police:

> Jack Ruby's cops were supposed to take care of Oswald, but Ruby bungled it. That's why he had to go in and finish the job on Oswald. If he didn't take care of Oswald, what do you think they would have done to him—put Ruby on a meat hook.[298]

The context of the "meat hook" is in reference to the fact that the Chicago Mob had recently murdered a suspected FBI informant—Chicago bookmaker

---

[296] *John F. Kennedy Tapes*, "Memoirs Dictation (w/ His Children) & Diem," November 4, 1963: youtube.com/watch?v=xEJdtodFcDQ

[297] Jack Anderson & Les Whitten, "Behind John F. Kennedy's Murder," September 7, 1976, *The Washington Post*: jfk.hood.edu/Collection/Weisberg%20Subject%20Index%20Files/R%20Disk/Roselli%20John/Item%2022.pdf

[298] Charles Brandt, *"I Heard You Paint Houses": Frank "The Irishman" Sheeran and the Inside Story of the Mafia, the Teamsters, and the Last Ride of Jimmy Hoffa* (Steerforth Press: 2005).

William "Action" Jackson—in a brutal torture killing that was meant to serve as an example to anyone who defied them. Jackson's body had been placed on a meat hook and gangsters around the country were well aware of the message.[299]

Whether it was the Mob or some other group, it was crystal clear to most people that somebody *did not* want Lee Harvey Oswald talking in a courtroom about the things that he knew. That sure as hell made a lot more sense to everyone who watched it happen, myself included, than what the Warren Commission made up! Wanna know what they said?

> The Commission has found no evidence that Lee Harvey
> Oswald or Jack Ruby was part of any conspiracy, domestic or
> foreign, to assassinate President Kennedy.[300]

Maybe they didn't *find* any because, as I said, they weren't looking for any! The Warren Commission also said that "Virtually all of Ruby's Chicago friends stated he had no close connection with organized crime."[301] And as historian John Simkin pointed out, "This information came from friends of Ruby, including Dave Yaras, a Mafia hitman."[302]

When Attorney General Robert F. Kennedy got a look at Ruby's phone records, he said it reminded him of his witness list of mobsters:

> The list was almost a duplicate of the people I called before the
> Senate Rackets Committee.[303]

So *come off it!* Ruby was up to his eyeballs with the mob and everyone knew it! What a joke. The whole scenario was obvious witness-silencing, and anyone with a functioning brain at the time concluded that.

The U.S. Congress disagreed with the Warren Commission, by the way, at least on that point. This is right from their final report:

---

[299] Sam Giancana & Chuck Giancana, *Double Cross: The Explosive Inside Story of the Mobster Who Controlled America* (Skyhorse Publishing: 2010).

[300] President Gerald R. Ford, *President John F. Kennedy: Assassination Report of the Warren Commission* (Flatsigned Press: 2005), 17.

[301] Ibid, 589.

[302] John Simkin, "Jack Ruby: Biography," *Spartacus Educational*, retrieved 3 May 2013: spartacus.schoolnet.co.uk/JFKruby.htm

[303] Talbot, *Brothers*, 21.

... Ruby's shooting of Oswald was not a spontaneous act, in that it involved at least some premeditation. Similarly, the committee believed it was less likely that Ruby entered the police basement without assistance, even though the assistance may have been provided with no knowledge of Ruby's intentions. ... The committee was troubled by the apparently unlocked doors along the stairway route and the removal of security guards from the area of the garage nearest the stairway shortly before the shooting... There is also evidence that the Dallas Police Department withheld relevant information from the Warren Commission concerning Ruby's entry to the scene of the Oswald transfer.[304]

And Jack Ruby said it himself:

I was framed to kill Oswald![305]

[304] House Select Committee on Assassinations, "HSCA Final Assassinations Report," 157–158.

[305] Don Freed, Jim Cookson & Jeff Cohen, "Jack Ruby: 'I was framed to kill Oswald!,'" May 10–16, 1975, *Los Angeles Free Press: jfk.hood.edu/Collection/White%20Materials/White%20 Magazines%20And%20Articles/LA%20Free%20Press%2005-10--16-75/Item%2001.pdf*

28

Jack Ruby Knew Lee Harvey Oswald

That's a *huge* point and one that they make a point of *not* telling you. The fact that Ruby and Oswald knew each other changes the whole context of everything!

And it's been established that they *did* know each other. The Warren Commission and the House Select Committee on Assassination both lied to us about that! And I can prove it.

Because how could they have not known, with any type of preliminary mediocre investigation, that these two guys obviously knew each other? Instead, all we get is some total B.S. story about Jack Ruby wanting to save Jackie Kennedy from the mental anguish of going through a horrible trial. Yeah right. I mean you have to just keep asking yourself: *How stupid do they think we are?* It gets to the point where it's all so obvious that it's actually insulting to your intelligence!

Jack Ruby, to me, is a key point because he didn't just know a few people, he knew *everybody*. He knew Lee Harvey Oswald, he knew the Dallas cops who let him into the police station when he killed Oswald, he knew the Mafia people, he knew the anti-Castro Cubans who were around Dallas—Jack Ruby knew 'em all!

Judyth Vary Baker is an author and someone I can personally vouch for; I've sat right next to her and gone back and forth over these issues, and I know that she's a person of high integrity. Judyth was a very close friend of Oswald in New Orleans just prior to the assassination. They were having a serious romantic affair. Her book, *Me & Lee*, tells the whole story about Oswald being set up to take the fall. It's big stuff, and she has extensive documentation to back up all of her claims.

I'll always remember the reaction of "Mancow" Muller when Judyth Baker and I were sitting there in the studio for his radio show and she told Mancow that Ruby absolutely knew Oswald. His reaction was of complete shock, as that changed everything. As Judyth shows in her book, Ruby had known Oswald since he was a kid.[306] Judyth's book pretty much fills in all the blanks of New Orleans and what was going on there:

> Jack Ruby visited David Ferrie's apartment one day when Judyth
> and Lee [Oswald] were there. Ferrie introduced him to Judyth
> as Sparky Rubenstein. Ruby recognized Lee, and said that he
> used to see him at parties when he was a boy.[307]

And there's a multitude of other eyewitnesses who saw the two of them together. For example, at least four of the dancers who worked in Jack Ruby's nightclub—in apparent risk of their own personal safety—came forward after the assassination and stated that they clearly remembered Oswald not only *being* in Jack Ruby's nightclub, but sitting there and talking to him. They were even introduced to Oswald by Jack Ruby! So how could they not remember? Those four Ruby employees were Melba Christine Marcades (also known as Rose Cheramie), Marilyn "Delilah" Walle, Beverly Oliver, and Janet "Jada" Conforto.[308]

---

[306] Judyth Vary Baker, *Me & Lee: How I Came to Know, Love and Lose Lee Harvey Oswald*, (TrineDay: 2011).

[307] Edward T. Haslam, *Dr. Mary's Monkey: How the unsolved murder of a doctor, a secret laboratory in New Orleans and cancer-causing monkey viruses are linked to Lee Harvey Oswald, the JFK assassination and emerging global epidemics* (TrineDay: 2007), 307, parenthetical comment in original; citing Judyth Baker, *Me & Lee*.

[308] Belzer & Wayne, *Hit List*, xiv, 49, 141, 310; "Did Ruby & Oswald Know Each Other?-Beverly Oliver," retrieved 29 April 2013: youtube.com/watch?v=Lgd_QY1c8q8

That makes perfect sense when you find out how Ruby would go down to the southern part of crime boss Carlos Marcello's territory to get dancers. It all adds up.

Beverly Oliver was one of Ruby's dancers. You can watch a video clip of her online. She simply tells her story about what she recollects very clearly. She's sincere and intelligent. Go watch it: youtube.com/watch?v=Lgd_QY1c8q8.

Bill Chesher was a car mechanic who had worked on Jack Ruby's car. Chesher and another mechanic, Robert Roy, said that they had both even seen Oswald in Jack Ruby's car.[309]

New Orleans District Attorney Jim Garrison had "solid evidence" Ruby, Oswald, and David Ferrie not only all knew each other, but—*get this*—that they were all working with the CIA in its anti-Castro operations:

> I have solid evidence indicating that Ruby, Ferrie, Oswald and others involved in this case were all paid by the CIA to perform certain functions: Ruby to smuggle arms for Cuban exile groups, Ferrie to train them and to fly counterrevolutionary secret missions to Cuba, and Oswald to establish himself so convincingly as a Marxist that he would win the trust of American left-wing groups and also have freedom to travel as a spy in Communist countries, particularly Cuba.[310]

That was what was actually going on, and *that* was what the government had to cover up! Garrison continued and he didn't mince his words either:

> We have evidence linking Ruby not only to anti-Castro exile activities but, as with almost everyone else involved in this case, to the CIA itself. Never forget that the CIA maintains a great variety of curious alliances it feels serve its purposes. It may be hard to imagine Ruby in a trench coat, but he seems to have been as good an employee of the CIA as he was a pimp for the Dallas cops.[311]

---

[309] James DiEugenio, "JFK: The Ruby Connection, Gary Mack's Follies-Part One," *Citizens for Truth about the Kennedy Assassination*, accessed 12 Nov. 21012: ctka.net/2009/ruby_mack. html

[310] *JFK Lancer*, "Jim Garrison's Playboy Interview, Part Three," retrieved 3 May 2013:. jfklancer.com/Garrison4.html

[311] Ibid.

They were all *knee-deep* in covert activities and Garrison figured out that it was precisely that relationship that made the U.S. government stonewall his investigation every step of the way:

> . . . Ruby was up to his neck with the plotters. Our investiga-
> tors have broken a code Oswald used and found Ruby's private
> unlisted telephone number, as of 1963, written in Oswald's note-
> book. The same coded number was found in the address book
> of another prominent figure in this case.[312]

As veteran JFK historian James DiEugenio points out, it was blatantly clear that Oswald and Ruby knew each other. The Warren Commission can refuse to talk about that huge elephant standing right there in the room if they choose to, but that doesn't make the damn thing disappear! Here's how DiEugenio described that "elephant" when commenting on a so-called "documentary" that failed to include some very basic facts which he detailed in his review of Gary Mack's film, who was a custodian of the JFK assassination museum now located on the sixth floor of the Book Depository building.

> All one needs to know about the latest Gary Mack fiasco is
> this: Almost none of the above is included in the hour. Noth-
> ing about the involvement of Ruby and Oswald in the Cuban
> conflict through the CIA and the Mafia; virtually none of the
> plentiful and multi-leveled connections of Ruby to the DPD;
> and none of the witnesses who indicate Oswald and Ruby knew
> each other.

> This, of course, is ridiculous. For if a program is trying to
> explore whether or not Ruby shot Oswald to conceal a plot to kill
> Kennedy, then it is fundamentally dishonest not to tell the viewer
> about the above. Because clearly those three areas of evidence
> would suggest the following:

> Ruby and Oswald shared connections to the CIA and the Mafia

> Ruby and Oswald knew each other through their experience in
> the Cuban crisis as extended into the USA

---

[312] Ibid.

> Ruby used his police contacts to enter the basement of City Hall
> and kill Oswald."[313]

Why would the Warren Commission hide the fact that they all knew each other if they were truly doing an authentic investigation and wanted to know the truth? Let me answer that for you—they *wouldn't* hide it and they didn't want you to know the truth! It wasn't about learning the truth; it was about taking the truth and trying to bury it where no one would ever find it.

> That was apparently the need for the whole cover-up—they
> were all involved together: Oswald, Ruby, Ferrie, Banister,
> Dr. Ochsner, Dr. Sherman—all tied inextricably together in the
> whole sordid story.[314]

Read Judyth Baker's book and Edward T. Haslam's book, *Dr. Mary's Monkey*, because that's another important one, too. They're a couple of real eye-openers.

Another thing that has been pointed out to me which I thought was very interesting—and I've never heard this brought out publicly before—was that when Ruby shot Oswald, did you notice that all of the detectives were dressed in dark black or blue suits; except for the guy actually escorting Oswald? He's dressed totally in white, with a big white cowboy hat. Well, that—according to a tip someone gave me—was to set up the shooter. Then, even with the big crowd of people, the shooter knows Oswald's going to be just to the right of the white cowboy hat. And you know who told me that? Judyth Baker. She said she noticed that when they brought Lee down . . . so the shooter can get on target. Obviously, there were *a lot* of strange things taking place with the whole Jack Ruby thing.

But the evidence is unmistakably clear on a huge point here. Jack Ruby and Lee Harvey Oswald definitely knew each other. And like I said, that's not just important; that's a fact that changes *everything*.

Listen to what the only District Attorney's office to *ever* investigate the JFK assassination concluded about the importance of the fact that Ruby knew Oswald:

> First of all, let me dispose of this concept of the 'temporarily
> deranged man.' This is a catchall term, employed whenever the

---

[313] DiEugenio, "JFK: The Ruby Connection, Gary Mack's Follies-Part One."

[314] Belzer & Wayne, *Hit List*, 294.

real motive of a crime can't be nailed down. In the overwhelming majority of instances, the actions of human beings are the direct consequences of discernible motives.

This is the fatal flaw of the Warren Report—its conclusion that the assassination of President Kennedy was the act of a temporarily deranged man, that the murder of Officer Tippit was equally meaningless and, finally, that Jack Ruby's murder of Oswald was another act of a temporarily deranged individual. It is, of course, wildly improbable that all three acts were coincidentally the aberrant acts of temporarily deranged men—although it's most convenient to view them as such, because that judgment obviates the necessity of relentlessly investigating the possibility of a conspiracy.[315]

Far from being an impulsive act, Jim Garrison described Ruby's murder of Lee Harvey Oswald like this:

> In Jack Ruby's case, his murder of Lee Oswald was the sanest act he ever committed; if Oswald had lived another day or so, he very probably would have named names, and Jack Ruby would have been convicted as a conspirator in the assassination plot. As it was, Ruby made the best of a bad situation by rubbing out Oswald in the Dallas city jail, since this act could be construed as an argument that he was 'temporarily deranged.'[316]

I agree with Jim Garrison.

---

[315] *JFK Lancer*, "Jim Garrison's Playboy Interview, Part Three."
[316] Ibid.

SECTION TWO

The Cover-Up

There were actually *two* conspiracies which are both scientifically provable: One that murdered President Kennedy, and the other that covered it up. No one is suggesting that Robert Kennedy was involved in the murder of his own brother. However, the fact that he helped to cover it up is, and should be, a highly significant indication of powerful post-assassination forces at work. The reason it had to be covered up was due to the very nature of the crime—the way the conspiracy was constructed.

And there's something else that needs to be said here. The word "conspiracy" has been much-maligned and that has apparently been very intentional. When you watch mainstream media, look very closely at how they ridicule that particular word. It's only a word, but the mere mention of it now stirs up childish controversy rather than intelligent inquiry. The evidence—and logic—dictate that a "lone nut" literally was not capable of engineering the highly complex and sophisticated assassination of the 35th President of the United States. The organized semantic ridicule of "conspiracy buffs" who "come out of the woodwork" with their "kooky theories" whenever someone famous is killed is a transparent effort at the marginalization of unwelcomed critical thinking. I have a news flash for those people: leaders have been killed throughout human history, and the facts have proved beyond a shadow of a doubt that it usually is a conspiracy! So read your history. And if the gatekeepers who are controlling what the American public does and does *not* have access to were really concerned with learning the truth about any particular issue, they would welcome critical commentary as a sign that *people are actually thinking* and are truly *participating in this Democracy*—exactly as the forebears of this country originally intended we do.

29

The Smoking Gun of
the Cover-Up

I've highlighted the memo from acting Attorney General Nick Katzenbach for a very good reason: Because it lays out the whole plan for the cover-up. If you want to read it again, it's at the front of this book, right where it belongs.

Keep in mind that it came from the U.S. Department of Justice—the Attorney General's office that Robert F. Kennedy himself was the head of— and it detailed exactly what had to be done.

That document *proves* that the whole U.S. government cover-up was not some idle occurrence and did not just evolve as the circumstances developed.

That was their plan from the start.

So look at the words and get yourself a good handle on the truth. It tells you what the plan was, straight from the get-go:

> The public must be satisfied that Oswald was the assassin; that he did not have confederates who are still at large; and that the evidence was such that he would have been convicted at trial.[317]

Is that clear enough for you? Because it's sure as hell clear to me.

---

[317] Nicholas deB. Katzenbach, Deputy Attorney General, "Memorandum for Mr. Moyers," November 25, 1963: maryferrell.org/wiki/index.php/Katzenbach_Memo

> We need something to head off public speculation or Congressio-
> nal hearings of the wrong sort.[318]

Yeah. We wouldn't want the public to wonder what actually happened to their President who just had his brains blasted to smithereens. We wouldn't want our duly-elected officials in Congress to conduct an actual investigation and try to figure out what actually happened. We wouldn't want *any* of those things, would we?

> The only other step would be the appointment of a Presidential
> Commission of unimpeachable personnel to review and examine
> the evidence and announce its conclusions.[319]

And *that's* why they formed the Warren Commission. That's the *real* reason:

Not to *find* the truth, *but to bury it!*

---

[318] Ibid.
[319] Ibid.

30

The Presidential Limousine
Was Crucial Crime Scene
Evidence

I f you've ever seen an actual police crime scene—or even watched television in the past twenty years—then you know that preservation of the crime scene is 101 at its most basic level. Everybody knows that.

Make no mistake about it: the open Lincoln limousine was the crime scene of the assassination of the President of the United States.

So let's take a little look at how they preserved that crucial crime scene. Did they wrap police tape around it so that everybody saw "Police Crime Scene Do Not Enter" and nobody touched the thing? Did they make any serious effort to maintain the integrity of that crime scene?

Nope. They didn't do any of those things that they clearly should have.

What did they do? Get a load of this:

JFK's limo was quickly shipped off to Detroit for a rapid make-over.

That's right. President Johnson & Co. had the crime scene immediately shipped away. Isn't that great? Does that tell you anything about the authenticity of the government's actual efforts to determine who killed our President? Maybe I should add *or the lack thereof.*

Believe it or not, that's what they actually did. What dummy doesn't know that a crime scene is not to be turned over or touched until the forensic team and detectives have gone over it? Here you have the very murder site as the car. How is it that wasn't even looked at? And no one questioned that and said, "Excuse me, we need to preserve that evidence"? That's Homicide 101. Again, how many standard procedures get violated, and it goes back to what Colonel L. Fletcher Prouty said: "When you look for a conspiracy, look for the violation of Standard Operating Procedures." Well, there's a *real beauty* for ya.

President Kennedy's assassination was on a Friday afternoon in Texas. By Monday morning before work hours—and probably much earlier—the President's limousine was already in Detroit sitting at the Ford plant and was already in the process of being destroyed and refurbished. In other words, the evidence was gone.

> George Whitaker Sr., a senior manager at the Ford Motor Company's Rouge Plant in Detroit, Michigan, told attorney [and professor of criminal justice] Doug Weldon in August of 1993, in a tape recorded conversation, that after reporting to work on Monday, November 25, he discovered the JFK limousine—a unique, one-of-a-kind item that he unequivocally identified—in the Rouge Plant's B building, with the interior stripped out and in the process of being replaced, and with the windshield removed. He was then contacted by one of the Vice Presidents of the division for which he worked and directed to report to the glass plant lab, immediately. After knocking on the locked door [which he found most unusual], he was let in by two of his subordinates and discovered that they were in possession of the windshield that had been removed from the JFK limousine.[320]

So when it came to preserving the most obvious evidence in the whole case, it was *Goodbye and Goodnight.* And that was *damn well* intentional.

---

[320] Douglas P. Horne, referencing Doug Weldon, "Photographic Evidence of Bullet Hole in JFK Limousine Windshield 'Hiding in Plain Sight'," June 4, 2012: lewrockwell.com/orig13/horne-d2.1.1.html

31

The Illegal Removal of the President's Body

A s Jim Garrison put it, the whole cover-up was enabled by the fact that:

The Government succeeded in accomplishing what, normally, it would not be able to accomplish in another city. It succeeded in getting the body of the President *out* of Dallas without an autopsy. In other words, Air Force One . . . didn't so much "take-off" as it made a "getaway" . . . The plane took off with the body of the President and no civilian autopsy had been conducted. Then the body was placed in a controlled environment—the military hospital at Bethesda. And *there* the autopsy was conducted. After the autopsy, Commander Humes, who conducted the autopsy, burned his notes, which was probably the first time in history that a serious autopsy resulted in the burning of the notes.[321]

At that time, legal jurisdiction over the body resided entirely with the authorities in Texas. There was no law on the books; no legal jurisdiction for

---

[321] *The Steve Allen Show*, 1971, KTLA-TV, (Golden West Broadcasters, Inc.): youtube.com/ watch?v=KXZfsbpa2kI

the "kidnapping" of the President's body. By law, it should have remained in Dallas for the autopsy. Not many people know that, but it's true.

The law was that local authorities had clear jurisdiction for the autopsy—not the Feds!

During that battle over the President's body—which was apparently at gunpoint right in the middle of a hospital—the Secret Service "won" and put the President's body on a plane.

Imagine that one, folks! There was a big battle over the President's body, and when things really started to get hairy, the Secret Service even had their guns drawn. Dallas authorities refused to release it to them, citing—quite correctly—that it was their legal jurisdiction to conduct the autopsy. As Secret Service specialist Vince Palamara noted:

> Also worthy of study are the widely reported violent actions of the Secret Service at Parkland. More than one commentator has stated that the agents protected JFK's corpse far more aggressively as they were stealing it from the local coroner—at gunpoint, who was merely trying to maintain the chain of evidence, than they had just moments before.[322]

Palamara has examined the facts surrounding the Secret Service issues of the assassination for decades and reaches a stark conclusion:

> Ironically, two of the agents who participated in that illegal seizure of the President's body at gunpoint were Roy Kellerman and Bill Greer, who rode in JFK's limousine and were paramount to his supposed security. Since the murder of a president was not then a federal crime, the agents had zero jurisdiction.[323]

That law was changed after the assassination—now the murder of a federal official is a federal matter. But it wasn't in 1963.

So whatever else there is to be said about it, the fact of the matter is that they *did* violate the law and they did so very aggressively.

---

[322] Palamara, *Survivor's Guilt*, citing Charles A. Crenshaw, M.D., *JFK: A Conspiracy of Silence: Headline-Making New Revelations from the Surgeon who tried to Save JFK and Oswald* (Signet: 1992).

[323] Vincent Michael Palamara, email to author, 10 May 2013.

32

Hoover and the FBI Assisted the Cover-Up

Get this: J. Edgar Hoover—twenty-four hours after the murder of President Kennedy—had already declared Oswald the killer. There hadn't been one shred of evidence. And when you look at the way the FBI was run back then, who's going to defy Hoover? When J. Edgar says Oswald did it, there ain't one agent that's gonna step out of line and say, "Wait a minute, maybe that's not right."

Historian Walt Brown summed it all up very well, describing how the cover-up would not have even been possible without the participation of Johnson and Hoover:

> Johnson's "actions were a virtual guarantee that the truth would
> be buried and" furthermore, "the assassination would not have
> been carried out if those behind it did not have the full acquiescence
> of the incoming President and the FBI Director. They controlled
> *everything* once the shots ended. They controlled *everything* but
> they did *nothing*.[324]

---

[324] Walt Brown, Ph.D., "Actions Speak Much Louder than Words—what, exactly, did Johnson and Hoover do?," *JFK Deep Politics Quarterly*, Vol. 17, #4, July, 2012 (emphasis in original).

That says it all. Their response to what we would call seeking justice was the same as what a poker player says to a losing hand: *Read 'em and weep*.

Hoover's FBI agents started badgering witnesses and controlling evidence shortly after the gun smoke lifted at Dealey Plaza. It's not only downright disturbing and frightening what they did to witnesses, it's totally outrageous. There are numerous substantiated cases of the FBI badgering witnesses to change their testimony and also of *changing* their testimony when it conflicted with the official government version.[325] Witnesses were shocked to see some of the things that the FBI had changed in their official statements and vehemently denied ever saying them![326]

That's what actually happened. And it wasn't just once or twice, because "numerous witnesses subsequently insisted that federal agents, or the Dallas police, or both, altered or even fabricated their statements."[327]

Isn't that great? They interview a witness, they don't like something the witness said, so what do they do? They just change it to fit with the way they prefer. To me, that's very serious; that's obstruction of justice, plain and simple.

Would you like a good example? A man named Warren Reynolds was a very clear case of that.

Mr. Reynolds was a solid, upstanding citizen who just happened to get a good close look at the man who shot Dallas Police Officer J. D. Tippit, forty minutes after the President was shot.

> He owned a car dealership and witnessed the shooting of Officer J. D. Tippit, and even gave chase to the man who escaped. However, he stated that the man was *not* Oswald, and he refused to be browbeaten into changing his testimony that it *may* have been a man looking like Oswald. Reynolds was shot in the head with a rifle on January 23, 1964, but, miraculously, he survived. Blatant intimidation continued and his ten-year-old daughter was almost kidnapped, but the abduction attempt failed; he received threats on his life and other intimidations, such as trespassers nosing

---

[325] Marrs, *Crossfire: The Plot That Killed JFK*.

[326] Sylvia Meagher, *Accessories After The Fact: The Warren Commission, The Authorities & The Report* (Random House: 1988); Marrs, *Crossfire: The Plot That Killed JFK*.

[327] Michael T. Griffith, "Where Was Oswald From 11:50 to 12:35 P.M. on the Day of the Assassination?," 1998: michaelgriffith1.tripod.com/where.htm

around outside his home at night. Finally, Reynolds had become a nervous wreck and told the FBI he had changed his mind and would identify Oswald as the shooter. After reversing his testimony, his harassment suddenly halted—but *surely*, that's just *one more incredible coincidence*.[328]

There are many other witnesses who experienced obvious intimidation.[329] We call ourselves a Democracy; a Republic that stands for something; where truth and integrity are values to uphold. So what the hell was that? Let me answer that for you. It was obstruction of justice. But when it's the Feds themselves doing the obstructing, then what happens? Then everybody just walks away and says *hey, that's the way it is—Hasta la vista, Baby!*

Hoover also obviously knew about Oswald's various roles with U.S. intelligence agencies. And that's not a *theory* or some conjecture on my part—the guy's *on record* as knowing about that.

Was there more than one Lee Harvey Oswald? Hoover obviously thought so. The following is the verbatim content of an FBI memorandum from Director J. Edgar Hoover, dated June 3, 1960; over three years prior to the assassination:

Date:	**June 3, 1960**
To:	**Office of Security Department of State**
From:	**John Edgar Hoover, Director**
Subject:	**LEE HARVEY OSWALD -INTERNAL SECURITY**

---

328 Belzer & Wayne, *Hit List*, 318.

329 Gary Richard Schoener, "A Legacy of Fear," *Fair Play Magazine,* #34, May–June 2000: acorn.net/jfkplace/09/Kelin34/fear.html ; Marrs, *Crossfire: The Plot That Killed JFK*; Bill Sloan & Jean Hill, *JFK: The Last Dissenting Witness* (Pelican: 2008).

Message	Since there is a possibility that an imposter is using Oswald's birth certificate, any current information the Department of State may have concerning the subject will be appreciated.[330]

Author Dick Russell established a lot of that linkage between Oswald, Ruby and U.S. intelligence agencies in his book, *On the Trail of the JFK Assassins*. For example, here's what Richard Schweiker, a United States Senator, exploded about when he dug around and found out how all the "alphabet" intelligence agencies had been scurrying around to cover up their obvious associations with Oswald *and* Ruby:

> Then there was Jack Ruby. "Why did the FBI withhold for
> twelve years that he'd informed for them on nine occasions?"
> Schweiker asks. "This wasn't national security information,
> so why were they so sensitive? Also I'm certain there were
> extenuating circumstances in his activities running guns to Cuba.
> We were really running a secret war against Cuba, and we know
> the CIA was heavily involved. Ruby had to have been at least
> working for someone who was working for the CIA."[331]

So all these guys—the Warren Commission, the FBI, other government agencies, the authorities in Texas—they *knew* that Oswald had intelligence connections. They even knew his damn informant number at the FBI:

> The Warren Commission knew, from Texas' Attorney General
> Waggoner Carr *and* District Attorney Henry Wade, that
> Oswald apparently had FBI informant No. 179 and was making
> a couple hundred dollars a month in wages from the Bureau![332]

---

[330] Ben A. Franklin, "1960 FBI Memo Warned Of Oswald Impostor," February 23, 1975, *The New York Times*: jfk.hood.edu/Collection/Weisberg%20Subject%20Index%20Files/O%20 Disk/Oswald%20Lee%20Harvey%20Russia%20Imposter/Item%2015.pdf

[331] Dick Russell, *On the Trail of the JFK Assassins* (Skyhorse Publishing: 2008), 44–45.

[332] Russell, *The Man Who Knew Too Much*, 20.

Wade's source said that Oswald had a CIA employment number as well.

When Oswald was living in Russia, a March 2, 1961, memo from the U.S. Passport Office to the State Department Security Office 'requested that the recipients advise if the FBI is receiving info about Harvey on a continuing basis.'[333]

That's big stuff. Oswald was an FBI informant. Ruby was an FBI informant and working with the CIA. You can see that there was a lot to cover up after the assassination.

A CI (Confidential Informant) for the FBI who was also a veteran U.S. military intelligence operative—who was a real-life real cloak-and-dagger double agent against the Soviets—actually *informed the Bureau by registered mail* about Oswald's specific involvement in a plot to kill the President. It's detailed specifically in the book, *The Man Who Knew Too Much* by Dick Russell. That gives you an idea of how much people trusted the FBI; he sent it to them registered mail so that he could have proof of it later! The guy was no dummy, that's for sure.

Oswald was brought into the conspiracy in July of 1963, deceived into thinking he was working for Castro. Soviet intelligence ordered Nagell either to convince Oswald he was being set up to take the rap—or kill him in Mexico City before the assassination could transpire. While both U.S. and Soviet intelligence agencies were aware of the conspiracy, it was the KGB—not the CIA or FBI—that attempted to prevent it. The Soviets, who had reached a growing accommodation with Kennedy after the 1962 Cuban missile crisis, were also afraid that the assassination would falsely be blamed upon them or the Cubans.[334]

How did the FBI respond to that? They said they're still looking for that letter! But hey, no problem; I guess they get a lot of mail.

Hoover knew all about Oswald's intelligence intrigues in Mexico City and we *know* that from the transcripts of Hoover's phone calls to President Johnson:

---

[333] Jesse Ventura & Dick Russell, *American Conspiracies* (Skyhorse Publishing: 2011), 33.
[334] Ibid, 212.

As recounted in these pages, FBI Director Hoover believed an
Oswald impostor had been at work in Mexico City. There is no
other way to construe Hoover's briefing of President Johnson, the
day after the assassination, when Hoover said:

"We have up here the tape and the photograph of the man who
was at the Soviet Embassy. That picture and the tape do not
correspond to this man's voice, nor to his appearance . . . it appears
that there is a second person who was at the Soviet Embassy."[335]

So Hoover is telling the President of the United States that Oswald was
even being impersonated by other intelligence agents? That has obvious implications in the field of intelligence; that means somebody's running an operation
and Oswald is somehow involved.

But Hoover didn't know anything about Oswald, right? These guys are
unbelievable; and I mean that literally *and* figuratively!

Still think Hoover didn't know anything? Well, in a way, that's sort of
right. Hoover apparently didn't think there was, in reality, much evidence
against Oswald; certainly not enough to convict him in a court of law. The following is a direct extract from a telephone conversation between Hoover and
President Johnson, held on November 23, 1963 at 10:01 a.m., in which Hoover
informs the new president about the alarming lack of substantive evidence
against Oswald. That was the day after the assassination. Look at what he says
about the case against Oswald:

**HOOVER: The evidence that they have at the present time is not
very, very strong. . . . The case as it stands now isn't strong enough
to be able to get a conviction...this man Oswald has still denied
everything. He doesn't know *anything* about *anything* . . .[336]**

U.S. Congressman Hale Boggs was the House Majority Leader and also
a member of the Warren Commission. Take a good look at what he *really*
thought:

---

[335] Summers, *The Kennedy Conspiracy?*, 386.
[336] "White House Transcripts of President Lyndon B. Johnson," November 23, 1963, excerpt
at: spartacus.schoolnet.co.uk/USAjohnsonLB.htm

A former aide to the late House Majority Leader has recently
recalled, 'Hale always returned to one thing:

Hoover lied his eyes out to the Commission—on Oswald, on
Ruby, on their friends, the bullets, the gun, you name it.'[337]

And the beat goes on and on:

> Speaking of the FBI, its deeply sinister strongman J. Edgar
> Hoover might have "lied his eyes out" to the Warren Commis-
> sion, as panel member Hale Boggs, the Louisiana congressman,
> memorably told an aide, pressuring and maneuvering the com-
> mission to reach a lone-assassin verdict. But again, in private,
> Hoover told another story. The summer after the assassination,
> Hoover was relaxing at the Del Charro resort in California,
> which was owned by his friend, right-wing Texas oil tycoon
> Clint Murchison. Another Texas oil crony of Hoover's, Billy
> Byars Sr.—the only man Hoover had called on the afternoon
> of November 22, 1963, besides Robert Kennedy and the head
> of the Secret Service—also was there. At one point, according
> to Anthony Summers, the invaluable prober of the dark side of
> American power, Byars' teenage son, Billy Jr., got up his nerve to
> ask Hoover the question, "Do you think Lee Harvey Oswald did
> it?" According to Byars, Hoover "stopped and looked at me for
> quite a long time. Then he said, 'If I told you what I really know,
> it would be very dangerous to this country. Our whole political
> system could be disrupted.'"[338]

So there you have it. They might as well have just said:
"We'd like to order one extra-large cover-up with everything. And can we
have that to-go, please?"

---

[337] Bernard Fensterwald & Michael Ewing, *Assassination of JFK: Coincidence or Conspiracy?*
(Kensington Pub Corp: 1977), excerpt at: spartacus.schoolnet.co.uk/JFKboggs.htm

[338] David Talbot, "The mother of all cover-ups: Forty years after the Warren Report, the
official verdict on the Kennedy assassination, we now know the country's high and mighty
were secretly among its biggest critics," September 15, 2004: salon.com/2004/09/15/warren/

33

The X-rays Showed That the Bullet Particles Were From Exploding Ammunition

It was originally researcher Harold Weisberg who proved something very important: The actual X-rays showed the bullet particles fragmented extensively in the President's head, which means the Mannlicher-Carcano couldn't have fired the bullet, as a Mannlicher only shoots a full metal jacketed bullet. All military weapons by NATO and the Geneva Convention—like the Mannlicher—are not allowed to shoot fragmented bullets from them. So the bullet out of the weapon would have to be a full metal jacket bullet, which does not break into pieces. So with Kennedy's actual X-rays showing particles of bullets, that tells you that the bullet was not from that gun!

The conclusion to reach from that is very simple: The bullet that hit President Kennedy in the head could not have come from the crime scene rifle that they said they linked to Oswald.

Other scientific studies substantiate the fragmentation. First of all, listen to the exact words of one of JFK's morticians, Tom Robinson, when testifying to Congress about that fatal bullet:

[Robinson said] that 'It exited in many pieces,' and then explained, 'They were literally picked out, little pieces of this bullet from all over his head.' In further support, moreover, we can go back to the statements of autopsy assistant James Curtis Jenkins and recall that in the exact spot where he claimed the doctors discovered a gray discoloration of the skull, Dr. Davis saw metallic fragments, which he assumed were in the scalp. A gray discoloration of the skull of course suggests the presence of lead. Lead is of course a metal. Two plus two equals four.

When one realizes that the largest fragments of an exploding bullet travel the furthest, and that the two largest fragments discussed at the autopsy were on the opposite ends of Kennedy's skull and equidistant from our proposed entrance, and adds this to the fact that, defying expectation, there were no small fragments surrounding the supposed in-shoot in the cowlick, then one should rightly conclude that the lateral x-ray demonstrates convincingly that a bullet broke up near the site of the supposed out-shoot, above the right ear.[339]

Fragmenting bullets that explode on impact—also known as "frangible" bullets or "hot loads"—are *not consistent* with the rifle alleged to be used in the assassination. "Oswald's rifle"—as the authorities liked to call it—was not of the type that handled frangible ammo.

But numerous bullet fragments were found inside the President's limo; some that were standard ammo, others that were apparently from frangible bullets.

Another factor—the measure of velocity of the shots—also shows that they are two different weapons.

Professor Jim Fetzer proved all of this in a scientific study of the weapons and the ammo. Here were his findings:

- The weapon that Oswald is alleged to have used could not have fired the bullets that killed JFK: the carbine was not a high-velocity weapon.

[339] Patrick J. Speer, *A New Perspective on the John F. Kennedy Assassination* (PatSpeer.com: 2007): patspeer.com/chapter18%3Ax-rayspecs

- Everyone, including [Gerald] Posner, agrees that the muzzle velocity of the Mannlicher-Carcano was 2,000 fps (feet per second). The death certificates, autopsy report, and Warren Commission declared he was killed by the impact of high-velocity bullets. High velocity would be 2,600 fps and up.

- The shot striking the right forehead was from a frangible or 'exploding' bullet, as evidenced by the extensive shockwaves of damage through the brain; Oswald's bullets were standard copper-jacketed military ammunition which could not have inflicted frangible damage.[340]

So "Oswald's rifle" *could not* have inflicted the specific type of damage present in the President's wounds, and "Oswald's bullets" *could not* have caused that specific type of damage or have left the type of bullet fragmentation that was found in that car.

---

[340] Belzer & Wayne, *Hit List*, 109, citing James H. Fetzer Ph.D., *Murder in Dealey Plaza: What We Know Now that We Didn't Know Then* (Open Court: 2000); James H. Fetzer Ph.D., "JFK and RFK: The Plots that Killed Them, The Patsies that Didn't," June 17, 2010, retrieved 10 May 2013: lewrockwell.com/spl2/jfk-rfk-plots.html

34

The Official Autopsy Photos
and X-Rays Were Altered

This one comes as a shocker to most people, but keep this point in mind as you read about the photos and X-rays: the evidence proves it, and I'm going to show you how.

> There are many contradictions in the publicly available autopsy images. Some of the photographs which were finally released to the public are inconsistent with the X-rays, and neither the photos nor the X-rays agree with what eyewitnesses [who were doctors and law enforcement professionals] described in Dallas or Bethesda. Some of the X-rays and photos have been identified as forgeries by experts.[341]

As I established in the very first entry of this book, literally dozens of highly credible eyewitnesses to President Kennedy's wounds *clearly document* a massive wound at the right rear portion of his head that could only have been from the exit of a bullet.

---

[341] Kent Heiner, *Without Smoking Gun: Was the Death of Lieutenant Commander William Pitzer Part of the JFK Assassination Cover-Up Conspiracy?* (TrineDay: 2004).

Here are some of their comments and please excuse the fact that some of
them are gory and graphic. Pretend you're on a jury and you have to weigh the
grisly evidence:

- SECRET SERVICE SPECIAL AGENT CLINT HILL: The
  right rear portion of his head was missing. It was lying in the rear
  seat of the car. His brain was exposed. There was blood and bits
  of brain all over the entire rear portion of the car. Mrs. Kennedy
  was completely covered with blood. There was so much blood you
  could not tell if there had been any other wound or not, except for
  the one large gaping wound in the right rear portion of the head.

- NURSE DIANA BOWRON: There was a gaping wound in the
  back of his head. It was gone. Gone. There was nothing there. Just
  a big gaping hole. There might have been little clumps of scalp,
  but most of the bone over the hole, there was no bone there. There
  was no damage to the front of his face, only wound in the back of
  his head and the entry wound in his throat. The wound was so
  large I could almost put my whole fist into it.

- NURSE DORIS NELSON (when shown the rear of head autopsy
  photo): There wasn't even hair back there. It was blown away. All
  that area was blown out.

- NURSE PAT HUTTON: A doctor asked me to place a pressure
  dressing on the head wound. This was of no use, however, because
  of the massive opening on the back of the head.

- DR. MALCOLM PERRY: There was blood noted on the car-
  riage and a large avulsive wound on the right posterior cranium.

- DR. RONALD JONES: There was a large defect in the back side
  of the head as the President lay on the cart with what appeared to
  be some brain hanging out of this wound with multiple pieces of
  skull noted next with the brain and with a tremendous amount of
  clot and blood.

- DR. PAUL PETERS: I noticed the head wound, and as I remember—I noticed that there was a large defect in the occiput. It
  seemed to me that in the right occipital parietal area that there
  was a large defect. There appeared to be bone loss and brain loss in

the area . . . we speculated as to whether he had been shot once or twice because we saw the wound of entry in the throat and noted the large occipital wound.

- DR. KEMP CLARK: I then examined the wound in the back of the President's head. This was a large, gaping wound in the right posterior part, with cerebral and cerebellar tissue being damaged and exposed.

- NURSE MARGARET HINCHCLIFF: The President had a gaping wound in the back of his head and an entrance wound in his throat.

- BETHESDA PHOTOGRAPHER FLOYD RIEBE: A big gaping hole in the back of the head.

- FBI SPECIAL AGENT FRANK O'NEILL: A massive wound in the right rear.[342]

So—here's the huge question: What happened to the rear head wound that all those witnesses saw but isn't in the autopsy photos?

You obviously can't miss a thing like that, especially when you're taking official autopsy photographs for the specific purpose of wound documentation. But in the official autopsy photos, there's no rear exit wound. That simply isn't possible. Unless the photos were altered, the wounds were altered, or all those emergency doctors and other personnel were lying.

Well, the doctors weren't lying. They know what they saw. They also documented it in a highly adequate and thoroughly professional manner.

I should point out that not only did they document the massive exit wound, they also documented the entry wound in the front that caused that huge exit at the back:

> Multiple witnesses, who were medically and otherwise credible, confirmed that they clearly saw an entry wound in the FRONT of President Kennedy's head, in his upper right forehead at the hairline.[343]

---

[342] Brad Parker, *First on the Scene: Interviews with Parkland Doctors* (JFK Lancer: 2005): jfklancer.com/parkland_drs.html

[343] Douglas P. Horne, *Inside the Assassination Records Review Board: The U.S. Government's Final Attempt to Reconcile the Conflicting Medical Evidence in the Assassination of JFK* (Douglas P. Horne: 2009).

So this is a no-brainer from a medical standpoint. Those doctors were there and they saw a small entry wound at the front and the big exit wound at the right rear. So how did that massive wound magically disappear?

As wild as it sounds—in the official U.S. government autopsy photos and X-rays, <u>there were different wounds on the body of the President</u>. And I emphasize that point because it's a point that *bears* emphasis. Imagine such a thing: The wounds were *changed*.

Well, there was further eyewitness testimony that indicated that what took place after the autopsy was—they basically patched that hole in the back the President's head:

- MORTICIAN THOMAS ROBINSON: About the size of a small orange . . . circular . . . ragged . . . directly behind the back of his head . . . they brought a piece of heavy duty rubber, again to fill this area in the back of the head . . . it had to be all dried out, packed, and the rubber placed in the hair and the skin pulled back over . . . and stitched into that piece of rubber.

- QUESTION: Can you give me some information on the head wound?

- FBI SPECIAL AGENT JAMES SIBERT: Oh, it was a good size, in the back part of the head there. Well, I think about three and a half inches one way, then quite a bit the other . . . now those two (Dr. Boswell and Dr. Humes, who performed the autopsy) stayed there till about 5:30 in the morning as I recall. That was their admission—that they stayed and helped the morticians. In other words, they must have taken some other pictures too, because they showed the pictures at that deposition that were neat in appearance, and boy, I don't remember anything like that . . . but my recollection of the way the head looked is nothing that would appear as this photograph shows. This photograph is too neat. Right back here is where you would have had that massive wound, right in here, and you see that's neat. My thought was that that was probably taken after reconstruction was done . . .[344]

---

[344] Parker, *First on the Scene: Interviews with Parkland Doctors.*

Some of the Navy personnel also seemed to have viewed photos from the "original" or "real" autopsy before the wounds were changed. Because the wounds they described in those photos did not exist in the official photos and the photos they referred to have completely disappeared:

> Petty Officer Saundra Spencer: They had one [autopsy photo] showing the back of the head with the wound at the back of the head. It was just a ragged hole.[345]

When the official version of the autopsy photos were shown to people who had viewed the body in Dallas or at Bethesda prior to the autopsy—solid eyewitnesses who saw the wounds—they said things like, "Those are not the wounds I saw."[346]

Douglas Horne was Chief Analyst for the Military Records Team of the Assassination Records Review Board in Washington, D.C. and oversaw the disposition of mountains of records related to the JFK assassination from 1995 to 1998. Horne then spent the next several years of his life writing his epic compilation of that project, a five-volume study totaling 1,807 pages, entitled *Inside the Assassination Records Review Board: The U.S. Government's Final Attempt to Reconcile the Conflicting Medical Evidence in the Assassination of JFK.* That book, released in 2010, is the most thorough and exhaustive study of the evidence in the JFK assassination in existence, particularly as it relates to the medical evidence in the case.

Horne's work—as well as that of Dr. David Mantik and others—have established that a lot of awful shenanigans took place during the autopsy of President Kennedy.[347] That was established by extensive scientific comparison of the official X-rays and photographs, with the placement of the wounds clearly substantiated by the doctors in Dallas. And they do not match.

Dr. Mantik examined the official materials many times and also found a number of other anomalies in the medical evidence which he explains in detail, complete with slides, in a study online called, "The JFK Autopsy Materials: Twenty Conclusions after Nine Visits" at: assassinationresearch.com/v2n2/pittsburgh.pdf.

---

[345] Ibid.

[346] Horne, *Inside the Assassination Records Review Board.*

[347] David W. Mantik, M.D., Ph.D., "The JFK Autopsy Materials: Twenty Conclusions after Nine Visits," November 20–23, 2003: assassinationresearch.com/v2n2/pittsburgh.pdf

First, the official skull X-rays do not show the condition of the skull or the brain as seen at Parkland.[348]

Stop and think about that for a second. The wounds in the official X-rays *did not match* the wounds documented by the emergency room doctors. They were dramatically different. They reflect an entry wound from the *rear*, whereas the wounds that were seen in Dallas clearly reflected an entry wound from the front.

Now read the following entry very carefully. It's written by a doctor, so it's in medical lingo, but play close attention to what he concludes:

> Instead, they [the official autopsy photos and X-rays] were taken after tampering by H&B [Dr. Humes and Dr. Boswell, the two physicians who performed the autopsy of President Kennedy], perhaps even after significant tampering, especially if Robinson and Reed are correct. Furthermore, the massive damage seen in the photographs and X-rays was not caused just by a bullet or even by multiple bullets, but instead by pathological hands. In particular, for a single, full metal-jacketed bullet—the Warren Commission's inevitable scenario—to generate such an enormous defect has always defied credibility. Likewise, Boswell's sketch [for the ARRB; Assassination Records Review Board] on a skull of this enormous defect only shows the condition of the skull after tampering by H&B—and does not reflect the skull as seen at Parkland [Hospital in Dallas]. The Parkland witnesses fully concur with this. On the other hand, many witnesses at Bethesda saw the condition of the skull before such tampering began. These witnesses, both physicians and paraprofessionals uniformly describe a right occipital blowout [right rear of skull], consistent with a shot from the front.[349]

In other words, the wounds didn't change by themselves. What that means in plain English is that they were altered and the massive exit wound at the rear

---

[348] David W. Mantik, M.D., Ph.D., *"Inside the Assassination Records Review Board (AARB)* by Douglas Horne: A Nearly-Entirely-Positive Review," 26 Feb. 2010. assassinationscience. com/HorneReview.pdf (accessed 6 May 2013).

[349] Ibid.

was disguised medically so that it could be represented in the official autopsy photos and X-rays as displaying the effects of a shot from the rear.

> At this point, Dr. Humes performed clandestine surgery on the head to enlarge the head wound to create 'evidence' of a temporal/ parietal exit and an incision was made to remove evidence of a right forehead entry. The scalp and skull were manipulated to conceal the size and location of the occipital 'blowout' and a 'wound' was created to simulate a small entrance wound on the back of the head.[350]

So, in even plainer English, there was illicit surgery at the Bethesda morgue.[351] They had to change the physical evidence to fit their lone gunman scenario of one shooter and a head shot from the rear. So, incredible as it sounds: Even though it was the body of the President of the United States, that's what they did. Gruesome, horrifying, outrageous, and also, by logical deduction, as Mr. Horne and Dr. Mantik have proved, necessarily true.

Chew on *that* one for awhile.

---

[350] Brian Rooney, "Burying The Truth—book review of Doug Horne's epic effort," April, 2010, *JFK: Deep Politics Quarterly.*

[351] Mantik, M.D., Ph.D., *"Inside the Assassination Records Review Board."*

35

Another Key Witness Conveniently Silenced: Navy Lieutenant Commander William Bruce Pitzer

A person who was very close to that bizarre autopsy of President Kennedy died a very "untimely" death; just as he was reportedly ready to go public about the altered autopsy materials.

They tried to say that United States Navy Lieutenant Commander William B. Pitzer committed suicide, but he didn't: he was murdered. The evidence of that case indicates that he was "eliminated" because of his impending intentions. An experienced U.S. Special Forces assassin even came forward and documented that the CIA had requested him to assassinate Pitzer due to a matter regarding classified national security materials. We'll get to that in a minute.

Lt. Commander Pitzer was the acknowledged "Head of the Navy TV Unit" at the National Naval Medical Center and was in charge of the Audio-Visual department at Bethesda.[352] He was called into work at the time of the Kennedy autopsy, and he handled film materials of that autopsy.[353]

---

[352] *Washington Post*, "Cmdr. William B. Pitzer, Head of Navy TV Unit," November 2, 1966: manuscriptservice.com/PitzerFiles/WBP_obits.pdf

[353] John Simkin, "William Pitzer: Biography," *Spartacus Educational*, retrieved 7 May 2013:

His Navy retirement was only days away and he had expressed excitement about his upcoming well-paying job running the educational television department at a college.

On October 29, 1966, Pitzer was found in a pool of blood of the floor of his office at the TV studio in Bethesda, dead from a gunshot wound to the head that authorities quickly ruled was self-inflicted, stating that he was depressed and had committed suicide.

But a new book, *Hit List*, details the many reasons that Pitzer's death was actually a "national security assassination" and not a suicide. The CIA even requested Daniel Marvin—an assassin with U.S. Army Special Forces—to "terminate" Pitzer for the stated reason that he was preparing to release "State secrets." Marvin refused to volunteer for that mission, but later realized that Pitzer had indeed been assassinated by a fellow member of Marvin's Special Forces team.[354] I'll show you the specific forensic evidence in a minute, but first, here's the case in a nutshell:

> Pitzer had a prime role in the documentation of records
> from President Kennedy's autopsy, was reportedly well
> aware that the wounds had been altered and was said to be
> planning to expose the problems with the JFK autopsy. He
> was also *not* suicidal according to reputable accounts. U.S.
> Army Special Forces Lieutenant Colonel Daniel Marvin
> was requested by the CIA to assassinate Pitzer for national
> security purposes:

> 'He was getting close to retirement and it was his plan that
> when he retired was when that information would be released
> to the public, 'cause they'd prove that the President was hit with
> more than one bullet in the head and he was hit from a different
> direction than they said.'[355]

spartacus.schoolnet.co.uk/JFKpitzerW.htm

[354] Lieutenant Colonel Daniel Marvin, US Army Special Forces (Retired), "The Unconventional Warrior Archives: Part Three—Orders to Kill," August 23, 2002,: expendableelite.com/UW_archives/UW_archive.0003b.html

[355] Belzer & Wayne, *Hit List,* 153–154, citing Lieutenant Colonel Daniel Marvin, US Army Special Forces (Retired); Simkin, "William Pitzer: Biography"; *JFK Assassination: 13 Version* (Documentary), 2003: youtube.com/watch?v=uWiMEQYt1n8

Pitzer had been privy to a lot of classified materials regarding what he had witnessed during that autopsy. Pitzer was sworn to secrecy about those events, like most of the people involved in the autopsy, because the U.S. government had invoked "National Security":

> After the completion of the autopsy report, Admiral Burkley, the late President's personal physician, requested written confirmation from Dr. Humes that he had burned his original notes. All Naval hospital staff who had been involved in the autopsy were called into the commanding officer's office several days after and required to sign orders acknowledging their obligation to remain silent about what they had seen and heard, under penalty of court-martial.[356]

Lt. Colonel Dan Marvin was an amazing man of much integrity—I have tremendous respect for the guy. When you talk about a true patriot, I think of somebody like him. This is a guy who led Special Forces teams in Laos when we weren't even technically *in* Laos. He saved a lot of soldiers' lives, performed complex duties with valor, and was awarded for them. Marvin was even requested to do a special mission at one time; the assassination of Cambodia's Crown Prince Sihanouk. He accepted that mission, but when President Johnson didn't hold up his end of the deal and announce the elimination of allowing safe havens for the enemy in Cambodia, Dan Marvin told the CIA that the deal was off.[357]

So that's the league this guy was in. He wasn't just the kind of guy that you could trust with his testimony; he was the type of guy that you could trust with *your life*! Dan passed away a short time ago and if you want to know what I think of him, it's the same thing Babe Ruth supposedly said: "Heroes get remembered, but legends never die." He's still with us in his books, though. There are also some clips online that convey the heroic humanity of this man. He was featured in "The Truth Shall Set You Free" episode of *The Men Who Killed Kennedy*. There's a long segment on his story, starting at about 17:50 and you owe it to yourself to watch him:[358] youtube.com/watch?v=iqpW89lhnE0.

---

[356] Heiner, *Without Smoking Gun.*

[357] Lieutenant Colonel Daniel Marvin, US Army Special Forces (Retired), *Expendable Elite: One Soldier's Journey into Covert Warfare* (TrineDay: 2005): mainemediaresources.com/ ffj_danmarvin.htm

[358] *The Men Who Killed Kennedy – Episode VI,* "The Truth Shall Set You Free," (Documentary), produced by Nigel Turner, A&E History Channel, 1995.

LTC Marvin goes into great detail—in that video clip and in his books and articles—about the specifics of that assassination.[359] He refused to volunteer for that mission, but he thought that a fellow assassin on his team, who went missing, was the one who killed Pitzer. But he remembered the name, and he remembered the mission and was positive that the assassination was requested by the CIA. As soon as he heard that Pitzer was shot, he knew it was an assassination—and that was a surety that he maintained till the day he died. He had nothing to gain by coming forward—and a lot to lose—but he did it anyway because that's the kind of man he was.

Here are some of the many reasons why the evidence *also* shows it was not a suicide.

- GSR testing for gunshot residue on the victim showed that he had not fired a weapon.[360]

- You can see why the government withheld the paraffin results for so long—even from Pitzer's family, by the way.[361] Once you read those results, it shows he had not fired a gun!

- "The paraffin tests of Pitzer's right palm and back of hand were negative, indicating the absence of nitrate, therefore no exposure to gunpowder. While false positives are not uncommon with this test due to contact with tobacco, cosmetics, certain foodstuffs etc., a negative result (as on Pitzer) is usually accepted as evidence of *no recent contact* with a discharged firearm."[362]

- The FBI paraffin tests also showed something else that proved he didn't shoot himself. They showed that the revolver was held at a distance of over 3 feet away from his head.[363] Think about it. That alone shows that he was murdered!

---

[359] Dan Marvin, "Bits & Pieces: A Green Beret on the Periphery of the JFK Assassination," May 1995, *The Fourth Decade*, Vol. 2, No. 4: maryferrell.org/mffweb/archive/viewer/showDoc.do?absPageId=519585; Marvin, *Expendable Elite*; Marvin, "The Unconventional Warrior Archives: Part Three—Orders to Kill".

[360] Heiner, *Without Smoking Gun.*

[361] Ibid.

[362] Allan R. J. Eaglesham & R. Robin Palmer, "The Untimely Death of Lieutenant Commander William B. Pitzer: The Physical Evidence," January 1998, emphasis added: manuscriptservice.com/Pitzer/Article-1.html

[363] Heiner, *Without Smoking Gun.*

Check out this point too:

> If we view all of Lieutenant Commander Pitzer's actions on his
> final day as a 'timeline' to discern his frame of mind, they are
> *dramatically* opposite to a troubled person contemplating suicide.
> Quite to the contrary, in fact, his final day was typical, even mun-
> dane. He was described as 'very cheerful.' He made breakfast,
> raked leaves, got a haircut, stopped at the store, checked things at
> the office—and was then shot in the head.[364]

And this one's my favorite. He wrote himself a note to remember to return
the revolver to the security office.[365] Now, if he was going to shoot himself in
the frigging head with that gun then *why in hell* would he have written that
note?

There are actually a lot more reasons than the ones I listed above. But I
think you get the idea.

**Lt. Commander William Bruce Pitzer did not commit suicide. It was a
national security assassination.**

---

[364] Belzer & Wayne, *Hit List*, 163, citing Heiner, *Without Smoking Gun.*

[365] Heiner, *Without Smoking Gun.*

36

The Zapruder Film Was
Apparently Altered

That film that was taken of the assassination as it happened *also* appears to have been altered.

General Charles Douglas (C. D.) Jackson was Managing Director of *Time-Life International*, which quickly purchased the very controversial film of the assassination by Abraham Zapruder, and then kept it under lock and key for many years, prohibiting the public from learning what actually happened.

When it was finally released, it was regarded as a perfect time-clock of the assassination and the one piece of evidence we could rely on. But what criminologists refer to as the "chain of evidence" of that film held some disturbing revelations.

Douglas Horne was Chief Analyst for Military Records for the Assassination Records Review Board. A dramatic finding came as a simple result of one of their public hearings. Horne explains:

> The Review Board held a public hearing which was televised
> by C-Span. One of the people watching happened to be one of
> two people who actually magnified individual frames from the
> Zapruder film the weekend of the assassination and made prints
> for three briefing boards for use in briefing high officials in the

government. The individual who watched the Z-film hearing on
C-Span was named Morgan Bennett Hunter, and his supervisor
in 1963 was Homer McMahon: both were then CIA employees at
NPIC, the National Photo Interpretation Center.[366]

The Secret Service brought that film to the CIA right after the assassination.

> The story that Homer and his assistant Ben told us was
> that, on the weekend of the assassination, they had a film
> brought to them by the Secret Service. . . . The Z-film
> was brought to them at NPIC on either Saturday night or
> Sunday night after the assassination, because they were
> positive it was before the president's funeral, which was
> on Monday. They said that (the agent) brought what he
> represented to them as being the original Zapruder film. He
> did not come from Dallas. He came from Rochester, New
> York, where he said the film had been developed. And he
> used a code word for a classified film laboratory that the
> CIA had paid Kodak to set up and run in Rochester, their
> headquarters and main industrial facility.[367]

That had huge implications and Horne realized it:

> This assertion by the Secret Service to two CIA film professionals
> that the original Zapruder film was developed in Rochester at a
> secret CIA-sponsored facility, instead of in Dallas, runs contrary
> to the paper trail that had traditionally been accepted as ground
> truth since 1967. We therefore now have an almost-too-good
> paper trail…which can no longer guarantee the authenticity of
> the film in the archives.[368]

The point is that if the film was already developed, it can't be developed
again, so the Secret Service wasn't bringing it to the CIA film specialists to have
it developed. And it's clear that the film was developed before it left Dallas. So
why was the Secret Service taking it to the CIA at a special lab?

---

[366] Russell, *On the Trail of the JFK Assassins*, 293–295.
[367] Ibid.
[368] Ibid.

The processing affidavits which attempt to establish the film's
chain-of-custody are all dated November 22, the day of the
assassination . . . these affidavits still do mean that the Kodak
lab in Dallas developed the original film; they establish that
Mr. Zapruder exposed three contact prints at the Jamieson film lab
in Dallas; and they further establish that he then returned to the
Kodak processing plant where the three copies were immediately
developed. All of these things happened on November 22, 1963.[369]

So that could be the way that what seems problematically absent from the
version of the Zapruder film we have been given—the stopping of the limousine that so many witnesses referred to, and the absence of blowout from the
gunshot to the head—were edited out of the original version:

If the authentic, original film was really shot in slow motion . . .
and you wanted to remove certain events such as the car stop on
Elm Street that over fifty Dealey Plaza eyewitnesses testified to,
you would need to remove several frames, and then recreate a
film that runs at normal speed, and that is much shorter than the
original in terms of total number of frames. Furthermore, if you
wanted to eliminate evidence of shots from the front you would
need to black out the exit wound in the back of the head in some
frames, and even remove some frames showing exit debris in mid-
air. . . . The image alteration in these frames would be done using
the technique called *aerial imaging* at a facility that possessed a
sophisticated optical printer.[370]

In other words, those changes would have to be made at a facility just like
the CIA plant where the film was quite possibly sneaked off to during that
broken chain of custody.

The bottom line, as Horne concludes, is that "anyone who believes that the
so-called original film in the archives today may be an altered, reconstructed
product, and not the true original mentioned in the Zapruder affidavit trail,
has valid grounds to be suspicious of it."[371]

---

[369] Ibid.
[370] Ibid.
[371] Ibid.

Not everyone in the JFK research community is convinced that the movie's been faked, but some are.

James Fetzer taught at university level as a Professor of Logic for several decades and has applied the proven principles of logical deduction and scientific inquiry to the study of the JFK assassination materials. He has written extensively about the alterations he believes happened to that film. Especially in his book, *The Great Zapruder Film Hoax*, he explores that theme in detail.

Upon frame-by-frame scientific examination of that film, Professor Fetzer concludes that while much of the film is genuine, it contains some frames that are scientifically impossible because they literally violate the laws of physics.[372]

Photographic expert Jack White studied the film for decades and arrived at the same conclusion. You can see an excellent video study online at "The Great Zapruder Film Hoax":[373] youtube.com/watch?v=dvLW3IBHHvA.

All I can say is this, if the head shot from the front was that obvious *before* they altered the film footage, imagine what it must have been like before it was modified!

---

[372] James H. Fetzer, Ph.D., *The Great Zapruder Film Hoax: Deceit and Deception in the Death of JFK* (Catfeet Press: 2003).

[373] "The Great Zapruder Film Hoax – 1/6," retrieved 8 May 2013: youtube.com/watch?v=dvLW3IBHHvA

37

The "Magic Bullet" Theory Has Been Proven False

And now we come to The Granddaddy of 'em all on the subject of conflicting evidence.

Ladies and gentlemen, introducing Arlen Specter and his world-famous "Single Bullet Theory," also known (mockingly) as the "magic bullet."

He *should* have called it the "Single Bullshit Theory." It almost defies description, but that didn't stop Mr. Specter. And by the way, it totally cracks me up that they refer to people like me and our crazy "theories" about conspiracy and then they have the nerve to come up with something as ridiculous as that "magic bullet."

Since the government clung to their official version of one gunman and three bullets after it was verified that a *separate* shot had hit bystander James Tague, the government effectively "ran out of bullets." There was a bullet hole in the back of the President's jacket—that's one. There was obviously a shot to his head—that's two. That only left one bullet to account for all the other damage.

So Arlen Specter, an attorney working at that time with the Warren Commission, devised a scenario where one bullet passed through President Kennedy, then changed course in mid-air and entered Governor Connally, went through-and-through Connally, then re-entered Connally again and lodged itself in his body. And the fact that it was impossible didn't stop Specter either.

To do true justice to this "theory"—and what a theory it is—you really need to see it as well as hear it. That's done well in Oliver Stone's film, *JFK*.[374] In two-and-a-half minutes, they totally demolish the entire thing. Here's the clip: youtube.com/watch?v=sBXjf8Jce10.

I pointed out a lot of these "long stretches" in *American Conspiracies*: the so-called "magic bullet" would have had to have caused seven separate wounds in President Kennedy and Governor Connally. Plus, when this bullet just happened to turn up on a stretcher at Dallas' Parkland Hospital, there weren't even any bloodstains on it. And how could that bullet be undamaged when the one that hit Connally left behind some permanent lead in his wrist?[375]

Take a good look at the almost total *lack* of damage to that bullet; it's ridiculous. There's a good photo of it online, with a good article, "The Magic Bullet: Even More Magical Than We Knew?" at: historymatters.com/essays/frameup/EvenMoreMagical/EvenMoreMagical.htm.

If that crazy theory had ever been subjected to the actual legal proceedings of a courtroom, it would have been rejected by a jury as laughably implausible.

That theory was also totally demolished from a scientific standpoint by respected forensic expert Dr. Cyril Wecht. He has investigated the assassination of President Kennedy in minute detail, and he is diametrically opposed to the findings of the Warren Commission. Many of his excellent works are available at his archives: cyrilwecht.com/journal/archives/jfk/index.php.

In his book, *Cause of Death*, Dr. Wecht rejects the single bullet theory as "an asinine pseudoscientific sham at best" that is "absolute nonsense."[376] I'd say that's pretty clear.

> One important question was whether or not a bullet could indeed strike a rib and a radius bone of a human being and emerge as a pristine bullet. Considering that this same bullet had supposedly gone through both the president and the governor, Wecht claims

---

[374] *JFK*, directed by Oliver Stone (Warner Home Video: 1991), youtube.com/ watch?v=sBXjf8Jce10

[375] Ventura & Russell, *American Conspiracies*.

[376] Cyril Wecht, M.D., J.D., Mark Curriden & Ben Wecht, *Cause of Death* (Onyx: 1995).

that no bullet could have caused all the wounds of these two men and emerged pristine.[377]

Also recall that Governor Connally—who, lest we forget, was even a *victim*—always maintained that he and JFK were hit by <u>separate bullets</u>.[378]

When FBI Special Agent James Sibert—who was present at the autopsy of President Kennedy—reflected on what he had seen, studied, and knew; here is his opinion:

I don't buy the single-bullet theory. I'm adamant in that statement.[379]

The phone transcripts of President Johnson reveal that the Warren Commission's invention of the premise that a single bullet was responsible for all the combined wounds was dismissed outright by many leaders, including members of the Commission itself.

In conversations with Senator Richard Russell (Senate Armed Services Committee Chairman and also a member of the Warren Commission), Senator Russell informs President Johnson of the utter unbelievability of the Warren Commission's "single bullet theory" and President Johnson immediately agrees with its absolute lack of plausibility.

SENATOR RUSSELL: They was tryin' to prove that the same bullet that hit Kennedy first, was the one that hit Connally and went through him and went through his hand and his bone and into his leg and everything else...But they said that...the Commission believe that the same bullet that hit Kennedy hit Connally. Well, I don't believe it!

PRESIDENT JOHNSON: I don't either.[380]

---

[377] Antoinette Giancana, John R. Hughes, DM OXON, MD, Ph.D.& Thomas H. Jobe, MD, *JFK and Sam: The Connection Between the Giancana and Kennedy Assassinations*, (Cumberland House: 2005).

[378] Russell Kent, "The Best Evidence Against the SBT," *Fair Play Magazine*, May–June 1998: acorn.net/jfkplace/09/fp.back_issues/22nd_Issue/sbt.html

[379] William Matson Law & Allan Eaglesham, *In the Eye of History: Disclosures in the JFK Assassination Medical Evidence* (JFK Lancer: 2004).

[380] White House tapes of September 18, 1964 at 7:54 P.M., cited in Donald E. Wilkes, Jr., Professor of Law, "JFK Killer Not Alone, UGA Professor Says," December 8, 1994, *The Athens Observer*, 1A: law.uga.edu/dwilkes_more/jfk_11alone.html

And I don't either.

Just watch the angles that magic bullet would have had to take in mid-air to do all that damage to Kennedy *and* Connally. Then they find it on a stretcher at the hospital, and guess what? It's like a new bullet! They called it a "pristine" bullet, because even after supposedly wreaking all that horrendous damage, the bullet still looks new. That's impossible!

In fact, that "pristine" bullet they found literally *could not* have done all that damage, for one simple reason: There was more bullet fragment recovered from Connally than was missing from that bullet.[381] Not possible, period.

---

[381] Kent, "The Best Evidence Against the SBT."

38

The U.S. Government Subverted the Investigation of New Orleans District Attorney Jim Garrison

There's people who'll disagree, but I think Jim Garrison was a true American hero. In 1966, the New Orleans District Attorney's Office uncovered evidence believed to be linked to the assassination of President Kennedy and opened up an official investigation of those facts that they were legally obligated to pursue. It was within their legal jurisdiction and could have—and *should* have—been pursued without obstruction of justice.

Take note here that the American people *welcomed* the District Attorney's investigation because it seemed that it was the first authentic look at it that anyone had taken. It was widely perceived that finally there was going to actually *be* an investigation.

If you want a good example of the American people's serious reservations about the Warren Commission and the way that they overwhelmingly welcomed Garrison's investigation, just listen to the District Attorney's appearance on *The Steve Allen Show* in 1971. And when you listen to Jim Garrison eloquently explaining what really happened, it's really amazing that—even

though the truth was available then—we're still being lied to now:[382] youtube.
com/watch?v=KXZfsbpa2kI.

Justice *was* obstructed. And it was obstructed by the very people who were
supposed to be guarding our rights to learn the truth.

It is now known that the U.S. government hindered the investigation
wherever it could. At first, few believed Garrison's claim that the CIA had
curtailed his investigation:

> Then . . . former CIA official Victor Marchetti revealed that high-
> level CIA conferences in early 1969 had determined to 'give help
> in the trial.' Said Marchetti: 'I sure as hell know they didn't mean
> Garrison.' Marchetti maintained that both [Clay] Shaw and David
> Ferrie, another of Garrison's prime suspects, had served the
> agency at one time.[383]

In fact, the wheels of power in the U.S. government impeded the investigation of Jim Garrison at every opportunity: electronically bugging his office,
smearing his name, and blocking extradition of witnesses Garrison sought after
they had fled to other states. His attempts to subpoena witnesses were struck
down by judges.[384] And then major media went after him, too; they launched
vicious and well-organized attempts against his investigations.[385]

So here's a very important question: Why did the U.S. government block
Jim Garrison's court case? That shows a government conspiracy, as Garrison
was a legitimate District Attorney prosecuting a local case; it was a murder
case so there's no statute of limitations on murder—it's *his* call. If he wants
to go after this case, why were subpoenaed witnesses halted by the federal
government? That point completely shows a government cover-up, government malfeasance to the worst degree. They worked against District Attorney
Garrison's trial. That had to come from the highest echelons of government.
Who makes the call to block Jim Garrison's trial? Is it the Attorney General?
Is it the President? It ain't gonna be some mid-level guy making a call like that

---

[382] *The Steve Allen Show*, 1971, KTLA-TV, (Golden West Broadcasters, Inc.): youtube.com/
watch?v=KXZfsbpa2kI

[383] Dick Russell, *On the Trail of the JFK Assassins*, 85.

[384] Joan Mellen, *A Farewell to Justice: Jim Garrison, JFK's Assassination, and the Case That Should
Have Changed History* (Potomac Books: 2005).

[385] William Davy, *Let Justice Be Done: New Light on the Jim Garrison Investigation* (Jordan Pub:
1999): ctka.net/nbc_cia.html

and over-ruling a legitimate local district attorney of Orleans Parish, you can bet on that.

Although the jury found that there was not sufficient evidence to convict Clay Shaw, who was the defendant in that trial, Garrison proved a lot of important things. He found strong assassination links to mobster Carlo Marcello's associates David Ferrie, Guy Banister, and Jack Ruby.

He also proved Oswald's intelligence linkage: Garrison's investigation found Shaw linked to a subterranean world of anti-Castro operations involving a bizarre pilot and paramilitarist named David Ferrie and a rabid John Birch Society member and ex-FBI agent named Guy Banister.

> Newly released government files, plus the results of digging
> by researchers William Davy, Peter Vea, and Jim DiEugenio,
> indicate that Oswald was frequently seen with Shaw, Ferrie, and
> Banister. In 1995, Lou Ivon, an investigator for Garrison, told
> Davy that in February 1967, he had met with a frightened David
> Ferrie, who admitted doing contract work for the CIA and who
> knew Oswald and Shaw. Four days after he told Ivon that Shaw
> worked for the CIA and that he hated Kennedy, Ferrie was found
> dead. Two unsigned suicide notes were found next to the body,
> but the autopsy cited a brain aneurysm as the cause of death.[386]

Garrison investigated Oswald's background more tenaciously and with much more thoroughness than did the Warren Commission.

Former FBI Special Agent William Turner, who had worked with the Garrison investigation, also shared some very interesting revelations in an excellent piece that detailed his experiences with that investigation. It was an article called, "The Garrison Commission on the Assassination of President Kennedy," and it really went in-depth about what they knew and how they knew it. A short excerpt follows, but if you have the time, the whole article is worth a read: wf.net/~biles/jfk/ramparts.txt

> [District Attorney] Garrison believes that Oswald was
> schooled in covert operations by the CIA while in the Marine
> Corps at the Atsugi Naval Station in Japan, a U-2 facility

---

[386] Roger S. Peterson, "Declassifed," August 1996, *American History Magazine*: assassinationweb.com/Peterson.htm

[interestingly, two possibly relevant documents, 'Oswald's
access to information about the U-2' {CD 931} and 'Reproduction of CIA official dossier on Oswald' {CD 692} are still classified in the National Archives]. Curiously, the miscast Marine
who was constantly in hot water had a Crypto clearance on
top of a Top Secret clearance and was given two electronics
courses. 'Isn't it odd,' prods Garrison, 'that even though he
supposedly defected to the Soviet Union with Top Secret data
on our radar nets, no action was taken against him when he
came back to the United States?'[387]

One of Garrison's major "finds" was Dean Andrews, a flashy Southern
attorney who was an established link between Lee Harvey Oswald and Clay
Shaw. Andrews knowingly concealed the fact that Clay Bertrand was an alias
for Clay Shaw, who—it has been proved—had ties to U.S. intelligence.[388]
The government clearly intimidated Dean Andrews into changing his testimony, as I'll show you below. But the CIA itself proved that Shaw was with
the Agency:

Now the CIA has admitted as much. Memorandums on a number
of the figures in Garrison's probe were prepared in 1967 and 1968
for the deputy director of plans . . . Garrison and Marchetti were
right. The CIA verified Shaw's background in an April 6, 1967,
file for the deputy chief, security research staff.[389]

But bear in mind that this was what researchers dug up later. At the
time, when Garrison was trying to conduct an authentic investigation, they
stonewalled him every step of the way. Make no mistake about it—the government lied and said there was no connection between Shaw and the CIA.

There's a clip online where you can see what a colorful character Dean
Andrews was. That was the jive-talking New Orleans attorney who John
Candy portrayed so well in Oliver Stone's film, *JFK*. That piece was also
one of the many "hatchet jobs" done on the Garrison investigation in the

---

[387] William W. Turner, "The Garrison Commission on the Assassination of President
Kennedy," *Ramparts Magazine*, January 1968: wf.net/~biles/jfk/ramparts.txt

[388] Russell, *On the Trail of the JFK Assassins*, 85.

[389] Ibid.

press, so it also shows you what Garrison was up against: youtube.com/watch?v=jCkw8zWmQD8.

Garrison documented the following conversation between him and Andrews for his book, *On the Trail of the Assassins*. For the film *JFK*, it was depicted almost verbatim. In the following exchange, the fear in Andrews's voice practically jumps off the printed page. Andrews was convicted of perjury, but in his opinion that was a much better choice than being killed.

GARRISON: If you lie to the Grand Jury as you have been lying to me, I'm going to charge you with perjury. Now am I communicating with you?

ANDREWS: (stunned) Is this off the off the record, Daddyo?

(Garrison nodded)

In that case, let me sum it up for you real quick. It's as simple as this. If I answer that question you keep asking me, if I give you the name you keep trying to get, then it's goodbye, Dean Andrews. It's bon voyage, Deano. I mean like permanent. I mean like a bullet in my head—which makes it hard to do one's legal research, if you get my drift. Does that help you see my problem a little better?

GARRISON: Read my lips. Either you dance in to the Grand Jury with the real moniker of that cat who called you to represent Lee Oswald, or your fat behind is going to the slammer. Do you dig me?

ANDREWS: [He stood up suddenly.] Do you have any idea what you're getting into, my man? You want to dance with the government? Is that what you want? Then be my guest. But you will get sat on, and I do mean hard.[390]

---

[390] Garrison, *On the Trail of the Assassins*, 91 – 95.

But the government torpedoed that witness and Garrison knew it. He also explained in his book how that came about:

> It had readily become apparent to me, however, that the more Andrews realized that his having received a phone call to defend Lee Oswald was a potential danger to him, the foggier the identity of Clay Bertrand became in his mind. By the time Andrews appeared before the Warren Commission in July of 1964, Bertrand's height had shrunk from six feet two all the way down to five feet eight inches. Apparently in response to subtle pressure from the FBI agents, Andrews told them, "Write what you want, that I am nuts. I don't care." The agents obligingly wrote in their final report that Andrews had come to the conclusion that the phone call from Bertrand had been "a figment of his imagination." This not only allowed the Bureau to conclude its investigation into Andrews but harmonized with its announced conclusion that Lee Oswald had accomplished Kennedy's assassination alone and unaided.[391]

And he proved that the Warren Commission altered witness testimony in a very corrupt manner. Another important witness whom the Garrison investigation found was Julia Ann Mercer:

> Some of the best witnesses to the assassination found their way to us after it became apparent to them that the federal agents and the Dallas police really were not interested in what they saw. Julia Ann Mercer was just such a witness. In fact, no other witness so completely illuminated for me the extent of the cover-up.

> Mercer had been but a few feet away when one of the riflemen was unloaded at the grassy knoll shortly before the arrival of the presidential motorcade. Consequently, she was a witness not only to the preparation of President Kennedy's murder but also to the conspiracy involved.

---

[391] Ibid, 92–93.

She gave statements to the FBI and the Dallas Sheriff's office, and
then returned to the FBI and provided additional statements, but
she was never called by the Warren Commission—not even to
provide an affidavit.[392]

Quite contrary to the attempted smear job done on her by author Gerald
Posner in his book, *Case Closed*, Julia Ann Mercer was a sophisticated woman and
very credible witness. Jim Garrison described his pleasant surprise at meeting her:

Then one day in early 1968, her husband called me at the office.
He said that he and his wife were in New Orleans on business and
had some things to tell me. I agreed to meet them at the Fairmont
Hotel, where they were staying.

Arriving at their suite, I found a most impressive couple. A
middle-aged man of obvious substance, he had been a Republican
member of Congress from Illinois. Equally impressive, she was
intelligent and well-dressed, the kind of witness any lawyer would
love to have testifying on his side in front of a jury.[393]

Ms. Mercer's statements were definitely altered, and she showed that to
Garrison in precise terms:

After he had departed on business, I handed her copies of her
statements as they had been printed in the Warren Commission
exhibits. She read them carefully and then shook her head.

'These all have been altered,' she said. 'They have me saying just
the opposite of what I really told them.'

It's not at all surprising that Mercer's testimony was a threat to the cover-
up. She was the eyewitness to an amazing event, and her recollection of it was
absolutely positive.

---

[392] Garrison, *On the Trail of the Assassins.*
[393] Ibid.

About an hour before the assassination, she had been driving west
on Elm Street and had been stopped—just past the grassy knoll—
by traffic congestion. To her surprise (because she recalled that the
President's parade was coming soon), she saw a young man in the
pickup truck to her right dismount, carrying a rifle, not too well
concealed in a covering of some sort. She then observed him walk
up 'the grassy hill which forms part of the overpass.' She looked
at the driver several times, got a good look at his round face and
brown eyes, and he looked right back at her.

Mercer also observed that three police officers were standing near a motorcycle on the overpass bridge above her and
just ahead. She recalled that they showed no curiosity about
the young man climbing the side of the grassy knoll with
the rifle.[394]

So, silly us, we think that the United States Government would actually
welcome upstanding citizens spending their own time to testify about important events that they witnessed, right?
Wrong, Charlie Brown!

After the assassination, when Mercer sought to make this information available to law enforcement authorities, their response
was almost frenzied. At the FBI office—where she went the day
after the assassination—she was shown a number of mug shots.
Among the several she selected as resembling the driver was a
photograph of Jack Ruby. On Sunday, when she saw Ruby kill
Oswald on television, she positively recognized him as the driver
of the pickup truck and promptly notified the local Bureau office.
Nevertheless, the FBI altered her statement so it did not note that
she had made a positive identification.

She laughed when she pointed this out to me. 'See,' she said, 'the
FBI made it just the opposite of what I really told them.' Then
she added, 'He was only a few feet away from me. How could

---

[394] Ibid.

I not recognize Jack Ruby when I saw him shoot Oswald on
television?'[395]

So that was what the Feds did. And guess what? The authorities in Dallas
did the same thing. They altered her testimony, too, in what Garrison aptly
describes as the "same fraud":

> The Dallas Sheriff's office went through the same laborious fraud
> and added an imaginative touch of its own. Although Mercer
> had never been brought before any notary, the Sheriff's office
> filed a sworn affidavit stating that she did not identify the driver,
> although she might, 'if I see him again,' and significantly chang-
> ing other facts.

> 'See that notarized signature?' she asked me. 'That's not my
> signature either. I sign my name with a big "A" like this.' She
> produced a pen and wrote her name for me. It was clear that the
> signature the Dallas Sheriff's office had on its altered statement
> was not even close to hers.[396]

It was obvious that Garrison actually cared about finding the truth, and as
a District Attorney, he certainly knew how to weigh the evidence, too:

> The implications of her experience were profound. First
> of all, Mercer's observations provided further evidence
> that there was another rifleman on the knoll ahead
> of the President.

> But to me the responses to her statements were even more chill-
> ing. They proved that law enforcement officials recognized early
> on that a conspiracy existed to kill the President. Both local and
> federal authorities had altered Mercer's statements precisely to
> conceal that fact.[397]

Jim Garrison described the Warren Report quite well:

---

[395] Garrison, *On the Trail of the Assassins.*
[396] Ibid.
[397] Ibid.

The twenty-six volumes is [sic] a domestic intelligence accomplishment.[398]

The following is straight from Garrison himself, regarding his interview of private investigator Jack Martin about the goings-on at Banister's office between Banister, Ferrie, and Oswald in the period prior to the JFK assassination.

MARTIN: There was Dave Ferrie—you know about him by now.

GARRISON: Was he there very often?

MARTIN: Often? He practically lived there.

GARRISON: And Lee Harvey Oswald?

MARTIN: Yeah, he was there too. Sometimes he'd be meeting with Guy Banister with the door shut. Other times he'd be shooting the bull with Dave Ferrie. But he was there all right.

GARRISON: What was Guy Banister doing while all this was going on?

MARTIN: Hell, he was the one running the circus.

GARRISON: What about his private detective work?

MARTIN: Not much of that came in, but when it did, I handled it. That's why I was there.

GARRISON: So, Jack. Just what was going on at Banister's office?

MARTIN: I can't answer that. I can't go into that stuff at all. I think I'd better go.

GARRISON: Hold on, Jack. What's the problem with our going into what was happening at Banister's office?

---

[398] *The Steve Allen Show*, 1971, KTLA-TV, (Golden West Broadcasters, Inc.): youtube.com/watch?v=KXZfsbpa2kI

MARTIN: *What's the problem? What's the problem?* The *problem*
is that we're going to bring the goddamned federal
government down on our backs. Do I need to spell it
out? I could get killed—and so could you.

But he went forward with that investigation anyway, and he deserves a lot
of credit for that.

As Jim Garrison put it himself:

One man with the truth constitutes a majority.[399]

---

[399] Jim Garrison, "Gerald Ford & Jim Garrison in 1967," retrieved 9 May 2013: youtube.com/watch?v=lixaRjLxadw

39

Another Key Witness Conveniently Silenced: David Ferrie

ust as Jim Garrison's investigation was getting started, his *star witness* died a "convenient" and very suspicious death. David Ferrie was a strange man; a homosexual during a macho period in history. But he was also an excellent pilot with tons of bravado and that came in handy when you were flying guns into Cuba on covert missions. He was also very well-connected, being both investigator and private pilot for Carlos Marcello, the crime boss of Texas and Louisiana.

And just like in Oliver Stone's *JFK*, Ferrie actually predicted his own death. After he was publicly named as an accused conspirator in the JFK assassination by the New Orleans District Attorney's office, Ferrie exploded at Jim Garrison's aide, Lou Ivon. These were his exact words:

> **You know what this news story does to me, don't you? I'm a dead man. From here on, believe me, I'm a dead man.**[400]

On the same day that Ferrie died, Garrison also lost *another* key witness: anti-Castro Cuban Eladio del Valle, who was brutally murdered in Miami.[401]

---

[400] Garrison, *On the Trail of the Assassins*, 138.
[401] Belzer & Wayne, *Hit List*, 168.

Just another coincidence, *right?* Right. His key witnesses were dropping like flies and he knew it:

> All I know is that witnesses with vital evidence in the case are bad
> insurance risks.[402]

I already documented his connections to Oswald and Guy Banister, so let's look at some of the inconsistencies surrounding Ferrie's death.

The Coroner ruled that his death was of natural causes; a brain aneurysm from a cerebral hemorrhage. But they *also* said they found two suicide notes in his apartment. And they were *typed*.[403]

Garrison's office found that rather strange and suspected poisoning.[404] With some dry wit and sarcasm, here's what the district attorney had to say about yet another amazing coincidence:

> I suppose it could just be a weird coincidence that the night Ferrie
> penned two suicide notes, he died of natural causes.[405]

Both of those so-called suicide notes were typed, undated, and unsigned.[406] The last person to see him alive reported that he had been in good spirits.[407] Others reported that his mood was combative, intent on fighting the charges against him.[408] Still sound like a suicide?

And get this: Those notes were not really suggestive of suicide. Instead, they were diatribes about things he was angered by; a man who knew he was about to be killed:

> They appear, instead, to be two notes written by a man who knew
> he was leaving this world—they were more the words of a man

---

[402] Donald W. Miller, Jr., MD., "Pursuing Truth on the Kennedy Assassinations," August 21, 2012: lewrockwell.com/miller/miller40.1.html

[403] Russell, *The Man Who Knew Too Much*, 182.

[404] Ibid.

[405] "Jim Garrison's Playboy Interview," *Playboy Magazine*, October 1967, Vol. 14 No. 10: jfklancer.com/Garrison2.html

[406] *John McAdams' The Kennedy Assassination Pages*, "David Ferrie's 'Suicide Notes,'" retrieved 10 May 2013: mcadams.posc.mu.edu/death10.htm

[407] Ibid.

[408] Ibid.

who was making his final statements; of words that he wanted
left behind.

One note to his best friend started out: 'When you read this I will
be quite dead and no answer will be possible.' It ended with the
words: 'As you sowed, so shall you reap.' The other letter started
out: 'To leave this life, to me, is a sweet prospect.' Then it com-
plained about the justice system and ended with: 'All the state
needs is "evidence to support a conviction." If this is justice, then
justice be damned.' The letters can be accessed in their entirety
online.

So they, indeed, do not appear to actually be notes regarding a
planned suicide.[409]

Garrison wasn't alone. A lot of people thought that Ferrie was murdered,
and among the authorities who did was Aaron Kohn, Managing Director of
the Metropolitan Crime Commission of New Orleans.[410] It was all just a *little
too convenient*.

---

[409] Belzer & Wayne, *Hit List*, 177, citing *McAdams*, "David Ferrie's 'Suicide Notes.'"

[410] John S. Craig, "The Mystery of David Ferrie," July, 1995, *Fair Play Magazine*: spot.acorn.
net/jfkplace/09/fp.back_issues/05th_issue/ferrie.html

40

Another Key Witness Conveniently Silenced: Dorothy Kilgallen

Here it is, short and not so sweet:

> Dorothy Kilgallen, the nationally-famous reporter who inter-
> viewed Jack Ruby in prison, died of unexplained causes after hint-
> ing at an explosive breakthrough in the Kennedy story.[411]

Actually, the causes *were* explained; they just made absolutely no sense! In fact, the official version is more full of holes than Swiss cheese.

Kilgallen was a nightmare for the government because she said she was sure the assassination of JFK was a conspiracy and wouldn't let the story die. She also vowed to stay on the case until she broke it and that she *would* indeed solve the case and prove the conspiracy as a result of the inside information she had acquired.

That claim had a foundation, as she was the only reporter in the country who was allowed to have a private interview with Jack Ruby and nobody knew

---

[411] Heiner, *Without Smoking Gun*, 113.

what he had told her. So when Kilgallen said that she was going to "bust this case wide open," everyone paid attention. And it's easy to see how that probably disturbed a lot of people in white shirts around Washington.

Kilgallen said it would all be in her new book that exposed the conspiracy behind the assassination, but that book was never published the way she intended, because she was soon found dead.

Sound suspicious? Well, keep reading, because it's so creepy it'll knock your socks off.

Official Scenario: She was found in bed in her ritzy, multi-level Manhattan townhome, the victim of an overdose. Having combined sleeping pills with alcohol, she succumbed to their effects and died. Either Suicide or Accidental Overdose.

Big problems with the official scenario.

It was medically estimated that Dorothy had the equivalent of fifteen to twenty pills in her body, in a triple combination of Nembutal, Seconal, and Tuinol, combined with alcohol, which supercharged their effects.

Yet it has been established that she was observed in a fine, coherent state a short time before her death occurred. She could *not* have taken that many pills—accidentally or otherwise—and still been walking around in a coherent state. Whatever did happen must therefore have happened very quickly.

And an even larger issue is the sterility of the crime scene. There was no vomit or mess of any kind. That would simply not be possible if she had swallowed fifteen to twenty pills and combined them with alcohol.

A person doesn't take that many pills *accidentally*. And she was happy that night; not the slightest bit suicidal. So that's why some think she was slipped a fast-acting "Mickey Finn" cocktail because—a short time later—she was *down*.

Whoever staged the crime scene made some *huge* mistakes. Check out some of these things; it's just like in a good thriller.

The bed that she was found in was actually the master bedroom, but all of her friends knew that the master bedroom was never used and contained a bed that she never would have gone to sleep in. It was just for show; it was off the living room, and when entertaining formally, was just used to maintain the false pretense that she and her husband were still a happy couple.[412]

She was found in bed with a book next to her, like she had been reading and then passed out. But the clothes she was wearing were something that friends and family knew she would never wear to bed: a blue bed jacket over a nightgown instead of her regular old pajamas.[413]

Even though she was supposedly ready for bed, she still had her makeup and false eyelashes on; two more things that friends and family knew she'd never wear to bed. Here's how Kilgallen's hairdresser, the one who discovered her body, explained it to a friend: "When I tell you the bed she was found in, and how I found her, you're going to know she was murdered."[414]

The book that was placed next to her on the bed was another mistake they made. It was a book that she had already read and had discussed it with friends.[415] So they picked a book that she wouldn't have been reading.

She also used reading glasses when she read, and there were no reading glasses near her. See what I mean about all the mistakes that the killers would have had no way of knowing?[416]

Another thing was that the air conditioning was left on, which was something she never did at night.[417]

When they ran lab tests on the drinking glass that was near the bed, it only showed traces of <u>one</u> barbiturate, but the autopsy showed that she was killed by a "cocktail" of small doses of <u>three different barbiturates</u>, which formed a lethal combination with alcohol.[418]

So somebody obviously tried to make it look like she had taken some pills, gone to bed, and quietly passed away. But then how did the other two barbiturates get into her body?

---

[412] Sara Jordan, "Who Killed Dorothy Kilgallen?," October 21, 2007, *Midwest Today*: midtod.com/new/articles/7_14_07_Dorothy.html

[413] Ibid.

[414] Ibid.

[415] Ibid.

[416] Ibid.

[417] Ibid.

[418] Cassie Parnau, "Archive/Medical Reports," *The Kilgallen Files*, retrieved 11 May 2013: kilgallenfiles.wordpress.com/category/official-reports/medical-reports/

And get a load of this little gem: All of Dorothy's notes on JFK for her upcoming book totally disappeared.

And if that's not bizarre enough for you, then get this: Dorothy was one smart cookie. She was aware that two other reporters who had been investigating JFK's murder had recently died very sudden and strange deaths.[419] So she usually carried her JFK notes with her. And she also even gave a backup copy of those notes to someone she knew she could trust: fellow journalist Flo Pritchett.

Well, *guess what Charlie Brown?* Her friend was dead two days later. And in case that's not crazy enough for you, the backup copy of the notes *also* vanished.

People have pointed out that her friend had a long-term illness, which was true. But what happened to the notes? Nobody has ever been able to explain that.

Kilgallen's book was published posthumously—*without* the chapter on JFK.

---

[419] Belzer & Wayne, *Hit List* (see Jim Koethe, Bill Hunter, Dorothy Kilgallen, Flo Pritchett).

41

Another Key Witness Conveniently Silenced: Lee Bowers

Lee Bowers was the best witness to multiple shooters in Dallas, as he had a bird's eye view of Dealey Plaza from a high spot looking down toward the grassy knoll. He was a solid citizen and witness and was sure about what he saw.

> One witness was in a better position than anyone else to observe suspicious activity by the fence at the top of the grassy knoll. This was railway worker Lee Bowers, perched in a signal box which commanded a unique view of the area behind the fence. Bowers said that, shortly before the shots were fired, he noticed two men standing near the fence.[420]

Here's how Bowers described the men he saw:

> One was 'middle-aged' and 'fairly heavyset,' wearing a white shirt and dark trousers. The other was 'mid-twenties

---

[420] Summers, *The Kennedy Conspiracy*.

in either a plaid shirt or plaid coat . . . these men were the
only two strangers in the area. The others were workers that
I knew.' Bowers also said that when the shots were fired
at the President 'in the vicinity of where the two men I
have described were, there was a flash of light, something I
could not identify, but there was something which occurred
which caught my eye in this immediate area on the embank-
ment . . . a flash of light or smoke or something which caused
me to feel that something out of the ordinary had occurred
there.'[421]

So I know you're probably saying to yourself, *Wow, what an incredibly valuable witness, and I'm sure the Warren Commission thought so, too*. Well, before
you get too excited, here's what they did:

Lee Bowers was questioned by the Warren Commission but was
cut off in mid-sentence when he began describing the 'something out of the ordinary' he had seen. The interrogating lawyer
changed the subject.[422]

Friends of Bowers said he hadn't told the whole story of everything he had
seen that day.

One of them, Walter Rischel, told reporters that his friend had been afraid
to talk about everything he had witnessed during the JFK assassination. Rischel
said that Bowers feared to 'go public' with the additional information, and for
some very good reasons. Bowers had also reportedly confided the same thing
in his minister.[423]

And then he was killed in what was, at first, reported as a one-car accident
on a long, open lonely stretch of road near Midlothian, Texas.

But there were eyewitness reports that another car ran Bowers off the
road.[424] That claim was investigated by a former member of the Texas

---

[421] Ibid.

[422] Ibid.

[423] Geraldo Rivera, "The Curse of JFK," May 6, 1992, *Now It Can Be Told*:
youtube.com/watch?v=mcXJJsZs7LE

[424] Robert J. Groden & Harrison Edward Livingstone, *High Treason: The Assassination of JFK
and the Case for Conspiracy* (Carroll & Graf: 1998).

Highway Patrol, Charles Good, who concluded that another car had indeed forced Bowers' car off the road.[425]

Bowers didn't die right away and apparently told emergency personnel that he thought he was drugged somehow when he had stopped for coffee a few miles back.[426]

So it's one of those cases where we just don't know. It's difficult to prove he was murdered. But a lot of things about the case just didn't add up and something sure didn't seem right.

---

[425] John Simkin, "Lee E. Bowers: Biography," *Spartacus Educational*, citing Charles Good, 1991, retrieved 11 May 2013: spartacus.schoolnet.co.uk/JFKbowers.htm

[426] Ibid.

42

Another Key Witness Conveniently Silenced: Mary Pinchot Meyer

Another new book you have to read is Peter Janney's *Mary's Mosaic*, which is a great study of the Mary Pinchot Meyer case and what it all meant from a historical standpoint. As the book shows, her murder was an assassination so professional that one CIA insider said it "had all the markings of an in-house rubout."[427]

Mary was an extremely intelligent, very attractive woman who—as fate would have it—was having a serious romantic affair with President Kennedy. As opposed to his many sexual "liaisons" with other women, this was apparently one of JFK's most serious relationships. And most of the people in Washington circles knew it.

After JFK's murder, Mary was one of the people who—like Dorothy Kilgallen—was sure that it was a conspiracy and was determined to prove it. She told friends she knew people at the CIA and that Agency people were involved:

> Meyer claimed to my friend that she positively knew that Agency-affiliated Cuban exiles and the Mafia were responsible for killing John Kennedy.[428]

---

427 Janney, *Mary's Mosaic*, 346–347.
428 Ibid, 314.

Then one day, she was out for her regular morning run and was murdered; two shots from a .38 at point blank range.

Police jumped all over the case, and against proper procedure, immediately said it was solved: random murder, possible sex crime. They came up with a great story that a middle-class black man who was found near the crime scene with his zipper undone was being held for the crime. That's exactly the type of thing that makes most people jump to conclusions, isn't it? Well, it almost worked.

Except that—in this particular case—the middle-class black man with the zipper undone actually managed to get a decent lawyer to come to his defense, and she totally demolished the case against him, right in open court for all to see. They found him not guilty, which left the case still unsolved.

Then other evidence started to materialize, a whole lot of "funny business" seeping into the light of day.

> Janney even uncovered direct evidence about the CIA's internal decision to 'terminate' Mary Meyer. Former killers who had been in the 'cleaning business' for the CIA have openly talked about it and revealed that it was done exactly how it looks like it was done; that they 'Had one of our cleaning men nail her down by the towpath while she was out for her daily jog.'

> 'She was eliminated because she knew too much.'[429]

They even figured out the assassin's operational code name, which was William L. Mitchell.

There's *tons* more on her case; way too much to go into here. But there's ample evidence that she was killed as a "national security assassination" to prevent her from divulging "highly sensitive information," like *the truth*.

---

[429] Belzer & Wayne, *Hit List*, 151, citing Janney, *Mary's Mosaic*, 355, 384.

43

Another Key Witness
Conveniently Silenced:
Sam Giancana

Sam Giancana was a top-level mobster linked to the CIA's anti-Castro assassination program. It was documented by Senator Frank Church's investigation that the CIA had gone to mobster Johnny Roselli to get the cooperation of Giancana and Santo Trafficante, another top Mafia leader, in their covert efforts to eliminate Castro once and for all.

Bear in mind that the guy who we're talking about here was a *ruling king of the mob*. Giancana—nicknamed "Sam the Man"—was not just a big name in Chicago where he was headquartered, but with big casinos in Nevada, giant hotels in Miami Beach, and a lot of major business interests in Hollywood and even Mexico, his name carried a lot of heat. His house was like a fortress, he knew everything about everybody because he knew that's what kept him alive, and you can bet he knew how to protect himself and what was his. His house had also been placed under twenty-four-hour FBI surveillance by the government and that came from a direct order from the Attorney General's office of Robert Kennedy.[430] Giancana was even followed by the Feds when he was on

---

[430] "Sam Giancana: Biography," retrieved 12 May 2013, *bio. True Story*: biography.com/people/sam-giancana-9542088?page=2

the golf course and bullied back at them about the harassment of the constant surveillance.

And even though he was extremely well-protected and under constant surveillance, they got him anyway. Here's how they did it:

> That night, while cooking in the kitchen of his Chicago home—which was described by many as a "fortress" or "bunker"—Giancana came under the gun. According to both his daughter and the police, who stated that Giancana was invulnerable in his own home due to the security systems and impregnability of the structure, only someone he knew or trusted could have gotten to him. Giancana would have to have let them in, gone back to cooking, and then been surprised when the assailant—or assailants—pulled a .22 pistol.[431]

Here's another description of that murder, and note the particular point that what Congress was specifically investigating was the CIA's use of the Mob for its anti-Castro black ops in Cuba:

> Giancana was next called to testify before a United States Senate committee investigating Mafia involvement in a failed CIA plot to assassinate Castro. Before he was scheduled to testify, Giancana flew to Houston, Texas, and underwent gall bladder surgery. He returned to his Oak Park home on June 17, 1975. Two days later, Sam Giancana was shot once in the back of the head and several more times up through the chin with a .22-caliber pistol while cooking in his basement. Though theories abounded as to who killed him [rival Mafiosi, CIA operatives nervous about his future testimony, one of many former girlfriends], no one was ever arrested in connection with the murder.[432]

A better question, actually, would be *how the hell* did somebody even get close enough to kill him without being picked off first by a Mafia bodyguard or a Federal agent?

This is exactly what happened—and when:

---

[431] Craig Roberts & John Armstrong, *JFK: The Dead Witnesses* (Cumberland Press International: 1994), 105.

[432] "Giancana: Biography," *bio. True Story*, A+E Networks.

June 19, 1975	Members of the U.S. Senate's Church Committee arrive in Chicago for the purpose of escorting Sam Giancana to Washington for his appearance before the committee.
June 19, 1975, 9:00 p.m.	Two "law enforcement officers" are observed outside Sam Giancana's home by his neighbors in Oak Park, a wealthy suburb of Chicago.
June 19, 1975, 11:15 p.m.	Three surveillance cars reportedly leave the area of Sam Giancana's home.
June 19, 1975, 11:30 p.m.	Sam Giancana is murdered inside his home.
June 20, 1975	The *Chicago Tribune* reports the murder of Sam Giancana. Allegations are made that the murder was sanctioned by the CIA.
June 21, 1975	The *Chicago Tribune* reports that Giancana's house was under surveillance on the night that he was killed.[433]

The murder of Sam Giancana right before he was to testify was big stuff and everyone knew it. And that was the elimination that set the stage for a major congressional investigation. But there were a few more "convenient witness deaths" of high-profile people, even while that investigation was being formed.

---

[433] Belzer & Wayne, *Hit List*, 218, citing Antoinette Giancana, John R. Hughes, DM OXON, MD, Ph.D. & Thomas H. Jobe, MD, *JFK and Sam: The Connection Between the Giancana and Kennedy Assassinations*, (Cumberland House: 2005).

44

Another Key Witness
Conveniently Silenced:
Johnny Roselli

After that high-profile witness elimination—Sam Giancana murdered the night before he was supposed to go to Washington to testify—it was pretty freaking obvious that it wasn't a coincidence.

Another high-ranking CIA official rumored to have gone "rogue" and participated in the assassination—William "Wild Bill" Harvey, head of the ZR/Rifle assassination unit linked to the use of U.S. mafia in attempts to kill Cuba's Fidel Castro—also died at that time.

So when Johnny Roselli's body washed up in an oil drum just as he was to be hauled before a Committee again and grilled about those same CIA/Mafia plots, it was so obvious that *even Congress had to do something about it*!

That's when they formed the House Select Committee on Assassinations; they knew they clearly had a "situation" and that it had to be addressed; or to at least have the *appearance* that it was being addressed, which is what it turned out to be.

Johnny Roselli was the man that the CIA's "Wild Bill" Harvey had used as the *key go-between* for the CIA's use of the Mafia in their assassination plots against Castro.

Roselli's body had been "garroted"—strangled from behind with a strong wire—stabbed, his legs sawn off and stuffed into an oil drum, and found off the coast of South Florida. It looked—or was *made* to look—like a typical mob "hit" on one of their own.

> The sudden deaths of Sam Giancana and Johnny Roselli and the alleged heart attack of the CIA's William Harvey, the official in charge of the CIA-mafia plot against Castro, helped to stimulate the formation of a committee to reinvestigate the Kennedy assassination.[434]

434 Giancana, Hughes, DM OXON, MD, Ph.D. & Jobe, MD, *JFK and Sam*, 145.

45

Another Key Witness
Conveniently Silenced:
George de Mohrenschildt

Another Chicago mobster closely linked to the Chicago Mob and its "business" arrangement with the CIA also soon got hit. Chuck Nicoletti, the top hit man for the Giancana organization, was murdered on March 29, 1977, right after the House Select Committee on Assassinations had determined that his testimony would be taken. On the same day, a shotgun blast killed George de Mohrenschildt, a man with ties to the CIA who was also a close friend of Lee Harvey Oswald—and was also being sought for testimony by the House Select Committee.

Think about *that* one: on *the exact same day* that Nicoletti was murdered, the man whom many referred to as Oswald's "handler" *also* died, just as he was being sought for testimony!

George de Mohrenschildt was a wealthy businessman with links to the U.S. intelligence community who befriended Oswald when he came back from Russia. But de Mohrenschildt was working with the government, or at least on their behalf. A military intelligence veteran, James Southwood, who had been told to get info on Oswald, reported to author Dick Russell that:

All the information I had about Oswald had been given to the
112th (military intelligence unit) by George de Mohrenschildt.[435]

So de Mohrenschildt obviously had some interesting information about
how and why he was feeding U.S. intelligence information about Lee Harvey
Oswald.

Robert Tanenbaum, Deputy Counsel to the House Select Committee
on Assassinations, was running that investigation. Tanenbaum quickly realized the importance of de Mohrenschildt's knowledge and sent investigator
Gaeton Fonzi to interview him for that purpose. In fact, as soon as Tanenbaum
learned of its importance, he responded, "We will have an investigator there
tomorrow."

But de Mohrenschildt was dead before that investigator could get to him.
He died from a shotgun blast to the face, which was quickly ruled a suicide. I
just have three words to say about that: <u>don't believe it</u>!

> On the morning of March 29, 1977, Gaeton Fonzi, the commit-
> tee's Miami-based investigator, arrived at the villa in Manalapan.
> He was told by de Mohrenschildt's daughter that her father was
> meeting with journalist Edward Jay Epstein at a Palm Beach
> hotel but would be back that night. At 1:00 p.m., de Mohren-
> schildt left by car and returned to his temporary residence. By
> 2:21 p.m., he was dead. Authorities determined the time by
> listening to a tape on which de Mohrenschildt's daughter was
> recording a TV soap opera while she was at work.[436]

An attorney, Mark Lane, believing the death to be far too coincidental,
realized that the tape recording made of that television show at the house
where de Mohrenschildt died could provide crucial evidence. He checked it
out and was right. Get a load of this: that tape shows that an intruder apparently entered the house during the time that de Mohrenschildt allegedly killed
himself with a shotgun.

Here's how that attorney described it:

---

[435] Russell, *The Man Who Knew Too Much*, 456.
[436] Russell, *The Man Who Knew Too Much*, 173.

They claimed he committed suicide. But if you listen to the tape, you hear this: You hear a little noise, then you hear silence and then you hear 'Beep-Beep-Beep-Beep-Beep,' a little more noise, and then you hear the shot. The 'Beep-Beep-Beep-Beep-Beep' was a security system, on medium mode. One mode is—if it's on fully armed—if anyone opens a door or window, a siren goes off and the police are notified. On another mode, it's off entirely. But on the *medium* mode, it goes 'Beep-Beep-Beep-Beep' to show that someone has opened the door and come into the house. Just before de Mohrenschildt was shot, that's what happened.[437]

Dick Russell investigated the case further and asked de Mohrenschildt's wife if she thought that her husband actually could have committed suicide:

Nobody that knew him does, that's my answer.[438]

There's another recent book out, titled *Hit List* by Richard Belzer and David Wayne, which goes into more detail on all these cases and how they all form a pattern. But I think you get the idea from just the ones I've shown you here.

So like I said, don't believe it. That was no suicide from a shotgun to the face, folks. He didn't leave a note for his daughter, and he *did* leave a huge bloodbath in the living room for her to come home and find. And by all reports, George de Mohrenschildt was *not* the kind of person to do that. Plus, it was just way, way too convenient. It doesn't pass the form of inductive reasoning known as 'The Duck Test': If it looks like a duck, walks like a duck, swims like a duck, and quacks like a duck—it's a duck.

George de Mohrenschildt was murdered and the fact that he died just as he was about to be interviewed by an investigator who actually cared about learning the truth was not another coincidence, but was in fact another witness elimination!

---

[437] Mark Lane, "G.DeMohrenschildt - The Security Alarm," retrieved 2 July 2013: youtube. com/watch?v=37dtEpvyUJU

[438] Russell, *The Man Who Knew Too Much,* 173.

46

The Warren Commission Structured the Evidence to Fit Its Pre-Formed Conclusions

The major problems that I have with the Warren Commission are the same problems most others who've really looked at it have had. Even some of the people who support the lone gunman theory agree with this assessment:

> The Warren Commission, it should be clear, never really conducted an investigation. They began with a conclusion and then worked fairly carefully to ensure that the available facts fit the pre-ordained determination.[439]

The Warren Commission blatantly and shamelessly obstructed justice. And I'm talking the kind of obstruction of justice that's a federal offense you're supposed to be prosecuted for. Instead, these people were rewarded; it was the best thing that ever happened to their careers. Arlen Specter, a mere attorney at that point, on the flying trapeze with his single magic bullet, went on to become

---

[439] Jim Moore, *Conspiracy of One* (Summit Publishing Group: 1997), 173.

an extremely powerful senator. Gerald Ford, then a U.S. representative for his state of Michigan, went from fabricating the placement of bullet wounds all the way to the White House. It was a real career-builder.

Let's take a quick look at some of their lies.

- **Jack Ruby knew Lee Harvey Oswald.**
  That's a *hugely relevant* point, as I covered earlier. So what did the Warren Commission do about that fact?
  They *lied* about it.

- **They knew that Oswald had connections to U.S. Intelligence.**
  So what they did do about that fact?
  They *lied* about it.

- **They knew that Oswald couldn't have done all the shooting.**
  Because they knew that *no one shooter* could have done all that shooting. And what did they do?
  They *lied* about that, too.

And here's another big lie that they got caught in. Gerald Ford—who, lest we forget, went on to become President of the United States after proving he could play ball for the fat cats—got himself caught in a whopper.

Buried in a batch of records that had been kept under lock and key for over thirty years, researchers discovered that the official location for placement of the bullet entry in the President's back was moved by a few inches in order to conform to the otherwise impossible Single Bullet Theory.[440]

That was the lie that made the ludicrous single bullet theory at least remotely—albeit *very* remotely—possible for attorney Arlen Specter to even argue with a straight face.

Gerald R. Ford took pen in hand and changed—ever so slightly— the Warren Commission's key sentence on the place where a bullet entered John F. Kennedy's body when he was killed in Dallas.

The effect of Ford's change was to strengthen the commission's conclusion that a single bullet passed through Kennedy and severely wounded Texas Governor John Connally—a crucial

---

[440] Mike Feinsilber, "Gerald Ford forced to admit the Warren Report fictionalized," July 2, 1997, *Associated Press*: whatreallyhappened.com/RANCHO/POLITICS/JFK/ford.html

element in its finding that Lee Harvey Oswald was the sole
gunman.[441]

And that was the big lie that gave birth to that ridiculous theory:

'This is the most significant lie in the whole Warren Commission
report,' said Robert D. Morningstar, a computer systems specialist
in New York City who said he has studied the assassination since
it occurred and written an Internet book about it.

The effect of Ford's editing, Morningstar said, was to suggest that
a bullet struck Kennedy in the neck, 'raising the wound two or
three inches. Without that alteration, they could never have hood-
winked the public as to the true number of assassins.'

If the bullet had hit Kennedy in the back, it could not have struck
Connolly in the way the commission said it did, he said.[442]

Arlen Specter also had an extremely successful career after his acrobatics
with the truth, supporting this crazy theory. I'm not suggesting that he was
rewarded for his "services"—or maybe I am. It's definitely something that
should be looked into, at the very least, because that's how high-level politics
seems to operate in this country these days.

Probably even more deceitful than those outright lies were the things that
they left out. It was the same scenario as I mentioned earlier in relation to eyewitnesses to the Tippit murder. Only the least credible witnesses were called to
testify, because they were the only ones that could be used to pin the blame on
Oswald. The best eyewitnesses to the assassination were ignored.

There were so many errors and omissions that historian Walt Brown actually named a book about that topic *The Warren Omission*!

Then, there were the subtle but very effective methods they used to control
what did and didn't get onto the official record. I'll explain.

As we now know, the magic act of the Great Arlen Specter could appear to
make bullets stop and change course in mid-air. But that's not *all* he could do!
He was also adept at formulating hypothetical questions in such a way that the

---

[441] Ibid.
[442] Ibid.

truth was nowhere to be found with his semantic genius at work. Don't believe me? Well, see for yourself:

Historian Walt Brown details the outright absurdities of the Commission in general and of (future President) Gerald Ford and Arlen Specter in particular:

> Another common technique . . . was the 'say now, prove later'
> argument. If someone asks you a question based on something
> they tell you will be proved later, your answer options are limited.
> Specter asked, 'I will hand you Commission Exhibit No. 684 and
> ask you if that is a picture of the reverse side of the coat, which
> we will later prove to have been worn by Governor Connally, the
> coat which is before you?' Dr. Shaw could have answered, 'Yes,'
> or 'Yes.'[443]

The ludicrous questioning methods—assuming facts *not* in evidence—that the Committee adopted literally created the testimony of the doctors rather than facilitating it via questions which would have actually solicited the doctors' own words. For example, consider the absurdity of the following question that Arlen Specter asked repeatedly to the doctors who had treated the President at Parkland Hospital:

> Mr. SPECTER: Permit me to add some fact which I shall ask
> you to assume as being true for purposes of having you express
> an opinion. First of all, assume that the President was struck by
> a 6.5mm copper-jacketed bullet from a rifle having a muzzle
> velocity of approximately 2,000 feet per second at a time when the
> President was approximately 160 to 250 feet from the weapon,
> with the President being struck from the rear at a downward
> angle of approximately 45 degrees, being struck in the upper right
> posterior thorax just above the upper border of the scapula 14 cen-
> timeters from the tip of the right acromion process and 14 centi-
> meters below the tip of the right mastoid process. Assume further
> that the missile passed through the body of the President striking
> no bones, traversing the neck and sliding between the muscles in
> the posterior aspect of the President's body through a fascia chan-
> nel without violating the pleural cavity, but bruising only the apex

---

[443] Walt Brown, Ph.D., *The Guns of Texas Are Upon You* (Last Hurrah Press: 2005), 200.

of the right pleural cavity and bruising the most apical portion of
the right lung, then causing a hematoma to the right of the larynx
which you have described, and creating a jagged wound in the
trachea, then exiting precisely at the point where you observe the
puncture wound to exist.

Now based on those facts was the appearance of the wound in
your opinion consistent with being an exit wound?'[444]

That's not how an investigation is properly conducted and it's pretty freaking obvious that the type of questions like the above are used to *control* the
evidence, not to uncover it.

Here's how an academic historian weighs the evidence on Mr. Specter's
methods:

From the time of the Truman Committee, through the McCarthy
witch hunts, to the Sherman Adams probe under Ike, to Watergate, Iran-Contra, and the 9/11 Commission, the . . . material
above is arguably the most vulgar degradation of truth ever
uttered in a federal inquiry.[445]
Senator Arlen Specter's ongoing lie is a massive disservice to a
man, an office, and a nation.[446]

Then there was Gerald Ford, who was such a verbal magician that
he could take a back wound— that highly credible eyewitnesses assured
him was being called a back wound because it was a wound that they had
seen *in the back*—and somehow turn that wound in the back into a "neck
wound." And, just to give you an idea of what was at stake here, he had
no problems at all "signing off" on that and defended his action till his
dying day.

Roy Kellerman was testifying to a frontal entry wound at a place
subsequently sealed with wax by the morticians forced to work

---

[444] Ibid, 205 (cited from 3H 362).
[445] Ibid, 205.
[446] Ibid, 195.

at Bethesda . . . [Secret Serviceman Clint] Hill would stay with
Mrs. Kennedy when the family was on the seventeenth floor of
Bethesda Naval Hospital, but would be called to the basement
morgue 'to view the body,' upon which he saw a wound six inches
below the shoulder, on the right side, which we now know,
thanks to Gerry Ford, was in the neck.

Special Agent William Greer . . . like Kellerman and Hill,
was clear about the placement of the wounds . . . Kellerman,
Hill, Greer—men whose lives were forever altered by a few
terrible seconds. One would think it logical that they would
remember the location of the wounds that destroyed their
careers. But they were all wrong. There was no entrance
wound in front of any ear, or in any shoulder. Trust in
Gerald Ford.'[447]

A true list of the errors and omissions of the Warren Commission would
literally be too long to go into here. But here's a few of the "highlights" for
you:

- The commission misrepresented the results of its own wound ballistics tests with regard to both the single-bullet theory and the
  fatal head shot.

- The commission never even mentioned that in the Zapruder film
  Kennedy's head and upper body snap violently backward and to
  the left when the fatal head shot occurs. In fact, when the commission printed the frames from the film, it reversed two key frames
  of the head shot sequence. When this fact was made public, the
  changing of the order of the frames was blamed on a 'printing
  error.'

- The commission accepted Ruby's doubtful story about how he
  gained access to the basement of the police department to shoot
  Oswald. The HSCA (House Select Committee on Assassinations)

---

[447] Ibid, 210–211, emphasis in original.

rejected Ruby's belated story, noting that the available evidence overwhelmingly indicated Ruby's story was false.

• The commission used faulty logic and unreasonable criteria to reject the accounts of witnesses whose reports suggested or proved a conspiracy was involved. Yet, when it came to witnesses whose stories at least seemed to support the lone-gunman theory, the commission bent over backwards to accept them.

• The commission erroneously claimed Jack Ruby did not have extensive ties to the Mafia. The HSCA later proved this claim to be utterly false.

• The commission failed to take testimony from numerous important witnesses.

• The commission's questioning of several key witnesses was inept, if not deliberately negligent.

• The commission failed to establish a motive for Oswald.

• The commission created the false impression that Oswald was proficient with a rifle and that he had ample practice with the alleged murder weapon.

• The commission brazenly misrepresented the results of its rifle tests. In those tests, which supposedly proved Oswald could have shot Kennedy in the manner alleged by the commission, three Master-rated marksmen *missed* the head and neck area of the target boards 20 out of 21 times, and some of their misses were far apart and even missed the human silhouette on the target boards, even though the target boards were *stationary*, even though the marksmen fired from an elevation of only 30 feet and were allowed to take as much time as they desired for the first shot, and even though two of them took longer than 6 seconds to fire their shots. Those rifle tests showed it was highly unlikely that a mediocre marksman like Oswald could have shot President Kennedy.

- In its attempt to bend the evidence to fit its conclusions, the commission contradicted itself.[448]

In summary, would you like to hear how President Richard Nixon summarized the Warren Commission? This is straight from his White House tapes:

It was the greatest hoax that has ever been perpetuated.[449]

That should make you angry, because the Powers That Be were obviously well aware—and still are—of all the crap that they have been force-feeding to us all these years.

---

[448] Michael T. Griffith, "The Warren Commission's Failed Investigation," February 19, 2002: michaelgriffith1.tripod.com/failed.htm

[449] Kevin Anderson, "Revelations and gaps on Nixon tapes," March 1, 2002, *BBC News*: news. bbc.co.uk/2/hi/americas/1848157.stm

47

The CIA Also Participated
in the Cover-Up

Like a true government agency, after the assassination of President Kennedy, the Central Intelligence Agency immediately went hard to work: covering their own rear ends!

> The Federal Bureau of Investigation and the Central Intelligence
> Agency engaged in a cover-up of highly relevant information
> when the Warren Commission was investigating President John
> Kennedy's assassination. . . . President Johnson and Attorney
> General Robert F. Kennedy became party to the effort which con-
> sisted of withholding key facts from the Warren Commission.[450]

Among that highly relevant information that the CIA closely guarded and/or destroyed, was evidence related to Lee Harvey Oswald and his actions on behalf of U.S. intelligence agencies. It's pretty easy to see why they did that,

---

[450] Tad Szulc, "FBI-CIA Cover-Up Alleged," May 28, 1976, *The Evening Bulletin*: jfk.hood. edu/Collection/Weisberg%20Subject%20Index%20Files/S%20Disk/Szulc%20Tad%20 New%20Republic%20The%20JFK/Item%2004.pdf

even though it's clearly obstruction of justice. Anything linking the President's assassin to the Agency would have been extremely embarrassing.

The CIA lied about Oswald not being debriefed after he returned from his "defection" to the Soviet Union. Researchers uncovered evidence in 1993 that Oswald had been debriefed by the Agency.

> Upon Oswald's return to the U.S. in 1962, he was, in fact, 'debriefed' by a CIA officer named Aldrin ['Andy'] Anderson. The debriefing report was read by CIA officer Donald Deneselya, who confirmed this in an interview for this book on May 25, 2007, as well as in the 1993 PBS *Frontline* program, "Who Was Lee Harvey Oswald?"[451]

Their diversionary tactics were employed right from the start too:

> Soon after the assassination, Johnson was led to believe by the CIA that Kennedy might have been the victim of a Soviet conspiracy.[452]

Here's another example of their "obfuscations" of the truth, from Berkeley Professor Peter Dale Scott:

> More importantly, the CIA and FBI conspired to suppress a major clue to the existence of a pre-assassination conspiracy. This was that an unknown person had falsely presented himself as Lee Oswald in a phone call to the Soviet Embassy in Mexico City. The FBI initially reported that the person making the recorded call 'was not Lee Harvey Oswald.' Later the FBI and CIA conspired, swiftly and clumsily, to conceal both the falsity of the impersonation and the fact that FBI agents had exposed the falsehood by listening to the tape.[453]

That might sound confusing but its ramifications are *huge*. And, as Scott points out, the way that the Agency covered their intelligence uses of Oswald at

---

[451] Janney, *Mary's Mosaic*, 430.
[452] Talbot, "The mother of all cover-ups."
[453] Peter Dale Scott, "Deep Politics III, Overview: The CIA, the Drug Traffic, and Oswald in Mexico," December, 2000: history-matters.com/pds/DP3_Overview.htm

the top secret CIA base in Atsugi, Japan, then as a "false defector" to the Soviet Union, and then in Mexico City probably explains what it was that they were actually covering up:

> It is important to understand that this suppression was entirely consistent with intelligence priorities of the period. This important clue had been planted in the midst of one of the most sensitive CIA operations in the 1960s: its largest intercept operation against the telephones of an important Soviet base. One can assume that this clue was planted by conspirators who knew that the CIA response would be to suppress the truth. As a result the CIA protected its sources and methods [in accordance with the responsibilities enumerated in its enabling statute]. The result was obstruction of justice in a crime of the highest political significance.[454]

And even after Oswald was eliminated, the CIA was still hard at work on damage control:

> Richard Helms, who was then in charge of clandestine operations for the CIA, sent a memo to the FBI on February 18, 1964. Helms was interested in a scar that Oswald was supposed to have had on his left wrist, after he allegedly attempted suicide in Moscow in 1959. Helms requested any FBI information, 'including the undertakers, copies of any reports, such as autopsy or other, which may contain information pertinent to this point. . . . The best evidence of a scar or scars on the left wrist would of course be direct examination by a competent authority and we recommend that this be done and that a photograph of the inner and outer surfaces of the left wrist be made if there has been no other evidence acceptable to the [Warren] Commission that he did in fact attempt suicide by cutting his wrist.'[455]

As I showed you earlier in this book, the CIA also played a role in "helping" the other side in the Jim Garrison investigation and in altering the Zapruder

---

[454] Ibid.

[455] Ventura & Russell, *American Conspiracies*, 37.

film of the assassination. They also worked with *Time-Life* to control that film and thereby manage the early information about the assassination:

> For many years, [chief of *Time-Life* media empire, Henry] Luce's personal emissary to the CIA was C. D. Jackson, a Time, Inc., vice president who was publisher of *Life Magazine* from 1960 until his death in 1964. . . . He also 'approved specific arrangements for providing CIA employees with Time-Life cover. Some of these arrangements were made with the knowledge of Luce's wife, Claire Booth.' [Herself a member of the Committee to Free Cuba, immediately after the assassination Mrs. Luce disseminated information implicating Oswald that she'd received from a group of CIA-backed Cuban exiles whom she supported.][456]

So the CIA and those acting on its behalf were very busy pointing fingers at Cuba and the Soviets and *away* from Oswald's links to intelligence.

These facts started to seep out eventually; you can only hide a skunk for so long before it starts to stink. Eventually even former staff attorneys of the Warren Commission started calling the CIA liars. Here's how former Warren Commission counsel Burt Griffin put it:

> I feel betrayed. I feel that the CIA lied to us, that we had an agency of government here which we were depending upon, and that we expected to be truthful with us, and to cooperate with us. And they didn't do it.[457]

Part of the Agency's concern was what Senator Frank Church figured out later anyway; that the CIA was using Mafia killers to try and assassinate Fidel Castro. They wouldn't reveal that earlier; it was a fact, but as Counsel Griffin noted, a fact that they withheld:

> The CIA concealed from us the fact that they were involved in efforts to assassinate Castro which could have been of extreme importance to us. Especially the fact that they were involved in working with the Mafia at that time.[458]

---

[456] Russell, *On the Trail of the JFK Assassins*, 35.
[457] Summers, *The Kennedy Conspiracy*, 376.
[458] Ibid.

Congressman Don Edwards, who was a Chairman of House committee hearings in 1975—and was himself a former FBI agent—reached some pretty dramatic conclusions about it all:

> There's not much question that both the FBI and the CIA are somewhere behind this cover-up. I hate to think what it is they are covering up—or who they are covering for.[459]

And as investigative author Anthony Summers summarized it at the end of his book on the Kennedy assassination:

> There is no longer any denying it. Above and beyond the information published in the main body of this book, documents now available confirm that the CIA and the FBI have long covered up what they knew about Oswald before the assassination.[460]

Even the CIA needed help for such a massive campaign of deception, which leads us to *Operation Mockingbird* and how the government really pulled off the outrage that President Nixon called the "greatest hoax ever perpetuated."[461] It was easy, as they had control of most of mainstream media!

---

[459] Ibid.
[460] Ibid.
[461] Anderson, "Revelations and gaps on Nixon tapes."

48

Mainstream Media Reinforced the False Conclusions of the Warren Commission

I t's a reality all-too-apparent—at least to those authors who have genuinely attempted to bring new evidence to public attention. Most of the mainstream media turns a blind eye to such new revelations while consistently welcoming, highlighting, and applauding quite publicly, the works which support the official government version of the assassination.

And I'm not talking about twenty or thirty years ago either. I'm talking about *now*, today. Because—believe it or not—even today, *The New York Times* refuses to even *review* my books (and many others who write about conspiracy). Which I find rather ironic because most of my books hit *The New York Times* bestseller list anyway!

But they won't touch it, unless it's in some critical format, usually mocking my work as "yet another conspiracy monger." Shouldn't we be asking ourselves why, in the year 2013, my bestselling books still are not even considered "reviewable" by the powers-that-run *The New York Times*? I find that very curious, don't you? Well, there's a lot of history behind decisions like that (by them), and it's a history intimately entwined with the Central Intelligence Agency.

234 JESSE VENTURA

I'll start at the beginning: *Operation Mockingbird*.

Starting in the early days of the Cold War [late 40s], the CIA
began a secret project called Operation Mockingbird, with the
intent of buying influence behind the scenes at major media outlets
and putting reporters on the CIA payroll, which has proven to be
a stunning ongoing success. The CIA effort to recruit American
news organizations and journalists to become spies and dissemi-
nators of propaganda was headed up by Frank Wisner, Allen
Dulles, Richard Helms, and Philip Graham (publisher of the
Washington Post).[462]

Pulitzer-winning journalist Carl Bernstein of Watergate fame detailed
that wide-scale intrusion of the intelligence community into the media in 1977.
Bernstein's work, *CIA and the Media*, is one of the most important articles ever
written, and you can read it online at: tmh.floonet.net/articles/cia_press.html

In 1953, Joseph Alsop, then one of America's leading syndicated
columnists, went to the Philippines to cover an election. He did
not go because he was asked to do so by his syndicate. He did not
go because he was asked to do so by the newspapers that printed
his column. He went at the request of the CIA.

Alsop is one of more than 400 American journalists who in the
past twenty-five years have secretly carried out assignments for
the Central Intelligence Agency, according to documents on file at
CIA headquarters.

Some of these journalists' relationships with the Agency were
tacit; some were explicit. There was cooperation, accommodation, and overlap. Journalists provided a full range of clandestine
services—from simple intelligence gathering to serving as
go-betweens with spies in Communist countries. Reporters
shared their notebooks with the CIA. Editors shared their
staffs. Some of the journalists were Pulitzer Prize winners, dis-

[462] Mary Louise, "Operation Mockingbird: CIA Media Manipulation," 2003: prisonplanet.com/
analysis_louise_01_03_03_mockingbird.html

tinguished reporters who considered themselves ambassadors-without-portfolio for their country. Most were less exalted: foreign correspondents who found that their association with the Agency helped their work; stringers and freelancers who were as interested in the derring-do of the spy business as in filing articles, and the smallest category, full-time CIA employees masquerading as journalists abroad. In many instances, CIA documents show journalists were engaged to perform tasks for the CIA with the consent of the managements of America's leading news organizations.[463]

Of course, they don't *admit* it; in fact, they hide it.

The history of the CIA's involvement with the American press continues to be shrouded by an official policy of obfuscation and deception. . . . Among the executives who lent their cooperation to the Agency were William Paley of the Columbia Broadcasting System, Henry Luce of Time Inc., Arthur Hays Sulzberger of the *New York Times*, Barry Bingham Sr. of the *Louisville Courier-Journal* and James Copley of the Copley News Service. Other organizations which cooperated with the CIA included the American Broadcasting Company, the National Broadcasting Company, the *Associated Press*, *United Press International*, Reuters, Hearst Newspapers, Scripps-Howard, *Newsweek* magazine, the Mutual Broadcasting System, the *Miami Herald*, and the old *Saturday Evening Post* and *New York Herald-Tribune*. By far the most valuable of these associations, according to CIA officials, have been with the *New York Times*, CBS, and Time Inc.[464]

This intermingling of the U.S. intelligence community with media has also been well-documented by the U.S. Congress. The following is an excerpt of the 1976 *Final Report of the Senate Select Committee to Study Governmental Operations with Respect to Intelligence Activities*:

---

[463] Carl Bernstein, "The CIA and the Media: How America's Most Powerful News Media Worked Hand in Glove with the Central Intelligence Agency and Why the Church Committee Covered It Up," October 20, 1977, *Rolling Stone*: tmh.floonet.net/articles/cia_press.html

[464] Ibid.

The CIA currently maintains a network of several hundred foreign individuals around the world who provide intelligence for
the CIA and at times attempt to influence opinion through the use
of covert propaganda. These individuals provide the CIA with
direct access to a large number of newspapers and periodicals,
scores of press services and news agencies, radio and television
stations, commercial book publishers, and other foreign media
outlets.

The Committee is concerned that the use of American journalists
and media organizations for clandestine operations is a threat to
the integrity of the press.[465]

That was in *1976*! Can you imagine how sophisticated that process is now?
The perceived need for subversion of the media originated as a by-product
of Cold War thinking. As a high-level CIA official explained it to Carl
Bernstein:

One journalist is worth twenty agents. He has access, the ability to
ask questions without arousing suspicion.[466]

The mainstream media certainly "played ball" with the government
and their official version of the JFK assassination. As I wrote in *American
Conspiracies*, this baloney began right away because, if you look back at the
original press coverage, the first reports indicated shots from the front!

The very first dispatch out of Dallas on November 22, 1963, came
from the *Associated Press*: 'The shots apparently came from a
grassy knoll in the area.' That was the news in most of the early
reports, though it was soon replaced with the Texas School Book
Depository.[467]

From the get-go, Oswald was damned as guilty by the media. The
headline in *The New York Times*: "Career of Suspect Has Been

---

[465] United States Senate, *Final Report, Select Committee to Study Governmental Operations with Respect to Intelligence Activities*, April 1976.

[466] Bernstein, "The CIA and the Media."

[467] Ventura & Russell, *American Conspiracies*, 38.

Bizarre." In the *New York Herald-Tribune*: "Left Wing Lunacy,
Not Right is Suspect." In *Time* magazine: "Evidence Against
Oswald Described as Conclusive."[468]

Then, Dan Rather either lied his eyes out or should have been declared
legally blind. You decide:

> Dan Rather, who was a local newsman in Dallas at the time, was
> the first journalist to see the twenty-second-long 'home movie'
> taken by dressmaker Abraham Zapruder. Rather then told a
> national TV audience that the fatal shot drove the president's
> head 'violently forward,' when the footage showed just the
> opposite! Later on, in his book *The Camera Never Blinks*, Rather
> defended his 'mistake' saying it was because his watching the film
> had been so rushed.

But nobody could question this at the time, because Time-Life
snapped up the Zapruder film for $150,000—a small fortune back
then—and battled for years to keep it out of the public domain.
The *Life* magazine publisher, C. D. Jackson, was 'so upset by
the head-wound sequence,' according to Richard Stolley, who
was then the magazine's L.A. bureau chief, 'that he proposed the
company obtain all rights to the film and withhold it from public
viewing at least until emotions calmed.'[469]

And then, to reverse the thinking on any of those authentic reports that
had slipped out about shots coming from the front, *Life* magazine came to the
rescue:

> *Life* published a story headlined "End of Nagging Rumors:
> The Critical Six Seconds" [December 6, 1963], that claimed to
> show precisely how Oswald had succeeded in hitting his
> target. Supposedly based on the Zapruder film, the magazine
> said that the president had been turning to wave to some-
> one in the crowd when one of Oswald's bullets hit him in

---

[468] Ventura & Russell, *American Conspiracies*, 39.
[469] Ibid.

the throat. But guess what? That sequence is nowhere to be
seen in the film.

> *Life* magazine devoted most of its October 2, 1964 issue . . .
> one of the articles was illustrated with eight frames from the
> Zapruder film. But Frame 323 turned out to contradict the War-
> ren Report's conclusion about the shots all coming from the rear.
> So the issue was recalled, the plates broken and re-set [this was
> all pre-computer], and Frame 313 showing the president's head
> exploding became the replacement. A second "error" forced still
> another such change. When a Warren Commission critic, Vin-
> cent Salandria, asked *Life* editor Ed Kearns about this two years
> later, Kearns wrote back: "I am at a loss to explain the discrepan-
> cies between the three versions of *Life* which you cite. I've heard
> of breaking a plate to correct an error. I've never heard of doing
> it twice for a single issue, much less a single story. Nobody here
> seems to remember who worked on the early Kennedy story . . ."[470]

Make no mistake about what they were doing—they were controlling the
information to jam the lone gunman theory right down our throats:

> Three months before the Warren Report appeared in September
> 1964, the *New York Times* ran a page one exclusive: "Panel to
> Reject Theories of Plot in Kennedy Death." They then printed
> the whole report as a forty-eight-page supplement and collabo-
> rated with Bantam Books and the Book-of-the-Month Club to
> publish both hardcover and paperback editions. "The commission
> analyzed every issue in exhaustive, almost archaeological detail,"
> according to reporter Anthony Lewis.

> The *Times* also put together another book, *The Witnesses*, which
> contained "highlights" from testimony before the Warren
> Commission. All these were aimed at shoring up the lone-
> gunman notion.

---

[470] Ibid.

In one instance, a witness who reported having seen a man with a rifle on the sixth floor had other portions of his testimony eliminated—namely, that he'd actually seen **two** men but been told to "forget it" by an FBI agent. Witnesses like Zapruder, who believed some of the shots came from in front, were left out entirely.[471]

As media critic Jerry Policoff put it:

Thus, the press' curiosity was not aroused when a 7.65 caliber German Mauser mutated into a 6.5 caliber Italian Mannlicher-Carcano; or when the grassy knoll receded into oblivion; or when an entrance wound in the President's throat became an exit wound [first for a fragment from the head wound and then for a bullet from the back wound]; or when a wound six inches below the President's shoulder became a wound at the back of the neck. The press was thereby weaving a web that would inevitably commit it to the official findings.[472]

As I have also pointed out, it was the mainstream media who ruthlessly attacked Oliver Stone's great film, *JFK*. Lord forbid anybody publicly suggested that maybe there were some questions about the assassination!

When Oliver Stone's movie *JFK* came out in 1991, the strongest attacks came from news outlets and journalists 'with the longest records of error and obstruction in defense of the flawed Warren Commission inquiry.' Are we surprised? They'll cheerlead for Posner and Bugliosi's books, but I'll bet you a free lunch they're not going to be reviewing this one anytime soon.[473]

The result of this highly questionable tangling of government and major media has been a very disturbing progression away from the notion of a free press.

---

[471] Ibid.

[472] Jerry Policoff, "The media and the murder of John Kennedy," *The New York Times*, August 8, 1975, Vol. 5 No. 3, pages 29–30: jfk.hood.edu/Collection/Weisberg%20Subject%20 Index%20Files/P%20Disk/Policoff%20Jerry/Item%20016.pdf

[473] Ventura & Russell, *American Conspiracies*, 43.

Many Americans still insist or persist in believing that we have a
free press, while getting most of their news from state-controlled
television, under the misconception that reporters are meant
to serve the public. Reporters are paid employees and serve the
media owners, who usually cower when challenged by advertisers
or major government figures. Robert Parry reported the first
breaking stories about Iran-Contra for *Associated Press* that were
largely ignored by the press and Congress, then moving to *Newsweek* he witnessed a retraction of a true story for political reasons.
In 'Fooling America: A Talk by Robert Parry' he said, 'The
people who succeeded and did well were those who didn't stand
up, who didn't write the big stories, who looked the other way
when history was happening in front of them, and went along
either consciously or just by cowardice with the deception of the
American people.'

Until the 1980s, media systems were generally domestically
owned, regulated, and national in scope. However, pressure
from the IMF, World Bank, and U.S. government to deregulate
and privatize the media, communication, and new technology
resulted in a global commercial media system dominated by a
small number of super-powerful transnational media corporations
[mostly U.S. based], working to advance the cause of global
markets and the CIA agenda.[474]

When it comes to the subject of the media and the JFK assassination, the
real story is the *absence* of any substantive story or investigative journalism.

If the assassination of John Fitzgerald Kennedy was one of the
darkest tragedies in the republic's history, the reporting of it has
remained one of the worst travesties of the American media.
From the first reports out of Dallas in November of 1963 to the
merciless flagellation of Oliver Stone's *JFK* over the last several
months, the mainstream media have disgraced themselves by
hewing blindly to the single-assassin theory advanced by the FBI

---

[474] Louise, "Operation Mockingbird."

within hours of the murder. Original, enterprise reporting has been left almost entirely to alternative weeklies, monthly magazines, book publishers, and documentary makers. All such efforts over the last twenty-nine years have met the same fate as Oliver Stone's movie: derision from the mainstream media. At first, the public bought the party line. But gradually, as more and more information slipped through the margins of the media business, and finally through the efforts of Congress itself, the public began to change its mind.

Today, according to a recent *New York Times*/CBS poll, an astonishing 77 percent of Americans reject the Warren Report's conclusions. How did such a tremendous credibility gap come about? And assuming that the majority of Americans are right, how did a free press so totally blow one of the biggest stories of the century.[475]

I obtained a copy of an amazing document: CIA document #1035-960, entitled *CIA Instructions to Media Assets: RE: Concerning Criticism of the Warren Report*. It was marked "DESTROY WHEN NO LONGER NEEDED" plus "PSYCH" and "CS" for Psychological Warfare unit of Clandestine Services Department of United States Central Intelligence Agency.

To those who say there's no evidence that the CIA controls the media in the United States—read it and weep:

1.	From the day of President Kennedy's assassination on, there has been speculation about the responsibility for his murder. Although this was stemmed for a time by the Warren Commission report, (which appeared at the end of September 1964), various writers have now had time to scan the Commission's published report and documents for new pretexts for questioning, and there has been a new wave of books and articles criticizing the Commission's findings. In most cases the critics have speculated as to the existence of some kind of conspiracy, and often they have implied that the Commission itself

---

[475] Robert Hennelly & Jerry Policoff, "JFK: How the Media Assassinated the Real Story," 2002: assassinationresearch.com/v1n2/mediaassassination.html

was involved. Presumably as a result of the increasing challenge to the Warren Commission's report, a public opinion poll recently indicated that 46 percent of the American public did not think that Oswald acted alone, while more than half of those polled thought that the Commission had left some questions unresolved. Doubtless polls abroad would show similar, or possibly more adverse results.

2. This trend of opinion is a matter of concern to the U.S. government, including our organization. The members of the Warren Commission were naturally chosen for their integrity, experience and prominence. They represented both major parties, and they and their staff were deliberately drawn from all sections of the country. Just because of the standing of the Commissioners, efforts to impugn their rectitude and wisdom tend to cast doubt on the whole leadership of American society. Moreover, there seems to be an increasing tendency to hint that President Johnson himself, as the one person who might be said to have benefited, was in some way responsible for the assassination.

Innuendo of such seriousness affects not only the individual concerned, but also the whole reputation of the American government. Our organization itself is directly involved: among other facts, we contributed information to the investigation. Conspiracy theories have frequently thrown suspicion on our organization, for example by falsely alleging that Lee Harvey Oswald worked for us. The aim of this dispatch is to provide material countering and discrediting the claims of the conspiracy theorists, so as to inhibit the circulation of such claims in other countries. Background information is supplied in a classified section and in a number of unclassified attachments.

3. Action. We do not recommend that discussion of the assassination question be initiated where it is not already taking place. Where discussion is active [business] addresses are requested:

   a.   To discuss the publicity problem with friendly elite contacts (especially politicians and editors), pointing out that the Warren Commission made as thorough an investigation as humanly possible, that the charges of the critics are without serious foundation, and that further speculative discussion only plays into the hands of the opposition. Point out also that parts of the conspiracy talk appear to be deliberately generated by Communist propagandists. Urge them to use their influence to discourage unfounded and irresponsible speculation.

b. To employ propaganda assets to [negate] and refute the attacks of the critics. Book reviews and feature articles are particularly appropriate for this purpose. The unclassified attachments to this guidance should provide useful background material for passing to assets. Our ploy should point out, as applicable, that the critics are (I) wedded to theories adopted before the evidence was in, (II) politically interested, (III) financially interested, (IV) hasty and inaccurate in their research, or (V) infatuated with their own theories. In the course of discussions of the whole phenomenon of criticism, a useful strategy may be to single out Epstein's theory for attack, using the attached Fletcher article and Spectator piece for background. (Although Mark Lane's book is much less convincing than Epstein's and comes off badly where confronted by knowledgeable critics, it is also much more difficult to answer as a whole, as one becomes lost in a morass of unrelated details.)

4. In private to media discussions not directed at any particular writer, or in attacking publications which may be yet forthcoming, the following arguments should be useful:

a. No significant new evidence has emerged which the Commission did not consider. The assassination is sometimes compared (e.g., by Joachim Joesten and Bertrand Russell) with the Dreyfus case; however, unlike that case, the attacks on the Warren Commission have produced no new evidence, no new culprits have been convincingly identified, and there is no agreement among the critics. (A better parallel, though an imperfect one, might be with the Reichstag fire of 1933, which some competent historians [Fritz Tobias, A. J. P. Taylor, D. C. Watt] now believe was set by Vander Lubbe on his own

initiative, without acting for either Nazis or Communists; the
Nazis tried to pin the blame on the Communists, but the latter
have been more successful in convincing the world that the
Nazis were to blame.)

b. Critics usually overvalue particular items and ignore others.
They tend to place more emphasis on the recollections
of individual witnesses (which are less reliable and more
divergent—and hence offer more hand-holds for criticism)
and less on ballistics, autopsy, and photographic evidence.
A close examination of the Commission's records will usually
show that the conflicting eyewitness accounts are quoted out
of context, or were discarded by the Commission for good and
sufficient reason.

c. Conspiracy on the large scale often suggested would be
impossible to conceal in the United States, esp. since informants
could expect to receive large royalties, etc. Note that Robert
Kennedy, Attorney General at the time and John F. Kennedy's
brother, would be the last man to overlook or conceal any
conspiracy. And as one reviewer pointed out, Congressman
Gerald R. Ford would hardly have held his tongue for the sake
of the Democratic administration, and Senator Russell would
have had every political interest in exposing any misdeeds on
the part of Chief Justice Warren. A conspirator moreover would
hardly choose a location for a shooting where so much depended
on conditions beyond his control: the route, the speed of the
cars, the moving target, and the risk that the assassin would
be discovered. A group of wealthy conspirators could have
arranged much more secure conditions.

d. Critics have often been enticed by a form of intellectual pride:
they light on some theory and fall in love with it; they also
scoff at the Commission because it did not always answer every
question with a flat decision one way or the other. Actually,
the make-up of the Commission and its staff was an excellent
safeguard against over-commitment to any one theory, or
against the illicit transformation of probabilities into certainties.

e. Oswald would not have been any sensible person's choice for a co-conspirator. He was a "loner," mixed up, of questionable reliability and an unknown quantity to any professional intelligence service.

f. As to charges that the Commission's report was a rush job, it emerged three months after the deadline originally set. But to the degree that the Commission tried to speed up its reporting, this was largely due to the pressure of irresponsible speculation already appearing, in some cases coming from the same critics who, refusing to admit their errors, are now putting out new criticisms.

g. Such vague accusations as that "more than ten people have died mysteriously" can always be explained in some natural way e.g.: the individuals concerned have for the most part died of natural causes; the Commission staff questioned 418 witnesses (the FBI interviewed far more people, conducting 25,000 interviews and re interviews), and in such a large group, a certain number of deaths are to be expected. (When Penn Jones, one of the originators of the "ten mysterious deaths" line, appeared on television, it emerged that two of the deaths on his list were from heart attacks, one from cancer, one was from a head-on collision on a bridge, and one occurred when a driver drifted into a bridge abutment.)

5. Where possible, counter speculation by encouraging reference to the Commission's Report itself. Open-minded foreign readers should still be impressed by the care, thoroughness, objectivity and speed with which the Commission worked. Reviewers of other books might be encouraged to add to their account the idea that, checking back with the report itself, they found it far superior to the work of its critics.[476]

About the nicest thing I can say is that at least they've put a lot of thought into how to distort our news and control the media!

The influence upon our "free press" is often overt, rather than covert. In fact, according to former media titan Katharine Graham, the public doesn't

---

[476] CIA Document # 1035-960, "RE: Concerning Criticism of the Warren Report," 1 April 1967: realhistoryarchives.com/collections/assassinations/jfk/cia-inst.htm

really need to know anyway; the following are her words from the 1988 speech to senior CIA employees at the Agency. So here's what those dirtbags really think; get a load of *this* one:

> We live in a dangerous and dirty world. There are some things
> the general public does not need to know and shouldn't.[477]

The death toll from that brand of arrogance has been astounding. And what's even more alarming than the information that *has* been widely disseminated to the American public, is the information that has *not* been.

It turns out the CIA has:

- Corrupted democratic elections in Greece, Italy, and dozens of other nations;

- Been involved to varying degrees in at least thirty-five assassination plots against foreign heads of state or prominent political leaders. Successful assassinations include democratically elected leaders like Salvador Allende (Chile) and Patrice Lumumba (Belgian Congo); also CIA-created dictators like Rafael Trujillo (Dominican Republic) and Ngo Dinh Diem (South Vietnam); and popular political leaders like Che Guevara. Unsuccessful attempts range from Fidel Castro to Charles De Gaulle;

- Helped launch military *coups* that toppled democratic governments, replacing them with brutal dictatorships or *juntas*. The list of overthrown democratic leaders includes Mossadegh (Iran, 1953), Arbenz (Guatemala, 1954), Velasco and Arosemena (Ecuador, 1961, 1963), Bosch (Dominican Republic, 1963), Goulart (Brazil, 1964), Sukarno (Indonesia, 1965), Papandreou (Greece, 1965–67), Allende (Chile, 1973), and dozens of others;

- Supported murderous dictators like General Pinochet (Chile), the Shah of Iran, Ferdinand Marcos (Philippines), "Papa Doc" and "Baby Doc" Duvalier (Haiti), General Noriega (Panama), Mobutu Sese Seko (Zaire), the "Reign of the Colonels" (Greece), and more;

---

[477] Louise, "Operation Mockingbird."

- Created, trained, and supported death squads and secret police forces that tortured and murdered hundreds of thousands of civilians, leftists, and political opponents in Guatemala, Honduras, El Salvador, Haiti, Bolivia, Cuba, Mexico, Uruguay, Brazil, Chile, Vietnam, Cambodia, Thailand, Iran, Turkey, Angola, and others;

- Helped run the "School of the Americas" at Fort Benning, Georgia, which trains Latin American military officers how to overthrow democratic governments. Subjects include the use of torture, interrogation, and murder;

- Conducted economic sabotage, including ruining crops, disrupting industry, sinking ships, and creating food shortages;

- Paved the way for the massacre of 200,000 in East Timor, 500,000 in Indonesia, and one to two million in Cambodia;

- Smuggled Nazi war criminals and weapon scientists into the U.S., unpunished, for their use in the Cold War;

- Conducted Operation MK-ULTRA, a mind-control experiment that gave LSD and other drugs to Americans against their will or without their knowledge, causing some to commit suicide;

- Kept friendly and extensive working relations with the Mafia;

- Actively traded in drugs around the world since the 1950s to fund its operations. The Contra/crack scandal is only the tip of the iceberg—other notorious examples include Southeast Asia's Golden Triangle and Noriega's Panama;

- The Association for Responsible Dissent estimates that by 1987, six million people had died as a result of CIA covert operations. Former State Department official William Blum correctly calls this an 'American Holocaust.'[478]

But hey, *no problem;* as long as all their friends in mainstream media *put the right spin on it*, or better yet, not even *cover* that type of stuff, everything's apparently fine. And, as far as the public, we can just go on with the stories they force-feed us and spend most of our so-called "news" time on the truly

---

[478] William Blum, *Killing Hope: U.S. Military and C.I.A. Interventions Since World War II* (Common Courage Press: 2008), cited in: Steve Kangas, "A Timeline of CIA Atrocities," 1998: huppi.com/kangaroo/CIAtimeline.html

big issues of the day: like who wore what on the Hollywood red carpet. Does it ever make you wonder why just about every evening newscast starts off with a murder or a kidnapping or an assault? So you either get nonsense or horror.

As a veteran who has defended what this country is *supposed* to stand for, I feel truly insulted by how the corporate-owned mainstream media has hijacked the real news in this country and replaced 90 percent of it with a bunch of *asinine crap* that not even a moron should be forced to watch.

If you want a *real* story, just try this one on for size: Corporatization has now centralized media ownership so much, that only *ten* companies now control everything that you see and hear on television *and* radio.[479] Ten companies?! And you can just bet that they're all "warm and cozy" with the CIA and their "official line" too.

> Massive corporations dominate the U.S. media landscape.
> Through a history of mergers and acquisitions, these companies
> have concentrated their control over what we see, hear, and read.
> In many cases, these companies are vertically integrated, control-
> ling everything from initial production to final distribution.[480]

They won't tell ya about that. But *remember this*:
That's how they control what you see, hear, and think!

---

[479] "Who Owns the Media," *Free Press*, retrieved 15 May 2013:freepress.net/ownership/chart
[480] Ibid.

SECTION THREE

The Witnesses

I t's a frequent observation that it could not really be a conspiracy that killed JFK, "because someone would have talked." They cite catchy sayings like: "Because three people can keep a secret—as long as two of them are dead." That's all very persuasive except for one very important fact: it simply isn't true; people *have* talked.

Contrary to common perceptions, many important witnesses have come forward and have had a lot to say, too. It's just usually drowned out in mainstream media, which would rather "engage our intellects" with nonsense than discuss the questions we ask of our government.

And by the way, that saying is actually: "Three can keep a secret if two are dead." It was on the door on the way out of the office of Mafia Godfather Carlos Marcello.[481] That's the same Carlos Marcello who was reportedly involved in the JFK assassination and was one of the people who "talked" (even though supposedly no one has, according to the government).

Marcello talked to a mob lawyer, Frank Ragano, who eventually went public with it. Right after the assassination—*gloating* about it—he talked to that attorney, and it was about one of the guy's own clients; he said: "When you see Jimmy [Hoffa], you tell him he owes me and he owes me big."[482] I have a hunch he wasn't talking about lunch that day either.

---

[481] Thomas L. Jones, "Big Daddy in the Big Easy," *Crime Library*, retrieved 14 May 2013: truTV.com/library/crime/gangsters_outlaws/family_epics/marcello/8.html

[482] Frank Ragano & Selwyn Raab, *Mob Lawyer* (Random House Value: 1996).

You'll find a lot of interesting things that people have said in this section. They've talked plenty . . . you just haven't heard it from all the puppets in the press. So stop looking at their sleight-of-hand attention diversions (because that's all they are) and pay attention to what some knowledgeable people have contributed to an intelligent appraisal of what really happened, often at great risk to themselves. In some cases, the "talk" came from FBI wiretaps and some other interesting sources, like that mob attorney. And almost all of it runs counter-current to what we've been told by our own government. But that seems to be a recurring pattern in this case, doesn't it?

49

A Special Team from Military Intelligence Was Sent to Dallas

Two veteran Military intelligence operatives—Richard Case Nagell, documented in the book *The Man Who Knew Too Much*, and William Robert Plumlee—have come forward with information dramatically changing the landscape surrounding the JFK assassination as we now know it.

The testimony of William Robert "Tosh" Plumlee contained some important revelations. It's authentic because he's the "real deal": I showed you his intelligence bona fides in the earlier entry in the evidence section, "Oswald was a U.S. intelligence operative."

Plumlee's background was profiled in the book, *Dead Wrong*. His testimony is *still* considered too hot to handle; most of it remains under seal and classified "Top Secret, Committee Sensitive," and it revealed some very important information that we had not known previously.

A "rescue team" was flown into Dallas by U.S. military intelligence.[483] The team members referred to it as an "abort team," because it was to abort an assassination attempt. You might be asking yourself the question: *Why didn't they just tell the Secret Service to stop President Kennedy's motorcade trip?* But as you'll soon see in the testimony of Secret Service Special Agent Abraham

---
[483] Belzer & Wayne, *Dead Wrong*, 111–115.

Bolden, for some reason there was a tight clampdown for national security purposes. In fact, in Chicago, the President's trip plans *were* cancelled—and then the Secret Service was ordered to destroy all evidence of the cancellation, as well as the foiled conspiracy plot that was the reason for the cancellation. So there were apparently other forces at work and—for whatever reason—in Dallas it apparently wasn't deemed feasible to simply "tell the Secret Service." After Chicago, there were also conspiracy plots in Miami and Tampa, and those were apparently foiled by successful U.S. intelligence intervention. So in Dallas, they apparently planned to successfully intervene again.

Instead they flew in a special team—military intelligence with CIA logistical support. They were well-trained and knew what to look for. Plumlee co-piloted that flight into Dallas on the morning of November 22, 1963, and went with team members into Dealey Plaza. He testified to all this in Congress. I can't show you his Congressional testimony, but Plumlee has also documented most of the facts in a sworn legal affidavit that was published in 2012. That testimony reads like a real spy thriller, made all-the-more real because of its historical significance in the JFK case:

> Upon reaching Dealey Plaza, the Intel Team split in three directions, looking for three or more shooters or teams that could form a triangulated crossfire. I was asked to act as a spotter, reconnoitering the south knoll in this operation with my friend and operational partner, "Sergio."

> We were also looking for a diversionary act, something that would give shooters an opportunity to secretly set up. Therefore, while people were congregating around Elm Street and the Book Depository and we heard sirens coming closer, instead of looking toward the commotion, we looked away from it, scanning the perimeter and looking for a shooter or shooters attempting to set up triangulation shooting in a kill zone that we had identified.

> We arrived at the plaza too late to abort the assassination; there was not enough time, our people were not in position and our communications between scattered team members were very poor.[484]

---

[484] Ibid.

That affidavit also showed us that Chicago mobster Johnny Roselli (whom Plumlee knew and transported on many occasions) was so well known in the CIA/military intelligence operations against Cuba that he was even given an operational cover name: Colonel Ralston. Plumlee flew Rosselli to locations many times and also took Roselli's fellow Chicago hit man, Chuck Nicoletti, to certain locations on behalf of U.S. intelligence:

> I piloted many covert missions for the United States government in the years just prior to the assassination of President Kennedy. John Roselli, also known to me by his intelligence codename "Colonel Ralston" a.k.a. "Rawlston" was a passenger on many of my flights in Florida, Cuba, and Texas. I knew Roselli was part of covert intelligence operations and I have personally had irrefutable confirmation on many occasions to that fact.
>
> Roselli was so well-known in covert Intel circles that he was usually referred to simply as "The Colonel." I was aware of the ongoing assassination attempts toward Fidel Castro at the time.
>
> I also transported Charles Nicoletti on two separate occasions; to Santa Barbara, California and Las Vegas, Nevada. I knew Nicoletti as "Raven"; a codename given to me by my case officer as the person I was to transport.[485]

Plumlee has a new book this year that details his actions even more; it's appropriately entitled, *Deep Cover, Shallow Graves*.[486]

Now *get* this: Mobster Johnny Roselli was <u>on that flight</u> into Dallas with the Special Team:

> I co-piloted a flight that infiltrated a Military intelligence team into Dallas on the morning of November 22, 1963, in an attempt to abort the assassination of President John F. Kennedy. This mission was at the direction of the Pentagon with CIA logistical support. John Roselli was a passenger on that flight. Intelligence for our mission, after some confusion, had identified Dealey

---

[485] Ibid.

[486] Robert Plumlee, *Deep Cover, Shallow Graves* (TrineDay: 2013).

Plaza as the sight for the operation of an assassination
attempt.[487]

Plumlee's description of the events of that day also confirms that there
were multiple shooters from multiple directions. It was a highly compart-
mentalized mission—this was big stuff.

> I do not know the names of most of the men who were on that
> mission because those type of operations are intentionally struc-
> tured in a manner that minimizes individual knowledge.

> In "Black Operations," one does not ask questions of others—
> that is an unwritten rule. The official post-mission debriefing
> took place at West Palm Beach, Florida on November 25, my
> birthday. That debriefing was conducted by Rex Beardsley, Bob
> Bennette and Tracy Barnes.[488]

So—we now know that U.S. intelligence was not only aware of the ear-
lier conspiracy plots against President Kennedy's life in Chicago, Miami, and
Tampa—it was *also* aware of the conspiracy plot in Dallas and even got a
Spec Op Team into Dealey Plaza that almost prevented the assassination.

And we *also* know that, just like with the earlier plots, for some reason even for the Secret Service, it was all very hush-hush; paper trails disappeared on all of those plots *and* on intelligence efforts to abort them. And
agents were told not to write anything down or say anything to anybody, but
to just forget it ever happened.[489]

---

[487] Belzer & Wayne, *Dead Wrong*, 111–115.

[488] Ibid.

[489] Bolden, *The Echo From Dealey Plaza*; Waldron & Hartmann, *Ultimate Sacrifice*; Belzer &
Wayne, *Dead Wrong*.

50

Conclusions of U.S. Intelligence Agents

Although it may not technically qualify them as a "witness" to an event, when an intelligence officer forms a conclusion about a specific event to which they may have direct knowledge, their testimony is valid, as in the case of courtroom expert witnesses. So I'll acknowledge right up front that not every one of the conclusions that follow is from someone who witnessed the crime. But I'll also point out that every one of them is an opinion that I'm damn interested in knowing.

Military intelligence operative Richard Case Nagell

Nagell, the main topic of *The Man Who Knew Too Much*, was the veteran military intelligence operative who was tracking Oswald's movements. Nagell was monitoring a JFK assassination plot which included Oswald, exiled anti-Castro Cubans, and probably conservative Texas millionaires. Nagell even went so far as confronting Oswald to convince him he was out of his depth and being set up by some very clever conspirators. Oswald didn't believe him.

Nagell realized that he himself had been set up in the process and that if he didn't take extreme action, he was destined to "take the fall" with Oswald.

So he sent a registered letter to J. Edgar Hoover and the FBI, warning them very specifically of a plot involving Oswald and two Cuban exiles.

Then he walked into a bank, fired two shots from his pistol up at the top of the wall, calmly walked out to his car, and waited to be arrested, so that he could talk to the FBI. Officially, nobody believed him and they threw him in prison. But at least he had his alibi.

And the FBI supposedly never got that letter; even though Nagell had kept proof it was sent.[490]

Why should we believe Nagell? When he got himself arrested, the FBI seized a notebook that he wanted them to find. When the Bureau finally let the contents become public in 1975, that notebook had listings remarkably similar to Oswald's—for the Fair Play for Cuba Committee and the Cuban Embassy in Mexico City, not to mention six names of CIA agents! And Nagell also turned over to his lawyer a military ID card for none other than Oswald himself—a card that had never surfaced publicly before! It even had a Department of Defense overstamp. You can see the card in the photo insert section of *The Man Who Knew Too Much*.[491]

Secret Service Special Agent Abraham Bolden

Bolden documented three previous attempts on the President's life in the weeks just prior to his death in Dallas. His book gives an excellent account of the details of that Chicago plot and how very closely it resembled the set-up of Oswald in Dallas.[492] You can also watch his story, told by himself, in this video clip: echofromdealeyplaza.net/id5.html

As his reward for coming forward to try to help the Warren Commission, Bolden was framed on false charges and thrown in prison.[493] His story is also detailed in the book, *Ultimate Sacrifice*.

Military intelligence operative William Robert "Tosh" Plumlee

In case you're wondering what happened to that military Intel veteran who was on that failed rescue mission, Tosh Plumlee was thrown in jail during that period as well, on a forged check charge that was totally trumped up.

---

490 Russell, *The Man Who Knew Too Much*, 11.

491 Russell, *The Man Who knew Too Much*, XVII.

492 Bolden, *The Echo From Dealey Plaza*; Waldron & Hartmann, *Ultimate Sacrifice*.

493 Ibid.

He figured it was to keep him "on ice"—prevent him from presenting any information that conflicted with the official government version—just like Nagell and Bolden. Starting to notice a pattern here?

CIA contract agent John Martino

Martino was an electronics expert who had worked with the mob, was imprisoned by Castro, and then wrote a book about the experience. You might say he was an anti-Castro writer for the CIA. He had Agency connections with their anti-Castro operations out of South Florida, was involved in some of those operations, and had close mob friends, such as Johnny Roselli, who were also directly involved in those black ops.[494]

At first, after the assassination, Martino was very public in trying to even further set up Oswald as a Castro pawn, spreading false stories about Oswald's ties to Castro's Cuba in the process.[495]

But later in life, when he knew death was near, Martino confessed his involvement several times.[496]

Martino's confession does two very important things:

1. It confirms Richard Case Nagell's appraisal of how Oswald was being set up as the patsy and hadn't figured that out;
2. It summarizes for us, in short form, the thinking behind some of the most important aspects of the assassination plot.

Here's what Martino said:

The anti-Castro people put Oswald together. Oswald didn't know who he was working for—he was just ignorant of who was really putting him together. Oswald was to meet his contact at the Texas Theatre. They were to meet Oswald in the theatre, and get him out of the country, and then eliminate him. Oswald

---

[494] Larry Hancock, *Someone Would Have Talked* (JFK Lancer: 2010): jfkfacts.org/tag/john-cummings/feed/ and *The Mary Ferrell Foundation,* "John Martino's Confessions," retrieved 16 May 2013: maryferrell.org/wiki/index.php/John_Martinos_Confessions

[495] Hancock, *Someone Would Have Talked*: jfkfacts.org/tag/john-cummings/feed/

[496] Ibid.

made a mistake . . . . There was no way we could get to him.
They had Ruby kill him.[497]

Martino also told his wife, Flo—*before* it happened— that a plot was on
to kill Kennedy in Dallas:

> Martino's wife also mentioned that she could tell, from over-
> hearing a flood of phone calls he received on the afternoon of
> the assassination, that her husband had been involved. Martino
> confessed his involvement—delivering money, serving as a cou-
> rier, other support activities—to a friend when Martino knew
> that he was dying.[498]

Martino's son said that on November 22, 1963, his father told him to
stay home from school and listen to the news on the radio instead—
they listened to the assassination reports together and his son said it
wasn't shock for his father: "It was more like confirmation."[499]

CIA Officer David Phillips

Phillips is often mentioned as a possible conspirator but it has never been
proven. It was believed by Gaeton Fonzi—investigator for the House Select
Committee on Assassinations—that Phillips was also known as "Maurice
Bishop," Oswald's intelligence handler for the CIA.[500]

In any event, Phillips was deeply involved in the CIA's anti-Castro efforts
out of Mexico City and its huge JM/WAVE station in South Florida and
rose to become Director of Western Hemisphere Operations at CIA. So he
obviously knew what the hell he was talking about. Here's what Phillips
concluded:

> **My final take on the assassination is there was a conspiracy,**
> **likely including American intelligence officers.**[501]

---

[497] Ibid.
[498] Ibid.
[499] Ibid.
[500] Gaeton Fonzi, *The Last Investigation* (Mary Ferrell Foundation: 2008).
[501] Hancock, *Someone Would Have Talked.*

CIA Officer E. Howard Hunt

Officer Hunt was dying of cancer and made tape recordings for his son's book, which effectively equate to his deathbed statement.

Hunt also said that the assassination was planned from the nexus of the CIA's anti-Castro operations and was referred to by those in the know as "The Big Event." Hunt confessed to his knowledge of the planning but maintained that his own role was basically just "on the sidelines" unless he was needed.

Hunt even diagrammed out a document in his own handwriting called "Chain of Command" which detailed who was behind the assassination, to the extent of his direct knowledge. Lyndon Johnson was at the top (as far as Hunt knew, at least) and was followed by veteran CIA official Cord Meyer. It's interesting to note that Meyer's ex-wife, Mary Pinchot Meyer, was having a serious affair with President Kennedy, which was common knowledge amid Meyer's Washington circles. That Chain of Command document reads as follows:

LBJ (Lyndon Johnson)
Cord Mayer (Meyer)
David Morales
Bill Harvey
French Gunman Grassy Knoll[502]

---

[502] Saint John Hunt, *Bond of Secrecy: My Life with CIA Spy and Watergate Conspirator E. Howard Hunt* (TrineDay: 2012).

I'd like to point out that one of the men on that list, William Harvey, was in charge of the CIA assassination unit codenamed ZR/RIFLE and is also on record as not only hating the Kennedys, but in preferring to use Corsican (French Mafia) killers for assassination purposes because they didn't lead as directly to the Mafia like Sicilians did.[503]

---

[503] Lamar Waldron & Thom Hartmann, *Legacy of Secrecy: The Long Shadow of the JFK Assassination* (Counterpoint: 2008).

CIA Agent David Morales

Morales—specifically named as a conspirator by Hunt—was also a high-ranking agent out of the CIA's JM/WAVE station who was on record as hating the Kennedys. He too had a great deal of experience in CIA black ops. Morales even alluded to his own probable involvement in the assassination in comments that he made about his hatred for JFK:

> Well, we took care of that son-of-a-bitch, didn't we?[504]

In reference to the assassinations of both JFK and RFK, Morales reportedly said:

> I was in Dallas when we got the son of a bitch and I was in Los Angeles when we got the little bastard.[505]

Los Angeles and "the little bastard" refer to the assassination of Robert Kennedy after he took the California primary during the 1968 race for the Democratic presidential nomination.

CIA Chief of Station, John Stockwell

John Stockwell was a CIA officer who became a station chief for the Agency and was awarded the CIA Medal of Merit for his work in Vietnam. But he became disenchanted with the Agency's policies as a result of his experiences and resigned from the CIA. Stockwell was openly critical of the CIA's "secret wars."

Stockwell had a military background and a lot of friends in the "spy trade"; he researched the JFK assassination very thoroughly and came to some very specific conclusions:

> A team of CIA, Cuban exile, and Mafia-related renegades organized a simple military ambush in Dallas and successfully gunned him down. The ambush and its cover-up were brazen and astonishingly open.[506]

---

[504] Fonzi, *The Last Investigation.*

[505] Shane O'Sullivan, "Did the CIA Kill Bobby Kennedy?," November 20, 2006, *The Guardian*: spartacus.schoolnet.co.uk/JFKmorales.htm

[506] John Stockwell, *The Praetorian Guard: The U.S. Role in the New World Order,* (South End Press, 1999).

You will probably start recognizing some names that keep popping up, as well as that infamous ZR/RIFLE assassination program:

> I personally believe, from my knowledge of the CIA that elements of the CIA's ZR/RIFLE program [an assassination group that was a component of OPERATION MONGOOSE] were probably involved in the conspiracy, along with Cuban exiles, and Sam Giancana, John Roselli, and Charles Nicoletti of organized crime. ZRRIFLE was exposed by the Senate Church Committee. The CIA's Chief of Operations, Richard Bissell, admitted to its existence as did its founder, a rough impetuous man named William Harvey, who boasted of his criminal connections.[507]

Colonel L. Fletcher Prouty

You know him as the mysterious "Mr. X" in Oliver Stone's film, *JFK* (the Colonel was a consultant for that movie). To say he knew his way around the intelligence community would be a pretty big understatement. Colonel Prouty was the main liaison between the CIA and United States Air Force, and at another time in his career, was Briefing Officer for the Secretary of Defense.

Suffice to say that he knew of what he spoke. And what did he say, you might ask?

Oswald was a patsy. There's no question about it.[508]

CIA Finance Officer James Wilcott

Wilcott was a finance officer for the CIA. He served in Tokyo during the time that Oswald was stationed in the Far East. Wilcott testified to the House Select Committee on Assassinations that Oswald had been recruited by the CIA for a double agent assignment in the Soviet Union. Wilcott said that he had handled funding for the project Oswald was on.[509]

---

[507] Ibid.

[508] Colonel L. Fletcher Prouty, "The Col. L. Fletcher Prouty Reference Site," retrieved 16 May 2013: prouty.org/

[509] Russell, *The Man Who Knew Too Much,* 83.

The CIA, Wilcott asserted, had some kind of 'handle' on Oswald and recruited him 'from the military for the express purpose of a double agent assignment to the USSR.'[510]

Gary Powers

When you think of Gary Powers, you usually think of the downed spy pilot incident with the Soviet Union, because his U-2 spy plane was brought down in Soviet territory in a highly publicized event usually referred to as the "U-2 Incident" in 1960.

But Powers was actually a veteran CIA agent who was one smooth operator. He was "Top Gun" way before anybody even thought of making the movie.[511] In fact, I love his line that he always used when reporters would ask him how high he was flying in his U-2 when he was brought down. Powers would just smile and say: *"Not high enough."*[512]

Powers—and many others—suspected Lee Harvey Oswald played a role in providing the Soviets the information about the U-2 to bring it down because Oswald had been at the CIA's Atsugi base where the U-2's were launched and then was in Russia in 1960 as a phony defector.[513] In any case, Powers *did not* believe the official version and found Oswald's role much too coincidental.[514]

---

[510] Ibid.

[511] *RoadrunnersInternationale*, retrieved 16 May 2013: roadrunnersinternationale.com/powers_gary.html

[512] Ibid.

[513] *COPA (Coalition on Political Assassinations)*, "Powers, U-2 Pilot Captured by Soviets, Awarded Silver Star," retrieved 16 May 2013: politicalassassinations.com/2012/06/powers-u-2-pilot-captured-by-soviets-awarded-silver-star/

[514] *COPA*, "CIA documents show US never believed Gary Powers was shot down," retrieved 16 May 2013: politicalassassinations.wordpress.com/2010/05/05/cia-documents-show-us-never-believed-gary-powers-was-shot-down/

51

Testimony and Wiretapped Conversations of Mobsters

Chauncey Holt

I covered Holt's role in the earlier section on the "three tramps," one of whom was Holt. But if you check that, you'll notice that the testimony of Holt strongly links Mafia and CIA members as having done "business" together for a long, long time.

Carlos Marcello and Santo Trafficante

Two Mafia Godfathers who were involved in that linkage between the CIA and the Mafia were Marcello, head of Louisiana and Texas and a major force nationally in the mob, and Trafficante, based in South Florida and also a major force. They were both the targets of FBI operations.

Federal wiretaps were instrumental in prosecution of the Mafia, and in the process, information pertaining to the JFK assassination was also obtained from numerous conversations. Government wiretaps and Mafia informants have provided detailed confessions to direct involvement in the assassination of President Kennedy.

FBI documents reveal that New Orleans Mafia Godfather Carlos Marcello confessed his involvement in the JFK assassination on several occasions.[515]

FBI wiretaps reveal that Florida Mafia Godfather Santo Trafficante expressed knowledge of his involvement in the assassination, even making a deathbed statement to his attorney, Frank Ragano.[516]

The following conversation took place between Santo Trafficante and his friend and Miami businessman, Jose Aleman, in 1963, shortly before the assassination of President Kennedy:

> TRAFFICANTE: Have you seen how his brother is hitting Hoffa . . . mark my word, this man Kennedy is in trouble and will get what is coming to him.

> JOSE ALEMAN: Kennedy will be re-elected.

> TRAFFICANTE: You don't understand me. Kennedy's not going to make it to the election. He is going to be hit.[517]

And here is what the Teamster boss—and avowed Kennedy hater—had to say about what his Mob brethren pulled off.

JIMMY HOFFA:

> I told you they could do it. I'll never forget what Carlos and Santo did for me.[518]

The New Orleans mob boss wanted to be sure that Hoffa never forgot.

CARLOS MARCELLO:

> When you see Jimmy, you tell him he owes me and he owes me big.[519]

[515] "FBI Document 124-10182-10430," Bradley S. O'Leary & L.E. Seymour, *Triangle of Death: The Shocking Truth About the Role of South Vietnam and the French Mafia in the Assassination of JFK* (WND Books: 2003); Waldron & Hartmann, *Ultimate Sacrifice*.

[516] Ragano & Raab, *Mob Lawyer*; Waldron & Hartmann, *Ultimate Sacrifice*.

[517] Waldron & Hartmann, *Ultimate Sacrifice*.

[518] Ragano & Raab, *Mob Lawyer*.

[519] Ibid.

Here, Marcello explains just why Hoffa owed him big—he'd gotten rid of JFK, whose brother Bobby was Hoffa's nemesis.

Carlos Marcello (from FBI records; spoken to an FBI confidential informant):

I had the little son-of-a-bitch killed, and I'd do it again…I wish I could have done it myself.[520]

Santo Trafficante (Spoken telephonically by Trafficante on FBI wiretap in 1975, shortly after the murder of Sam Giancana):

> Now there's only *two* people alive who know who killed Kennedy,
> and *they* ain't talkin'.

Santo Trafficante (Deathbed statement of Trafficante to his attorney, Frank Ragano; spoken in Sicilian, days before Trafficante's death):

> Carlos fucked up. We should not have killed John. We should
> have killed Bobby.[521]

Johnny Roselli:

Columnist Jack Anderson befriended Roselli and, gradually over time, important facts came out of that relationship. Anderson wrote the following about it, in this case with Roselli trying to point the finger back at Castro.

> Before he died, Roselli hinted to associates that he knew who
> had arranged President Kennedy's murder. It was the same con-
> spirators, he suggested, whom he had recruited earlier to kill
> Cuban Premier Fidel Castro.

> According to Roselli, Castro enlisted the same underworld
> elements whom he had caught plotting against him. They suppos-
> edly were Cubans from the old Trafficante organization. Working
> with Cuban intelligence, they allegedly lined up an ex-Marine

---

[520] "FBI Document 124-10182-10430," O'Leary & Seymour, *Triangle of Death.*

[521] Ragano & Raab, *Mob Lawyer.*

sharpshooter, Lee Harvey Oswald, who had been active in the
pro-Castro movement.

According to Roselli's version, Oswald may have shot Kennedy
or may have acted as a decoy while others ambushed him from
closer range. When Oswald was picked up, Roselli suggested the
underworld conspirators feared he would crack and disclose information that might lead to them. This almost certainly would have
brought a massive U.S. crackdown on the Mafia. So Jack Ruby
was ordered to eliminate Oswald making it appear as an act of
reprisal against the President's killer.[522]

So there's a lot of documentation—from the FBI's own files—linking those
guys to the assassination:

Trafficante 'had been recruited in the CIA' plots to kill Castro
months before JFK became president.[523]

Like Marcello, Trafficante later confessed his involvement in
JFK's assassination.[524]

Recently declassified FBI documents confirm that just a few
years before his own death, Carlos Marcello confessed on three
occasions to informants that he had had JFK killed.[525]

---

[522] Jack Anderson, "JFK plot: Did mobster's death cover up secret," September 8, 1976: news.
google.com/newspapers?nid=2002&dat=19760908&id=3PYuAAAAIBAJ&sjid=QtsFAAAA
IBAJ&pg=4912,1845880

[523] David Talbot, "The man who solved the Kennedy assassination," Salon.com, 11-22-03:
ultimatesacrificebook.com/outline.html

[524] Jack Newfield, "I want Kennedy killed," May 1992, *Penthouse*; Ragano and Raab, *Mob Lawyer*,
346–354, 361; Waldron & Hartmann, *Ultimate* Sacrifice: ultimatesacrificebook.com/outline.html

[525] FBI DL 183A-1f035-Sub L 3.6.86 and FBI Dallas 175-109 3.3.89, cited by A. J.
Weberman; CR 137A-5467-69, 6-9-88, cited by O'Leary & Seymour, *Triangle of Death*:
ultimatesacrificebook.com/outline.html

James Files

James Files is a man in prison who says he was a shooter that day on the grassy knoll. He's still alive and has been interviewed in custody. Some people in the JFK research community have questioned his veracity but, if you take a close look, most of the attacks on him are suspiciously weak (like saying he was doing covert ops in Laos before we were actually in Laos). Much of his story matches up with the actual evidence. For example, he says he was wearing a reversible plaid jacket—which matches up precisely with Lee Bowers' testimony of the man he saw with a rifle on the grassy knoll. There are a lot of other corroborations like that, too.

Wim Dankbaar, a Dutch businessman, constructed a great website with a lot of research, specializing in Files, Holt, and tons of other information: jfkmurdersolved.com/index1.htm.

Dankbaar also hired former FBI Special Agent Zack Shelton to look into the Files case like he had investigated Chauncey Holt and his connections. Zack had tons of experience in the FBI organized crime unit, so he checked out everything about Files' story, friends, and history; checking his background and then checking and double-checking every little part of his testimony. He verified Files' bona fides with the mob in general and Chuck Nicoletti (Files' boss) in particular. That alone makes what he has to say well worth listening to.

You can see Files' testimony online; like Chauncey Holt's testimony, he ties together the links between the Mafia and elements of the CIA: youtube.com/watch?v=tFhu-yeyb_Y.

Also online, you can see FBI vet Zack Shelton discussing the case in general and Files in particular. This is a great clip that details the findings of his ten-year, unbiased, professional investigation: jfkmurdersolved.com/index1.htm.

52

Other Witnesses

Judyth Vary Baker

Judy Baker is someone I can personally vouch for; I've sat right next to her and gone back and forth over these issues, and I know that she's a person of high integrity. Judy was a very close friend of Oswald in New Orleans just prior to the assassination, and they were having a serious romantic affair.

Her book, *Me & Lee*, tells the whole story about Oswald being set up to take the fall. It's incredible stuff, and she has extensive documentation for her claims:

> Judyth shows the evidence and relates—from her first-hand experience—all she knows about the Kennedy assassination, her love affair with Lee Oswald over the summer of '63, her conversations with him as late as two days before JFK's death, his role as a deep-cover intelligence agent who was framed for an assassination he was actually trying to prevent, and how he was silenced by his old friend Jack Ruby.[526]

---

[526] Judyth Vary Baker, *Me & Lee: How I came to know, love and lose Lee Harvey Oswald* (TrineDay: 2011): meandlee.com/

There's also a good recent video from her 2012 interview by CBS News that captures her integrity, in my opinion.[527] Just Google "Judyth Vary Baker 60 Minutes" or go to: cbsnews.com/video/watch/?id=50135979n.

So—as a result of her direct knowledge—she doesn't just *think* Oswald was U.S. intelligence; she *knows* he was. And she doesn't just *think* he was set up as a patsy, she knows that one, too.

Madeleine Duncan Brown

Ms. Brown had a twenty-one-year romantic affair with Lyndon Johnson and gave birth to a child from him. Her book, *Texas in the Morning*, details those events and there's also an excellent documentary on her testimony, "The Clint Murchison Meeting—November 21, 1963" that goes into all the details: youtube.com/watch?v=POmdd6HQsus.

But to summarize briefly right here, Ms. Brown was present with Lyndon Johnson at a party at the home of Texas oil millionaire, Clint Murchison. Present there were Murchison, FBI Director J. Edgar Hoover, Dallas Mayor R. L. Thornton, future President Richard Nixon, John McCloy (chairman of Chase Manhattan Bank and head of the Ford Foundation, as well as future Warren Commission member), oil baron H. L. Hunt (reportedly the "world's richest man" at that time), George Brown (founder of Brown & Root, which later became Halliburton), and various others whom she recognized as members of the "8F Group."[528]

At the end of the evening, there was a clandestine meeting where the plot to kill JFK was finalized. Johnson despised John and Robert Kennedy—he referred to them as "the Irish Mafia"—and the group's plans against JFK were apparently finalized on November 21, 1963. Madeleine Brown describes Johnson's arrival at Murchison's:

> Tension filled the room upon his arrival. The group immediately went behind closed doors. A short time later Lyndon, anxious and red-faced, re-appeared.

[527] "Lee Harvey Oswald's 'ex-girlfriend' talks conspiracy," *CBS News*, November 28, 2012: cbsnews.com/video/watch/?id=50135979n

[528] Madeleine D. Brown, *Texas in the Morning: The Love Story of Madeleine Brown and President Lyndon Baines Johnson* (Conservatory Press: 1997), 166; John Simkin, "Suite 8F Group," *Spartacus Educational*, retrieved 20 May 2013: spartacus.schoolnet.co.uk/JFKgroup8F.htm

I knew how secretively Lyndon operated. Therefore, I said
nothing ... not even that I was happy to see him. Squeezing my
hand so hard it felt crushed from the pressure, he spoke with a
grating whisper—a quiet growl into my ear not a love message,
but one I'll always remember:

'After tomorrow those goddamn Kennedys will never embarrass
me again—that's no threat—that's a promise.'[529]

When you take the time to listen to a witness like this, who has come
forward at no benefit to herself, you get an idea of how much valid information is actually out there that we are not given access to. You can witness her
intelligence and sincerity online in the documentary, *The Clint Murchison
Meeting*[530]: youtube.com/watch?v=POmdd6HQsus.

And here's a *real* eye-popper from her book. This is from a conversation
with LBJ that she remembered well on New Year's Eve, 1963—six weeks
after the assassination. And please excuse his language, but that's the way
the guy talked:

'Lyndon, you know that a lot of people believe you had something to do with President Kennedy's assassination.'

He shot up out of the bed and began pacing and waving his
arms screaming like a madman. I was scared!

'That's bullshit, Madeleine Brown!' he yelled. 'Don't tell me you
believe that crap!

'Of course not,' I answered meekly, trying to cool his temper.

'It was Texas oil and those fucking renegade intelligence bas-
tards in Washington.'[531]

---

[529] Brown, *Texas in the Morning*, 166, emphasis in original.
[530] RIE & Robert Gaylon Ross, Sr., "The Clint Murchison Meeting—November 21, 1963,"
(Documentary), retrieved 18 May 2013: youtube.com/watch?v=POmdd6HQsus
[531] Brown, *Texas in the Morning*, 189.

Marina Oswald

In later years, Marina—Russian-born wife of the accused assassin, Lee Harvey Oswald—went public with her opinion that her husband definitely was being used by the U.S. intelligence community. And being so close to the matter, her views are very relevant.

Marina said that he must have been a government agent:

> Porter [her name after remarrying] said that in retrospect, Oswald seemed professionally schooled in secretiveness 'and I believe he worked for the American government.'

> 'He was taught the Russian language when he was in the military. Do you think that is usual that an ordinary soldier is taught Russian? Also, he got in and out of Russia quite easily, and he got me out quite easily.'[532]

Marina also observed something important that I've been pointing out to you throughout this book:

> 'It was a very complicated plot, brilliantly executed. Could any intelligent person believe that kind of thing was organized by one man?'[533]

I'd like to mention that Marina was also severely mistreated by the U.S. government. She was lied to and betrayed, and those were her exact words on the subject, not just mine.[534] It wasn't fair, it wasn't right, and I think they still owe the woman a formal apology.

There's an excellent interview of Marina online from an NBC interview with Tom Brokaw, and you can observe for yourself the intelligence with which she states her case; even while being bullied around by Mr. Brokaw:[535] youtube.com/watch?v=swHZ0DxB8n8.

---

[532] Lee Harvey Oswald's widow believes he didn't act alone," *Associated Press*, September 28, 1988: news.google.com/newspapers?nid=1310&dat=19880928&id=mOdVAAAAIBAJ&sjid =r-EDAAAAIBAJ&pg=6750,6875130

[533] Ibid.

[534] "Marina Porter (Marina Oswald) interview, NBC, 1993," retrieved 18 May 2013: youtube. com/watch?v=swHZ0DxB8n8

[535] Ibid.

Marguerite Oswald

The mother of Lee Harvey Oswald, it should be said, was convinced right from the start that her son was a pawn of U.S. intelligence agents, and she never wavered from that opinion. It's logical to presume that she probably knew a thing or two about that matter as well. Here's part of Oswald's mother's testimony before the Warren Commission:

> I think Lee was an agent. I cannot *prove* Lee was an agent. But I have facts that may lead up to them . . . I have as much circumstantial evidence that Lee was an agent, as the Dallas police have that he was a murderer.[536]

Good point, Marguerite!

---

[536] John Kelin, "Fair Play for Oswald," November 1993: acorn.net/jfkplace/09/fp.back_issues/03rd_Issue/fp_Oz.html

53

Fabian Escalante and Conclusions of Cuban Intelligence Study

I n 1960, Fabian Escalante was Chief of Counterintelligence with Cuba's Department of State Security—Cuba's counterpart of the CIA, known as G-2. He actively oversaw counterintelligence tactics regarding efforts to "double" Cuban intelligence agents and otherwise falsified intelligence matters regarding Castro and Cuba.

In 1976, Escalante became head of the whole Department of State Security—the equivalent of CIA Director. In that capacity, which coincided with the investigations being conducted by the House Select Committee on Assassinations, Escalante cooperated with U.S. investigators who were sent to meet with him.

In 1995, Escalante authored the book, *The Secret War: CIA Covert Operations Against Castro, 1959–62*. He then published *JFK: The Cuba Files* in 2006, detailing reports from Cuban counterintelligence agents who had successfully infiltrated anti-Castro groups in Miami.

He had also become head of the Cuban Security Studies Center in 1993. In that capacity, Escalante led a major study based on information that was available to him from his unique positions of power. So the conclusions of such a serious intelligence study are not something to be taken lightly.

Here's what happened according to our judgment. The hawks
never supported, they didn't understand this strategy, didn't agree.
Anything that didn't agree with a new invasion of Cuba, they
didn't agree with. We think the hawks felt themselves betrayed.
According to our judgment there were two strategies to be followed by the US: (1) from the administration; (2) and one from the
CIA, the Cuban exiles, and the Mafia—and even they had their
own independent objectives. Around that on the part of this latter
group, there developed this need to assassinate Kennedy. It seemed
to them that Kennedy was not in agreement to the new invasion.[537]

Author Dick Russell attended a special conference in Nassau between
U.S. researchers and Fabian Escalante and detailed some of his revelations:

The most intriguing news to come out of the Nassau conference,
however, was Escalante's revelation about what another leader of
the Alpha 66 group allegedly told him. As we have seen, [agent
Richard Case] Nagell would never reveal the true identities of
'Angel' and 'Leopoldo'—the two Cuban exiles who he said had
deceived Oswald into believing they were Castro operatives.
Instead, on several occasions when I prodded him, Nagell had
cleverly steered the conversation toward a man named Tony
Cuesta—indicating that this individual possessed the knowledge that he himself chose not to express. Cuesta, as noted earlier, had been taken prisoner in Cuba during a raid in 1966.

"Cuesta was blinded [in an explosion] and spent most of his time
in the hospital," Escalante recalled. In 1978, he was among a group
of imprisoned exiles released through an initiative of the Carter
Administration. "A few days before he was to leave," according
to Escalante, "I had several conversations with Cuesta. He volunteered, 'I want to tell you something very important, but I do
not want this made public because I am returning to my family in

---

[537] Fabian Escalante, *Cuban Officials and JFK Historians Conference*, December 7, 1995:
spartacus.schoolnet.co.uk/JFKescalante.htm

Miami—and this could be very dangerous.' I think this was a little bit of thanks on his part for the medical care he received."

Escalante said he was only revealing Cuesta's story because the man had died in Miami in 1994. In a declaration he is said to have written for the Cubans, Cuesta named two other exiles as having been involved in plotting the Kennedy assassination. Their names were Eladio del Valle and Herminio Diaz Garcia.[538]

---

[538] *The Man Who Knew Too Much*; dickrussell.org/articles/richard.htm

SECTION FOUR

The Why, Who, and How

54

The "Military-Industrial Complex," JFK's Foreign Policy & the Joint Chiefs of Staff

H e may have been President of the United States, but John F. Kennedy was at war with his own national security structure.

On July 20, 1961, President Kennedy stormed out of a formal meeting of the National Security Council because he was thoroughly disgusted at the fact that he had just been seriously requested to approve a plan for a surprise nuclear attack against the Soviet Union; a plan that was presented "as though it were for a kindergarten class" by General Lemnitzer, Chairman of the Joint Chiefs of Staff, and Allen Dulles, Director of the CIA.[539]

Kennedy told his Secretary of State about the incident and then said bitterly:

And we call ourselves the human race.[540]

So it's no secret that JFK was having huge trouble with his own people in Washington—especially the Joint Chiefs of Staff.[541] Those difficulties were

---

[539] Talbot, *Brothers,* 68–69.

[540] Talbot, *Brothers,* 69.

[541] Talbot, *Brothers.*

extreme and were related to what they perceived as his "too soft" position on communism and his foreign policy overall, as well as his attempts to avoid military interventions that the Joint Chiefs saw as necessary and desirable.

It is very well-documented that JFK not only intended on withdrawing troops from Vietnam, but also on sharply reducing the nuclear threat by going full steam ahead on a nuclear test ban treaty, to be followed by serious negotiations on arms reduction between all the world's nuclear powers—and accompanied by serious efforts of détente with the Soviet Union, Cuba, and the entire Eastern Bloc.[542]

These efforts made JFK about as unpopular with the CIA and the Joint Chiefs as a fox in a chicken coop. They hated his guts, openly and intensely. They also opposed his efforts in every way possible to them, including disobeying specific Presidential directives to cease and desist in all covert actions against Cuba. It didn't stop them; they conducted their raids and black ops anyway, and just failed to notify the President about it.[543] It was a war right here at home in Washington.

President Eisenhower, who preceded Kennedy in office, apparently saw the whole thing coming. His farewell address to the nation contained a specific warning that few understood at the time but which now, in retrospect, seems uncanny and very eerie. These were his exact words:

> This conjunction of an immense military establishment and a large arms industry is new in the American experience. The total influence—economic, political, even spiritual—is felt in every city, every state house, every office of the federal government. We recognize the imperative need for this development. Yet we must not fail to comprehend its grave implications. Our toil, resources and livelihood are all involved; so is the very structure of our society.
>
> In the councils of government, we must guard against the acquisition of unwarranted influence, whether sought or unsought, by the military-industrial complex. The potential for the disastrous rise of misplaced power exists and will persist.

---

[542] James W. Douglass, *JFK and the Unspeakable: Why he died and why it matters* (Touchstone: 2010); Talbot, *Brothers*.

[543] Ibid.

We must never let the weight of this combination endanger our liberties or democratic processes. We should take nothing for granted. Only an alert and knowledgeable citizenry can compel the proper meshing of the huge industrial and military machinery of defense with our peaceful methods and goals, so that security and liberty may prosper together.[544]

Those were strangely direct and harshly chosen words for an outgoing President of the United States.

The clash between those forces—an outgoing President's warning of the imminent dangers and increasing powers of a "Military-Industrial Complex"; versus the traditional principles of our Republic embodied in the Democratic principles of diplomacy and negotiation—quite clearly came to the *flash point* of confrontation during Kennedy's presidency.

---

[544] President Dwight D. Eisenhower, "Farewell Address," January 17, 1961: pbs.org/wgbh/americanexperience/features/primary-resources/eisenhower-farewell/

55

The Kennedy Administration's War on Organized Crime & Big Oil

As if the Kennedy Administration didn't have enough enemies on the foreign policy and military fronts, its domestic and economic policies also angered a lot of other very powerful people.

As amazing as it sounds, even though there had been many Mafia killings during Prohibition, FBI Director J. Edgar Hoover refused to even acknowledge the existence of organized crime.[545] Hoover flatly denied that the Mafia operated in the United States. It was not until a big mob meeting in upstate New York made national headlines in 1957, proving that the mob had actually flourished in the U.S.—largely due to the total lack of the FBI's attention and resources—that the Bureau finally directed some attention toward organized crime. Hoover was also a "closet" homosexual which apparently led to his being blackmailed by the mob.[546]

Robert Kennedy—Attorney General of the United States in his brother's administration—was the exact opposite of that. He launched open war against the Mafia in the United States after his brother took office.

---

[545] Carl Sifakis, *The Mafia Encyclopedia* (Facts on File: 1999), 127.

[546] Anthony Summers, *Official and Confidential: The Secret Life of J. Edgar Hoover* (Ebury: 2012)

The Enemy Within, a book by Robert Kennedy, had exposed the extent of Mafia influence throughout American culture and its dangers and insidious effects.[547]

Then, under his directorship as Attorney General, for the first time in history, the Department of Justice launched a serious offensive against organized crime, using every legal device in the book (and a few that weren't) to get them off the streets and limit their abilities to conduct what had been "business as usual." It was a very organized and effective assault, putting dozens of high-level mobsters in federal prisons.

But there were persistent rumors that the mob was now being double-crossed by John and Robert Kennedy because it was Mafia help that had given them political victory. It has been reported that Joseph Kennedy cut the deal that got his son elected. According to author Seymour Hersh:

> In the 1960 presidential election, Joe Kennedy made a deal with
> Sam Giancana. This former Al Capone hit man was the most
> influential gangster in the powerful organized crime syndi-
> cate in Chicago. The deal was for Giancana to get out the JFK
> vote among the rank and file in the mob controlled unions and
> siphon campaign funds from the corrupt Teamsters union fund.
> What Giancana would get in return is unknown. JFK's stolen
> win in Illinois was crucial to his narrow general election victory
> of less than one tenth of one percent of the popular vote.[548]

Frank Sinatra—closely linked to Sam Giancana and organized crime in Chicago—and many of his Hollywood pals, had also played a major support role in helping to get Kennedy elected.

So the mob in general—and "the boys in Chicago" in particular who had "brokered" the deal with Joe Kennedy and reportedly held up their end of the deal—felt that they should have, at the very least, received some preferential treatment from the Kennedy Administration's Department of Justice. Instead, they got the heat turned up on them higher than it had

[547] Robert F. Kennedy, *The Enemy Within: The McClellan Committee's Crusade Against Jimmy Hoffa and Corrupt Labor Unions* (De Capo Press: 1994)

[548] Seymour M. Hersh, *The Dark Side of Camelot* (Back Bay Books: 1998): bztv.typepad.com/Winter/DarkSideSummary.pdf

ever been in history, and they perceived it as a betrayal and a ruthless double-cross.[549]

Add to all that, the fact that—in a highly controversial deportation proceeding—U.S. Marshals practically kidnapped the sophisticated Carlos Marcello and then dumped him in a Guatemalan jungle; and you can see how there were some very upset gangsters running around and wishing nasty things on the Kennedy brothers.[550]

> On the afternoon of April 4, 1961, eight years after he was ordered deported, Carlos Marcello was finally ejected from the United States. As he walked into the INS office in New Orleans for his regular appointment to report as an alien, he was arrested and handcuffed by INS officials. He was then rushed to the New Orleans airport and flown to Guatemala. Marcello's attorneys denounced the deportation later that day, terming it "cruel and uncivilized," and noted that their client had not been allowed to telephone his attorney or see his wife.[551]

Marcello was livid and always referred to the incident as his "kidnapping":

> Marcello referred to his 1961 deportation as an illegal 'kidnapping' . . . he testified that 'two marshals put the hand-cuffs on me and they told me that I was being kidnapped and being brought to Guatemala, which they did, and in thirty minutes time I was in the plane.' He further testified that 'they dumped me off in Guatemala, and I asked them, let me use the phone to call my wife, let me get my clothes, something they wouldn't hear about. They just snatched me and that is it, actually kidnapped me.'[552]

So the Kennedys were not very popular with Mr. Marcello.

---

[549] Sam Giancana & Chuck Giancana, *Double Cross: The Explosive Inside Story of the Mobster Who Controlled America* (Skyhorse Publishing: 2010).

[550] G. Robert Blakey, Chief Counsel and Staff Director, Gary T. Cornwell, Deputy Chief Counsel & Michael Ewing, Researcher, "Appendices to Final Report of Select Committee on Assassinations, U.S. House of Representatives, 95th Congress, Second Session," January 2, 1979: jfkassassination.net/russ/jfkinfo/jfk9/hscv9e.htm#threat

[551] Ibid.

[552] Ibid.

Similarly, the Kennedy Administration was also going after a prize of the oil and gas industry: their favored tax treatment known as the depletion allowance. The issue about changes in the oil depletion allowance sounds complicated but it was simply this; oil millionaires were receiving gigantic tax breaks, and JFK decided that the pigs had been feeding at the trough at public expense for too long and decided to put an end to it. President Kennedy was said to be disturbed by the fact that a man like Texas oil baron H. L. Hunt had an annual income of thirty million dollars and hardly paid any taxes on it.[553]

> Just before John F. Kennedy was assassinated he upset people like Clint Murchison and Haroldson L. Hunt when he talked about plans to submit to Congress a tax reform plan designed to produce about $185,000,000 in additional revenues by changes in the favorable tax treatment until then accorded the gas-oil industry.[554]

Those Texas oil barons already had *huge differences* with the "Kennedy liberals from Massachusetts"—in the form of dramatic differences in "fighting communism" and "treatment of Negroes," among many others. Moving publicly to eliminate their highly prized oil depletion allowance made Kennedy about as popular in Texas as a thief at a bridal shower.

So, when you add it all up, you can see that there was some extremely high-octane hatred that was targeted on JFK; and much of it was centered right in Texas.

---

[553] John Simkin, "Theory: Texas Oil Men," *Spartacus Educational*, retrieved 20 May 2013: spartacus.schoolnet.co.uk/JFKSinvestOil.htm

[554] Ibid.

56

Complicity of the CIA

I'd like to look at the area of specific evidence of CIA involvement. People often speculate that "the CIA did it" but fail to really provide any evidence; and without evidence, it's just a vague assertion.

Here's what we now know. The CIA-Mafia plots to kill Fidel Castro were somehow related to JFK's murder. The CIA conducted a cover-up after the assassination, hiding a now obvious role in the relationship between alleged assassin Lee Harvey Oswald and U.S. intelligence, particularly in regard to his false defection to the Soviet Union during the Cold War. But those points are broad and pretty general. So what do we know *specifically*?

The large CIA station in South Florida known as JM/WAVE appears to have played a major role in the organization phase of the conspiracy. Specifically, William "Wild Bill" Harvey and David Morales from JM/WAVE, and CIA officer Cord Meyer were named in the deathbed confession of CIA Officer E. Howard Hunt as having directly participated in the JFK assassination.[555] Anti-Castro exile groups apparently involved in the assassination, such as the "Alpha 66" group, were also affiliated with JM/WAVE, as were mobsters Johnny Roselli and John Martino.[556]

---

[555] Hunt, *Bond of Secrecy*.
[556] Hancock, *Someone Would Have Talked*.

The fact that Johnny Roselli was even brought into Dallas to abort the assassination, with the special team from military intelligence, is another strong indication that the plot to kill Kennedy was hatched out of those anti-Castro black ops based in Florida.[557]

CIA Officer David Phillips handed us another such clue. As Phillips put it in an unpublished manuscript found after his death that mirrored the roles of both Oswald and Phillips in the weeks leading up to the assassination:

> I was one of the two case officers who handled Lee Harvey
> Oswald. After working to establish his Marxist bona fides, we
> gave him the mission of killing Fidel Castro in Cuba . . . I don't
> know why he killed Kennedy. But I do know he used precisely
> the plan we had devised against Castro.[558]

The CIA was also obviously involved in the visits of an Oswald "double" to Mexico City. As has been observed by investigators who've delved into the matter, the purpose of that double was apparently to link Oswald to KGB assassin Valeriy Kostikov, thereby building an intelligence "legend" whereby JFK's assassination could be blamed on the Soviets and Cubans.[559]

> [At] 9:20 a.m. on the morning of November 23, CIA Director
> John McCone briefed the new President. In [historian Michael]
> Beschloss' words: 'The CIA had information on foreign connec-
> tions to the alleged assassin, Lee Harvey Oswald, which suggested
> to LBJ that Kennedy may have been murdered by an interna-
> tional conspiracy.' It would be wrong however to think that the
> CIA cover-up was limited to defusing this Phase-One impression
> of an international conspiracy. The CIA, by covering up the falsity
> of the alleged Oswald phone call to the Soviet Embassy, actually
> helped strengthen a spurious supposed link between Oswald and
> an alleged Soviet assassination expert, Valeriy Kostikov.[560]

---

[557] Ibid.

[558] Morley & Scott, *Our Man in Mexico: Winston Scott and the Hidden History of the CIA.*

[559] Scott, "The CIA, the Drug Traffic, and Oswald in Mexico".

[560] Scott, "The CIA, the Drug Traffic, and Oswald in Mexico," citing Michael Beschloss, ed., *Taking Charge: The Johnson White House Tapes, 1963–1964* (Simon & Schuster: 1997): history-matters.com/pds/DP3_Overview.htm

That reported visit by Oswald to Kostikov was false, but nevertheless was information that made it all the way from the CIA to the President of the United States, where it was considered vitally important and formed the basis of the national security cover-up:

> It is not certain whether the conspiracy [CIA Director John] McCone referred to on November 23 involved Cuba or the Soviet Union. Beschloss's account implies that McCone's "information" concerned Oswald's alleged visit in September 1963 to the Soviet Embassy in Mexico City:
>
> 'A CIA memo written that day reported that Oswald had visited Mexico City in September and talked to a Soviet vice consul whom the CIA knew as a KGB expert in assassination and sabotage. The memo warned that if Oswald had indeed been part of a foreign conspiracy, he might be killed before he could reveal it to U.S. authorities.'
>
> Johnson appears to have had this information in mind when, a few minutes after the McCone interview, he asked FBI Director J. Edgar Hoover if the FBI 'knew any more about the visit to the Soviet embassy.'[561]

To sum up: That false intelligence legend of Oswald as a communist—with links to the KGB's assassination apparatus as well as to Castro via the Fair Play for Cuba Committee—were a ploy to justify a U.S. retaliatory air strike against Cuba.

As Peter Dale Scott noted:

> We know from other sources that Bobby Kennedy, on the afternoon of November 22, was fearful of a Cuban involvement in the assassination. Jack Anderson, the recipient of much secret CIA information, suggests that this concern may have been planted in Bobby's head by CIA Director McCone.

---

[561] Scott, "The CIA, the Drug Traffic, and Oswald in Mexico," citing Beschloss, *Taking Charge* and National Archives.

'When CIA chief John McCone learned of the assassination, he
rushed to Robert Kennedy's home in McLean, Virginia, and
stayed with him for three hours. No one else was admitted. Even
Bobby's priest was turned away. McCone told me he gave the
attorney general a routine briefing on CIA business and swore
that Castro's name never came up. . . . Sources would later tell
me that McCone anguished with Bobby over the terrible possibility that the assassination plots sanctioned by the president's own
brother may have backfired. Then the following day, McCone
briefed President Lyndon Johnson and his National Security
Advisor McGeorge Bundy.

Afterward McCone told subordinates—who later filled me
in—what happened at that meeting. The grim McCone shared
with Johnson and Bundy a dispatch from the U.S. embassy in
Mexico City, strongly suggesting that Castro was behind the
assassination.'[562]

Cuba was continually "promoted" by U.S. intelligence, as the probable perpetrators of the murder of President Kennedy.

Three days later the [Mexican] Ambassador, Thomas Mann, the
CIA Station Chief, Winston Scott, and the FBI Legal Attaché,
Clark Anderson, enthusiastically promoted wild allegations that
Oswald's act had been plotted and paid for inside the Cuban
Embassy.[563]

Key CIA officials spread stories immediately after the assassination that
Cuba's Fidel Castro was behind the President's murder.[564] So, as Colonel
Fletcher Prouty also observed, a whole *false legend* about "the President's assas-
sin" was quickly being force-fed to everyone by the CIA. There were people in

---

[562] Scott, "The CIA, the Drug Traffic, and Oswald in Mexico," citing Jack Anderson, with Daryl
Gibson, *Peace, War, and Politics: An Eyewitness Account* (Tom Doherty Associates: 1999), 115–16.

[563] Ibid.

[564] Jack Anderson, "JFK plot: Did mobster's death cover up secret," September 8, 1976: news.
google.com/newspapers?nid=2002&dat=19760908&id=3PYuAAAAIBAJ&sjid=QtsFAAAA
IBAJ&pg=4912,1845880

the Agency who wanted it to quickly be assumed that the Communists were
responsible for the assassination of President Kennedy.

And in addition to "controlling the spin" on those events, persons with
CIA connections were also reportedly directly involved in the assassination.
District Attorney Garrison's office had no doubts about that:

> His investigation led Garrison to believe that, regardless of
> whoever actually fired the shots in Dealey Plaza, the assas-
> sination was the result of a plot hatched in New Orleans
> by persons with CIA connections. Furthermore, Garrison
> concluded, following the assassination the CIA engaged in
> a cover-up to protect itself and the assassins. . . . Garrison
> thought that 'the assassins were CIA employees who were
> angered at President Kennedy's posture on Cuba following
> the Bay of Pigs disaster, and that the CIA was frustrating his
> investigation, although the agency knew the whereabouts of
> the assassins.'[565]

Jim Garrison made it very clear that his investigation concluded that
Kennedy was killed by men who had worked with the CIA from its anti-
Castro operations:

> The thesis Garrison has set forth is that a group of New Orleans-
> based, anti-Castroites, supported and/or encouraged by the CIA
> in their anti-Castro activities, in the late summer or early fall
> of 1963 conspired to assassinate John F. Kennedy. This group,
> according to Garrison, included [Clay] Shaw, [David] Ferrie,
> [Lee Harvey] Oswald . . . and others, including Cuban exiles and
> American anti-Castroites. . . . Their plan was executed in Dallas
> on November 22, 1963. At least part of their motivation . . . was
> their reaction to Kennedy's decisions at the Bay of Pigs and the

---

[565] Donald E. Wilkes, Jr., Professor of Law, "Destiny Betrayed: The CIA, Oswald, and the
JFK Assassination," December 7, 2005, *Flagpole Magazine*, 8, citing Fred Powledge, "Is
Garrison Faking?," June 17, 1967, *The New Republic*, 13–18: law.uga.edu/dwilkes_more/
jfk_22destiny.html

changes in U.S. policy toward Cuba following the missiles crisis of 1962.[566]

So to clarify, the CIA *as an agency* does not appear to have acted overtly in the assassination itself, but several "rogue" or "renegade" CIA agents, acting on their "off-the-books" mission, do appear to have been involved.

PLAYBOY: How could your probe damage the prestige of the CIA and cause them to take countermeasures against you?

GARRISON: For the simple reason that a number of the men who killed the President were former employees of the CIA involved in its anti-Castro underground activities in and around New Orleans.[567]

---

[566] Wilkes, Jr., "Destiny Betrayed," citing Richard H. Popkin, "Garrison's Case," September 14, 1967: nybooks.com/articles/archives/1967/sep/14/garrisons-case/?pagination=false

[567] "Jim Garrison's Playboy Interview," *Playboy Magazine*, October 1967, Vol. 14 No. 10: jfklancer.com/Garrison2.html

57

Complicity of Military-Industrial Complex

I t's a practice with some writers to make thinly veiled accusations about U.S. military involvement in the assassination but not to offer anything concrete in the way of substantiation.

So instead of vague assertions that reinforce those currents we already know, I'd like to concentrate here on some specific information that I will detail.

Lieutenant Colonel Robert E. Jones, 112th Military Intelligence Group, Fort Sam Houston, San Antonio, Texas

Of all the evidence of an intelligence nature, by far the most important came—and came very quickly—from the 112th military intelligence group in Texas. A document containing this information was finally released on May 16, 1973, and it revealed that it was the 112th that had quickly named Oswald as the President' assassin:

> On November 22, the 112th MIG file was instrumental, perhaps
> crucial, in clinching the superficial case against Oswald as an
> assassin. For both the rifle said to have killed the President and

the pistol said to have killed Officer Tippit had been ordered
by 'A.J. Hiddell.' Almost immediately after the assassination,
the name 'was fed into various circuits that transmitted it to
government agencies that might yield pertinent information.'
By 3:15 p.m., Colonel Robert E. Jones of the 112th MIG at Fort
Sam Houston contacted the FBI in Dallas and linked Hidell to
Oswald.[568]

That single action by Colonel Jones had rapid interpretations and huge
implications:

Army intelligence declassified an extraordinary army telegram
about Oswald dispatched late in the evening of November 22,
1963. The cable, from the Fourth Army Command in Texas to
the U.S. Strike Command at MacDill Air Force Base in Florida,
linked Oswald to Cuba via Cuba's alleged Communist 'propaganda vehicle,' the Fair Play for Cuba Committee. It also transmitted two statements about Oswald, both false, which had come
via Army intelligence from the Dallas police:

'Assistant Chief Don Stringfellow, Intelligence Section, Dallas
Police Department, notified 112th Intelligence Group, this Head-
quarters, that information obtained from Oswald revealed he
had defected to Cuba in 1959, and is a card-carrying member of
Communist Party.'[569]

As a direct result of that false Oswald info which was disseminated very
quickly after the assassination and apparently came from Colonel Robert Jones
of the 112th MIG in Texas, we almost went to war.

- USSTRICOM, the U.S. Strike Command, is an extraordinary
  two-service command (Army and Air Force) set up in 1961 in
  response to the 'Lebanon crisis' of 1958. Designed to provide a
  swift strike force on short notice, its location in Florida made it
  singularly appropriate for a surprise attack on Cuba.

---

[568] Peter Dale Scott, *Deep Politics and the Death of JFK* (University of California Press: 1996),
258.

[569] Ibid.

- There is a flavor of *Seven Days in May* to this cable of November 22, which USSTRICOM intelligence requested, since the distribution list (although confusing) suggests that it may not have reached head-quarters in Washington until four days later."

- . . . one can see the abundance of reasons behind the consensus, apparently generated by Hoover, for establishing that Oswald was just a nut who acted alone.[570]

The threat of a large-scale military confrontation as a result of the JFK assassination was much more concrete than is commonly believed. According to FBI agent James Hosty (who handled Oswald for the FBI), he learned from two independent sources that shortly after Oswald's arrest:

> . . . fully armed warplanes were sent screaming toward Cuba. Just
> before they entered Cuban airspace, they were hastily called back. With
> the launching of airplanes, the entire U.S. military went on alert.[571]

So it's highly plausible that it was not the assassination of the 35th President of the United States that the cover-up subverted; what the cover-up precluded was the military confrontation which was designed to be the *result* of the assassination.

> These planes would have been launched from the U.S. Strike
> Command at MacDill Air Force Base in Florida. We have a cable
> from U.S. Army intelligence in Texas, dated November 22, 1963,
> telling the Strike Command [falsely] that Oswald had defected
> to Cuba in 1959 and was 'a card-carrying member of the Com-
> munist Party.' As discussed below, these allegations are incom-
> patible with the present Phase-Two account of Oswald's life, but
> were corroborated at the time. At 4:00 p.m. on the afternoon of
> November 22, Hoover told Bobby Kennedy that Oswald 'went to
> Cuba on several occasions, but would not tell us what he went to
> Cuba for.' [There is nothing in FBI files on Oswald, as released
> to the public, to suggest either that Oswald had visited Cuba, or
> that he had been interrogated about such visits by the FBI.][572]

---

[570] Ibid.

[571] James P. Hosty Jr. & Thomas Hosty, *Assignment Oswald: From the FBI agent assigned to investigate Lee Harvey Oswald prior to the JFK assassination* (Arcade Publishing: 1997).

[572] Scott, *Deep Politics and the Death of JFK*, 258.

Many among those anti-Castro groups, in the military and elsewhere, had longed for serious military action against Cuba. It looks like they almost got it, too—by blaming the assassination on that set-up intelligence legend of Lee Harvey Oswald.

George L. Lumpkin, Military Intelligence

As Chris Matthews pointed out on his show, *Hardball*, it was really the changing of the President's motorcade route that made the assassination happen in the first place.[573] Without that, you don't have the victim in the kill zone where everything was set to go. But Chris Matthews never tells you who was *responsible* for that change in the parade route . . . and I will.

It was reportedly the Assistant Police Chief of Dallas: George Lumpkin. He's the one who recommended that route to the Secret Service.[574] But there was more to Assistant Chief Lumpkin than first met the eye:

> Lumpkin was also a Colonel in Army intelligence and rode in the pilot car of the Kennedy motorcade that day; he was also the officer who ordered that the Texas School Book Depository Building be sealed off after the assassination, as well as the man who specifically chose Ilya Mamantov to be Marina Oswald's Russian interpreter following the assassination.[575]

So as far as being involved in some very important things that enabled the assassination of President Kennedy and the frame-up of Lee Harvey Oswald, the virtually unknown Colonel Lumpkin was actually a man who was very close to some crucial pieces of the puzzle.

Army Cryptographer Eugene Dinkin

Dick Russell documented the testimony of Eugene B. Dinkin, who had been a cryptographic code operator for the U.S. Army in France in 1963. Dinkin intercepted secret military codes which he said were specific to a plot to kill President Kennedy. The coded information was very specific; a plot to kill the

---

[573] Chris Matthews, *Hardball with Chris Matthews,* May 29, 2007, *NBC News*: nbcnews.com/id/18941406/ns/msnbc-hardball_with_chris_matthews/t/hardball-chris-matthews-may/#.UaLfjEDVCyA

[574] Palamara, *Survivor's Guilt.*

[575] Belzer & Wayne, *Hit List*, 290.

President on November 28, 1963, that was to be blamed on a Communist or Negro who would be designated as the assassin.[576]

Dinkin's duties were deciphering and analyzing cable traffic messages in Western Europe, i.e. a code-breaker for the NSA (National Security Agency). In that capacity, Dinkin monitored the cable traffic in relation to the French OAS (Secret Army Organization, a radical group intent on the overthrow of France's government), especially insofar as their attempts to assassinate French President Charles De Gaulle.[577]

Dinkin intercepted two messages, in mid-October and on November 2, 1963, announcing the assassination of John F. Kennedy. On the basis of the cable traffic he intercepted and was able to interpret, Dinkin mailed a letter to Robert Kennedy on October 22, 1963, stating that:

> **An attempt will be made to assassinate President Kennedy on November 28, 1963, and its blame will be placed on a Communist or Negro, who will be designated as the President's assassin.**[578]

Dinkin clearly believed that a conspiracy to kill President Kennedy was being engineered but was unable to gain the attention of anyone in command. After breaking the code and interpreting the second message and having not heard anything from Robert Kennedy, Dinkin was so concerned that he then went AWOL from his base and visited the U.S. Embassy in Bonn, Germany, repeating his highly specific warning to an official there.

> On November 13, Dinkin was "hospitalized" in a closed psychiatric ward. On December 5, 1963, after the assassination of President Kennedy, Dinkin was transferred to Walter Reed Army Hospital where he was given "therapy" to help him understand that his warning of the assassination had been "coincidental" and represented a projection of his hostility toward authority figures. Left with no other realistic option to secure his freedom, Dinkin eventually "accepted" their diagnosis, was released, and given a medical discharge from the Army.[579]

---

[576] Russell, *The Man Who Knew Too Much,* 552–557.
[577] Ibid.
[578] Ibid.
[579] Ibid.

Journalist Hugh Turley also covered the story:

> On October 16, 1963, when Dinkin was stationed in Metz,
> France, he wrote a letter to Attorney General Robert F. Kennedy
> warning that the president would be assassinated on or about
> November 28, and requesting an interview by the Justice Depart-
> ment. Dinkin sent the letter registered mail, and to prevent it
> from being intercepted, used the return address of an Army
> friend, Pfc. Dennis De Witt. He did not receive an answer.

> Dinkin later changed the predicted assassination date to
> November 22, and said it would happen in Texas. He believed the
> military was involved in the plot and that a Communist would
> be blamed. The day after the murder, the *Washington Evening
> Star* reported that the alleged assassin Lee Harvey Oswald was a
> 'pro-Castro Marxist.'[580]

It was also later learned that a French assassin from the Corsican Mafia and
associated with the French OAS, Michel Mertz, was in Dallas on November 22,
1963, using the alias "Jean Souetre" and was arrested and deported shortly
after the assassination.[581] Was Dinkin's code-breaking linked to a "French
connection"?

Now, also recall what Bill Harvey, the "assassin manager" at the CIA's
ZR/RIFLE program said about his preference for Corsicans because they're
less likely to lead to the Mafia; and suddenly that all seems very important.

So how did they "handle" Eugene Dinkin?

Dinkin was treated with strong drugs, psychological reconditioning, and
threatened with electric shock treatments if he didn't respond to the "therapy."
Nice, huh?[582]

Tosh Plumlee confirmed he believes it was Dinkin's message that was the
intelligence actually responsible for sending the Military intelligence abort
team mission into Dallas on November 22:

---

[580] Hugh Turley, "Assassination Enablers?," May 2013, *Hyattsville Life & Times*: dcdave.com/
article5/Dinkin1.pdf

[581] Waldron & Hartmann, *Ultimate Sacrifice.*

[582] Russell, *The Man Who Knew Too Much*, 352.

It was because of Dinkin's info on November 8, 1963, that the Military Intelligence Abort Team was sent to Dallas to abort the hit.[583]

Jim Southwood, Military Intelligence

After Jim Southwood's thirty-year secrecy agreement (which he signed with the U.S. Military upon his retirement) finally expired, he contacted Dick Russell, author of the saga on Richard Case Nagell, *The Man Who Knew Too Much*. While in the military, Southwood had a top-secret clearance in Military intelligence.

In September of 1962, Southwood received what he was told was "a very important assignment" at the 502nd Military Intelligence Battalion in South Korea. The order came from the 112th MIG (Military Intelligence Group) in San Antonio, Texas—the same 112th from which Lieutenant Colonel Robert E. Jones, the afternoon of the same day as the assassination of JFK, immediately provided files on Lee Harvey Oswald/Alek Hidell.

The request given to Southwood from the 112th MIG was specific: for any and all information in the files on "Lee Harvey Oswald," a.k.a. "Harvey Lee Oswald" and "Alek James Hidell." Note that the request from the 112th MIG came over two months prior to the assassination. The request also sought any and all information on Jeanne and George de Mohrenschildt and anything the files had on Polish fighter pilots in World War II and the Teutonic Knights.

Southwood stated the following for the historical record:

> All the information I had about Oswald had been given to the
> 112th by George de Mohrenschildt. It was basically that Oswald
> was a peculiar guy, that he had strange sexual practices, that he
> was constantly in trouble with his wife, and that he should be
> watched closely. The request from the 112th said that de Mohren-
> schildt talked about being a member of this Teutonic Knights
> organization, and so was Oswald.[584]

There was not much in the files on Oswald's activities in Korea.

But there were numerous references and copies of files that came out of Japan on Oswald, as well as references and some copies of

---

[583] Robert Plumlee, Email to author, May 18, 2013.

[584] Ibid.

ONI [Office of Naval Intelligence] reports. This guy was under constant surveillance by both ONI and army intelligence when he was stationed in Japan. Also by the Japanese National Police. Sometimes he'd been known to frequent homosexual bars. One of the reports was that he was suspected of being involved in a homosexual relationship with a Soviet colonel. When I read the name 'Eroshkin' in your book, it came back to me: *That* was the colonel. There were also reports about his having defected to Russia.[585]

Southwood collected the information in the files and gave it to his Commanding Officer, Major Dominic Riley, who asked him if he knew who General Carter was. Southwood responded that he did not. His Commanding Officer then told him that General Carter was a friend of his, was Deputy Director of the CIA, and "This is going to him personally. They have an intense interest in this guy Oswald."[586]

General Marshall S. Carter was Deputy Director, CIA from April 3, 1962 to April 28, 1965 and went on to become Director of NSA.[587]

When asked his opinion on the matter by his Commanding Officer, Southwood stated:

SOUTHWOOD: Major, all I know is that this is a very unusual person. It would seem to me that he's involved in some kind of intelligence operation.

MAJOR RILEY: Why do you think that?

---

[585] Ibid, emphasis in original.

[586] Ibid.

[587] Grace Vale, "Clifton C. Carter: Intelligence Agent," March 1975, *Computers* and People: groups.google.com/forum/#!topic/alt.conspiracy.jfk/Gvy06-KgkHA and *Central Intelligence Agency,* "Marshall Sylvester Carter, Lieutenant General, US Army," retrieved 27 July 2013: cia.gov/library/center-for-the-study-of-intelligence/csi-publications/books-and-monographs/directors-and-deputy-directors-of-central-intelligence/carter.html

SOUTHWOOD: Well, this guy's eighteen years old, involved with
a Russian colonel, goes into the Soviet Union,
and comes back out.[588]

Dick Russell was fascinated by Southwood's recollections:

Here, unprompted, were further details substantiating Oswald's
murky relationships with intelligence operations in the Far East.
An unusual file check apparently places Oswald in liaison with
Colonel Nikolai Eroshkin. Could this have been Oswald's alleged
role in the aborted Eroshkin defection plan? To somehow ply
himself as homosexual "bait" in an effort to blackmail and coerce
the Soviet colonel?[589]

Southwood saw the name Oswald yet again:

It was some weeks afterwards when I saw Oswald's name again. It
also came out of the 112th. They wanted any background we had
on Richard Case Nagell . . . I'm certain that the code name "Laredo"
was in that file. Because I remember asking an Army buddy of
mine, 'What's that refrain, *Streets of Laredo*.' It stuck in my mind. At
the time I just figured, 'Well, they're watching Oswald like a hawk.
And this guy Nagell is the guy who's doing it.'[590]

"Laredo" happened to be a code name Nagell told author Russell he'd used
in 1963. The moment that Southwood learned of the assassination of President
Kennedy, it all came quickly together in his mind:

I was in downtown Boston on November 22. When I heard
Oswald's name, I came right out of my chair.[591]

So Southwood was certain that Oswald was an intelligence operative
for the U.S. government and was specifically of special interest to the 112th
Military Intelligence Group in Texas.

---

[588] Ibid.
[589] Ibid.
[590] Ibid.
[591] Ibid.

General Ed Landsdale

Colonel Fletcher Prouty has confirmed that—after intensive study of the photographic evidence—General Ed Landsdale was present in Dealey Plaza during the assassination.

That confirmation was also made by others in the military who were familiar with Landsdale and studied the photographs. For example, U.S. Marine Corps Lieutenant General Victor Krulak knew both Landsdale and Prouty very well. In his response to Colonel Prouty, who had sent him the photo, General Krulak wrote back, as follows:

> That is indeed a picture of Ed Landsdale. The haircut, the stoop,
> the twisted left hand, the large class ring. It's Landsdale. What in
> the world was he doing there?[592]

The following is from the website of Colonel Prouty and Len Osanic:

- Col. Fletcher Prouty and Gen. Victor Krulak both worked with Gen. Ed Landsdale in the Pentagon.

- Both men identify him being in Dealey Plaza, November 22, 1963.

- Gen. Landsdale specialized in political-psychological warfare operations and manipulation of governments.

- He worked for Allen Dulles, the Director of Central Intelligence. Although his cover story title was always Colonel and later General, he was always working for the CIA.

- The photo of him reveals deep involvement with certain members of the CIA in the planning, removal, cover story and cover-up of the assassination of President Kennedy in Dallas on November 22, 1963.

- Planning and cover story for such manipulation of government personnel was Landsdale's forte.

- Documents shown here are available at prouty.org.[593]

---

[592] Lieutenant General Victor H. Krulak, "Letter to Colonel Fletcher Prouty," March 15, 1985: ratical.com/ratville/JFK/USO/appD.html

[593] "Col. L. Fletcher Prouty on Ed Landsadle being in Dealey Plaza on Nov. 22," retrieved 23 May 2013: federaljack.com/col-l-fletcher-prouty-on-ed-lansdale-being-in-dealey-plaza-on-nov-22-1963/

The above conclusion has led to speculation that Ed Landsdale may have been "C-Cube" for the assassination operation: Command, Control and Communications. General Landsdale also happened to be the man who sent Colonel Prouty on a military expedition to Antarctica, which coincided with the JFK assassination. Prouty found it highly suspicious that he and many other experienced Washington veterans had been sent out of town at that time for a variety of low priority reasons.

I prefer to see professional forensic confirmation, like in the case of Lois Gibson confirming the "three tramps'" identities. But for whatever it's worth, Colonel Prouty and General Krulak were certain in their confirmations—and were also well aware of the gravity of the implications.

58

Complicity of the Mafia

Johnny Roselli and John Martino confessed to their involvement in setting up the JFK assassination through the anti-Castro intelligence operations in South Florida. If you want to see their specific statements on it, look back at the entry on mobsters in the witness section of this book. Roselli in particular figured prominently in the whole assassination plot, evidenced by the fact that the rescue team that was rushed into Dallas from military intelligence *brought Roselli in* with them, apparently for the purpose of calling it off with his co-conspirators.[594]

Links to three Mafia godfathers have also been well-established:

GODFATHER:	MAFIA FAMILY
Sam Giancana	Chicago (plus major strength in Nevada, Miami Beach, Hollywood)
Carlos Marcello	New Orleans (plus major strength in Texas, Cuba)
Santo Trafficante	Florida (plus major strength in Cuba)[595]

---

[594] Belzer & Wayne, *Dead Wrong*, 111–153.

[595] Waldron & Hartmann, *Legacy of Secrecy*, Waldron & Hartmann, *Ultimate Sacrifice*.

Chauncey Holt's testimony revealed how a fourth Mafia family was involved in the assassination—the Detroit family of Peter Licavoli also provided substantial support in the set-up operations of the assassination plot.[596]

Holt also detailed how professional assassin Chuck Nicoletti was brought into Dallas. Nicoletti himself verified his whereabouts that day, too; in his assassination "work book" for November 22, 1963, he wrote the following entry: "Dallas-JFK."[597]

We also know from Holt's verified testimony, as well as from the photographic evidence and professional determinations from forensic artist Lois Gibson, that two other assassins were with Chauncey Holt in Dealey Plaza—Charles Harrelson and Charles Rogers (also known as Richard Montoya).[598]

The testimony of James Files also ties together the actions of Nicoletti, Roselli, and others in Dallas. Files' credibility is supported by several former FBI agents who investigated his claims. He cross-confirms the movements of Nicoletti and Roselli.[599] The testimony of military intelligence veteran Tosh Plumlee cross-confirms the actions of Roselli as well.[600]

Jack Ruby also played a key "supporting role" in the operation and had established links to many mobsters.[601] Mobster Jim Braden (also known as Eugene Hale Brading) was in Dallas, apparently in a support role.[602] Frank Sturgis of Watergate fame is also frequently named as having apparently had a support role.[603]

Many recent books—mobster's memoirs, you could call them—have documented the mob's participation in the JFK assassination. In fact, that participation is now so taken for granted within organized crime that, at this point, it has become widely accepted folklore.[604]

---

[596] Holt, *Self-Portrait of a Scoundrel.*

[597] Wim Dankbaar, *Files on JFK* (TrineDay: 2008); Zack Shelton, Interview with author, 2006.

[598] Holt, *Self-Portrait of a Scoundrel.*

[599] Dankbaar, *Files on JFK.*

[600] Belzer & Wayne, *Dead Wrong*, 111–114.

[601] Garrison, *On the Trail of the Assassins.*

[602] Eagelsham, Allan "Familiar Faces in Dealey Plaza," November 21, 2004, *The Education Forum*: educationforum.ipbhost.com/index.php?showtopic=2313.

[603] Hunt, *Bond of Secrecy.*

[604] Bill Bonanno, *Bound by Honor: A Mafioso's Story* (St. Martin's: 2000); Brandt, *I Heard You Paint Houses;* Giancana & Giancana, *Double Cross;* Giancana, Hughes, DM OXON, MD, Ph.D.& Jobe, MD, *JFK and Sam.*

59

Complicity of Anti-Castro Cubans

Manuel Rodriguez Quesada and Gilberto Rodriguez Hernandez

Rodriguez Quesada was a bodyguard of a major exile leader, Rolando "El Tigre" Masferrer, a man with an army—Los Tigres—that was ready and willing to fight Castro.

Rodriguez Hernandez was a military coordinator for the Cuban government-in-exile groups.

A professional assassin used by U.S. intelligence—John O'Hare—reportedly said that he was ordered to kill both Rodriguez Quesada and Rodriguez Hernandez because of exile leader Eladio del Valle's fear that they would expose the identities of those responsible for the JFK assassination.

O'Hare reportedly killed them both.[605]

Angel and Leopoldo

Richard Case Nagell, the military intelligence spy who was tracking Lee Harvey Oswald's movements before the assassination, figured out that Oswald

---

[605] Belzer & Wayne, *Hit List*, 165–169, citing Robert D. Morrow, *First Hand Knowledge* (S.P.I. Books: 1992) and Craig Roberts & John Armstrong, *JFK: The Dead Witnesses* (Consolidated Press: 1994), 98.

was being deceived into believing he was working in an intelligence operation with pro-Castro agents. In reality, Nagell learned, they were involved in anti-Castro intelligence operations, but Oswald refused to believe it when confronted with the information by Nagell.

Nagell knew the two Cuban agents only by their "war names" (false names for intelligence operations)—which were "Angel" and "Leopoldo"— but it is believed they may have been two dangerous commandos from the aggressively anti-Castro exile group, Alpha 66.

Cuban exiles using those same "war names" showed up on the Dallas doorstep of Silvia Odio in late September of 1963. They were accompanied by a quiet young American who they introduced as "Leon Oswald." Forty-eight hours later, "Leopoldo" telephoned Odio and asked what she thought of "Leon." She remembered "Leopoldo" saying:

> He's kind of loco kind of nuts. He could go either way. He could
> do anything—like getting underground in Cuba, like killing Cas-
> tro. The American says we Cubans don't have any guts. He says
> we should have shot President Kennedy after the Bay of Pigs. He
> says we should do something like that.

But Silvia Odio's testimony before the Warren Commission was dismissed because the commission had already concluded Oswald was on his way to Mexico City at the time he supposedly showed up at her door.[606] Well, Oswald's "double" was either at Odio's door to set him up, or in Mexico City visiting the Soviet/Cuban embassies, *also to set him up*.

Tony Cuesta, Eladio del Valle and Herminio Diaz Garcia

Tony Cuesta was a founding member of Alpha 66, a highly combative paramilitary exile group that hated Castro with a vengeance. Cuesta was taken prisoner after a failed covert operation into Cuba in 1966.

When his team was captured, Cuesta pulled the pin on a grenade in a final attempt to take out his Cuban enemies and was blinded and lost a hand. Cuesta then spent many years in a Cuban prison, and his political positions softened somewhat as he grew older.

Years later, Cuesta actually admitted his participation in the JFK assassination—*personally*—to Fabian Escalante, head of Cuban Counterintelligence.

---

[606] Russell, *The Man Who Knew Too Much*, p. 309.

Cuesta also reportedly provided Escalante with a voluntarily written declaration to that effect, which also stated that Cuesta had direct knowledge that two other Cuban exiles—Eladio del Valle and Herminio Diaz Garcia—also were involved in plotting the assassination of President Kennedy.[607]

Diaz Garcia was a hired killer who had been a bodyguard for Santo Trafficante and also worked for Tony Varona.[608] He died in combat during a raid into Cuba in 1966.

Eladio del Valle was a brutal exile leader who was brutally murdered himself in Florida. He was known to have links to Florida Godfather Santo Trafficante, himself a key suspect in the assassination of President Kennedy.[609] In addition to being named as a conspirator in the JFK assassination by Tony Cuesta, a friend of del Valle's also claimed that del Valle was murdered because of his involvement in the assassination.[610]

The murder of del Valle was just as he was being sought for testimony by the investigation of District Attorney Jim Garrison. In fact, del Valle was killed the *exact same day* that another crucial witness, David Ferrie, was found dead under circumstances that Garrison also found suspicious.[611]

Tony Varona and Rolando Masferrer, Alpha 66

Tony Varona was a loyal supporter of former Cuban President Carlos Prío Socarrás (the leader overthrown by a military coup just before the Cuban Revolution" see; spartacus.schoolnet.co.uk/JFKprio.htm). He worked at efforts to reinstate Prío Socarrás, which included assassination attempts on Fidel Castro.

Varona worked closely with Prío Socarrás and another extremely popular exile leader, Manuel Artime. But he *also* worked closely with mobsters Johnny Roselli and Santo Trafficante in the CIA-Mafia attempts to assassinate Fidel Castro.[612]

---

[607] Russell, *The Man Who Knew Too Much*: dickrussell.org/articles/richard.htm

[608] John Simkin, "Herminio Diaz Garcia: Biography," *Spartacus Educational*, retrieved 25 May 2013: spartacus.schoolnet.co.uk/JFKgarciaH.htm

[609] Anthony Summers, *Not in Your Lifetime* (Marlowe & Co.: 1998), 319, 491.

[610] *Reference Center for Marxist Studies*, "Eladio del Valle: Biography," retrieved 25 May 2013: marxistlibrary.org/eladio-del-valle-biography/

[611] Belzer & Wayne, *Hit List*, 167–179.

[612] John Simkin, "Tony Varona: Biography," *Spartacus Educational*, retrieved 25 May 2013: spartacus.schoolnet.co.uk/JFKvarona.htm

Tony Varona was the key connection for Roselli to hardcore Cuban killers like Herminio Diaz Garcia.[613]

Colonel C. William Bishop, senior Military member of an elite assassinations unit, told author Dick Russell that, from direct personal knowledge, he could name Varona and Masferrer as conspirators in the JFK assassination:

> By 1963, the Cuban element—see, Kennedy had gone to Miami, to the Orange Bowl down there, and made this statement that the brigade's flag would fly over Cuba and all this crap. That was a stopgap. The exiles for a time believed him. Then shortly after that, a presidential executive order came out that no military-style incursions into Cuba based from the United States would be tolerated. The end result was complete distrust and dislike for Kennedy and his administration by the Cuban exiles. You take Tony Varona and Rolando Masferrer to name but two—and there were many, many more—when serious talk began to happen about the possibility of assassinating Kennedy.[614]

Rolando Masferrer was a killer with his own private army who was closely associated with mobster Santo Trafficante's organization and was brought into CIA-Mafia anti-Castro operations by Johnny Roselli and John Martino.[615]

As Colonel Bishop of the CIA's Executive Action assassination program put it, in addition to Masferrer being a "key bagman" for the militant Alpha 66 group:

> He also had different ties with Jimmy Hoffa. As far back as 1962, I think. But Rolando, from time to time when it came to large sums of money, had sticky fingers. I think that's why he was killed, eventually. Either that, or the Kennedy assassination. Because he knew about it.[616]

Masferrer was killed when his car was blown to bits by a very professional car bomb in 1975.

---

[613] Hancock, *Someone Would Have Talked.*

[614] Russell, *The Man Who Knew Too Much,* dickrussell.org/articles/richard.htm.

[615] Waldron & Hartmann, *Ultimate Sacrifice*: ultimatesacrificebook.com/documentation.html

[616] Russell, *The Man Who Knew Too Much*, 333.

Antonio Veciana

Veciana was the exile leader who founded the extremist anti-Castro group, Alpha 66. He was involved in attempts to kill Castro and testified that the CIA secretly funded some of their military and intelligence operations against Cuba in secret because the Kennedy Administration was in strong opposition to such raids and black ops.[617]

Veciana's testimony was also enlightening because he said that he was certain he saw Lee Harvey Oswald with his CIA handler, known to Veciana only by his operational name of Maurice Bishop. Congressional investigators suspected that Maurice Bishop was actually David Phillips, but were never able to prove it completely.[618]

Manuel Artime

Artime was another popular Cuban exile leader. But in addition to working with the CIA to help try and regain Cuba from Communist control, he was playing both sides of the fence by also working with the Mafia.[619]

Like many close to the CIA-Mafia plots, Artime died just as he was being sought to testify before a Congressional committee in 1975. He died from rapid-onset cancer but it should be noted that a strain of rapid-onset cancer was being developed in the nexus of anti-Cuban operations to be used as a potential bioweapon against Fidel Castro.[620]

It's beyond the realm of coincidence to look at how many witnesses with information about the CIA-Mafia plots against Castro died sudden deaths just as they were about to be pressed by investigators concerning what they knew. That list includes Artime, Rolando Masferrer, David Ferrie, Johnny Roselli, Sam Giancana, Chuck Nicoletti, George de Mohrenschildt, Carlos Prío Socarrás, and Eladio del Valle. Others with inside information about those intelligence operations and their apparent link to the JFK assassination were killed before investigators had even figured out who they were: Herminio Diaz Garcia, Manuel Rodriguez Quesada, and Gilbert Rodriguez Hernandez.[621]

[617] John Simkin, "Antonio Veciana: Biography," *Spartacus Educational*, retrieved 26 May 2013: spartacus.schoolnet.co.uk/JFKveciana.htm

[618] Fonzi, *The Last Investigation*

[619] Waldron & Hartmann, *Ultimate Sacrifice*: ultimatesacrificebook.com/documentation.html

[620] Haslam, *Dr. Mary's Monkey*; Baker, *Me & Lee*.

[621] Belzer & Wayne, *Hit List*, 165–183, 301.

Carlos Prío Socarrás

Prío Socarrás was President of Cuba from 1948 to 1952. Even though he was "elected" as opposed to being a dictator, his presidency was considered one of the most corrupt eras in Cuban history, with many links to organized crime and political corruption.[622]

He was involved in the CIA's Bay of Pigs operation that tried to overthrow Castro and was also linked to two other persons of "keen interest" to the Congressional committee investigating the assassination: mobsters Jack Ruby and Frank Sturgis.[623]

It was also believed that Prío Socarrás had relevant information about the JFK assassination, and he was being sought as a witness by Congress. But before he could testify, he died from gunshots outside the garage of his Miami home on April 5, 1977. It was ruled another suicide, but some investigators say that he was murdered to keep him from testifying.[624]

---

[622] Russell, *On the Trail of the JFK Assassins*, 136.

[623] John Simkin, "Carlos Prio: Biography," *Spartacus Educational*, retrieved 26 May 2013: spartacus.schoolnet.co.uk/JFKprio.htm

[624] Ibid, citing David Miller, "Did the CIA Kill Carlos Prio."

60

Complicity of Lyndon Johnson

Conclusions of Soviet KGB

I discovered an amazing document while I was writing this book. Get a load of this:

By September 16, 1965, the Soviet KGB had concluded that Lyndon Johnson was responsible for the JFK assassination.[625]

Stop for a minute and imagine the *gravity* of that! I already told you about how slick the Russian KGB were. They had figured out—in 1963—that Oswald was part of a plot to kill President Kennedy. And since Kennedy as President was their best option at that time, they *acted on that intelligence* to try and "eliminate" the Oswald threat and save President Kennedy, even if that meant having Oswald killed.[626]

Their conclusions, therefore, are very important. In a sense, it seems they knew what was going on better than our U.S. intelligence agencies did!

So I found this document from U.S. intelligence which wasn't even released until the 1990s; it was buried in millions of documents—literally *millions* of pages that researchers studied for years. And buried in all those documents was

---

[625] Robert Morrow, "The LBJ-CIA Assassination of JFK," November 28, 2012: lyndonjohnsonmurderedjfk.blogspot.com/2012/11/lbj-cia-assassination-of-jfk-112912.html also see: Anna K. Nelson, American University, "JFK Assassination Review Board Releases Top Secret Documents," 1998: indiana.edu/~oah/nl/98feb/jfk.html

[626] Russell, *The Man Who Knew Too Much*, 282–283, 464.

one that contained a real gem; a true game-changer. At first, it was apparently just passed over as "foreign intelligence" matters. But JFK researcher Robert Morrow has been attempting to bring the deeper meaning of that intelligence into the light of day where it belongs. This is a verbatim excerpt from the FBI memo:

> **Our source added that in the instructions from Moscow, it was indicated that 'now' the KGB was in possession of data purporting to indicate President Johnson was responsible for the assassination of the late President John F. Kennedy.**[627]

The above intelligence was in a high-level FBI internal memorandum—entitled "REACTION OF SOVIET AND COMMUNIST PARTY OFFICIALS TO THE ASSASSINATION OF PRESIDENT JOHN F. KENNEDY"—and also states the following:

> On September 16, 1965, this same source reported that the KGB Residency in New York City received instructions approximately September 16, 1965, from KGB headquarters in Moscow to develop all possible information concerning President Lyndon B. Johnson's character, background, personal friends, family, and from which quarters he derives his support in his position as President of the United States.[628]

Another statement in that FBI document revealed the broader conclusions of Soviet leadership:

> According to our source, officials of the Communist Party of the Soviet Union believed there was some well-organized conspiracy on the part of the 'ultraright' in the United States to effect a 'coup.' They seemed convinced that the assassination was not the deed of one man, but that it rose out of a carefully planned campaign in which several people played a part. They felt those elements interested in utilizing the assassination and playing on anticommunist sentiments in the United States would then utilize

---

[627] Anna K. Nelson, American University, "JFK Assassination Review Board Releases Top Secret Documents," 1998:indiana.edu/~oah/nl/98feb/jfk.html

[628] Ibid.

this act to stop negotiations with the Soviet Union, attack Cuba
and thereafter spread the war.[629]

Like I said, the Russians were some pretty slick customers and drew some
very cogent conclusions. There's a lot of other circumstantial evidence that
Johnson was involved in the conspiracy.

Madeleine Brown

I covered Ms. Brown's testimony earlier—you can find it in the section on "Other
Witnesses." But she stated very clearly for the historical record that her lover of
many years and father of her child, Lyndon Johnson, told her on the night before
the assassination in no uncertain terms that '**After tomorrow those goddamn
Kennedys will never embarrass me again—that's no threat—that's a promise.**'[630]

Billie Sol Estes

The testimony of Billie Sol Estes detailed that his former business partner,
Lyndon Johnson, was directly responsible for the murder of several individuals
and that one of those was the murder of John F. Kennedy.

> To convey an idea of the extent of pervasive corruption wreaked
> by Lyndon Johnson's political organization in Texas, one need
> look no further than the trial of his henchman, Mac Wallace.
> Described as Johnson's hit man, Wallace was found guilty of First
> Degree Murder with eleven jurors recommending the death pen-
> alty and the twelfth juror recommending life imprisonment.

> But in an incredibly obvious example of a corrupt system known
> at the time as "Texas Justice," the judge over-ruled the jury, tech-
> nically sentencing Wallace to five years imprisonment, which was
> "suspended" by the judge, and Wallace was immediately freed.[631]

Douglas Caddy, Esq., a Texas attorney formally representing Billie Sol
Estes, contacted the United States Attorney's Office on August 9, 1984, inform-
ing them of the following:

---

[629] Ibid.

[630] Brown, *Texas in the Morning*, 166, emphasis in original.

[631] Belzer & Wayne, *Dead Wrong*, 22.

My client, Mr. Estes, has authorized me to make this reply to your
letter of May 29, 1984. Mr. Estes was a member of a four-member
group, headed by Lyndon Johnson, which committed criminal
acts in Texas in the 1960s. The other two, besides Mr. Estes and
LBJ, were Cliff Carter and Mac Wallace. Mr. Estes is willing to
disclose his knowledge concerning the following criminal offenses:

   I. Murders

     1. The killing of Henry Marshall

     2. The killing of George Krutilek

     3. The killing of Ike Rogers and his secretary

     4. The killing of Harold Orr

     5. The killing of Coleman Wade

     6. The killing of Josefa Johnson

     7. The killing of John Kinser

     8. The killing of President J. F. Kennedy[632]

The statement sent to the U.S. Department of Justice included the following: "Mr. Estes is willing to testify that LBJ ordered these killings, and that he
transmitted his orders through Cliff Carter to Mac Wallace, who executed the
murders."[633]

Mac Wallace

A fingerprint identified at the so-called sniper's nest in Dealey Plaza was positively identified by a certified expert in that field who determined clear fourteen-
point identification, far exceeding the legal requirement of proof for a match.[634]

    That fingerprint belonged to the notorious Mac Wallace, a convicted killer
who, for many years, took care of the "dirty work" for Lyndon Johnson.[635]

---

[632] Douglas Caddy, Esq., "Letter to Mr. Stephen S. Trott, Assistant Attorney General,
Criminal Division, U.S. Department of Justice," August 9, 1984: home.earthlink.
net/~sixthfloor/estes.htm

[633] Ibid.

[634] Alan Kent, "Mac Wallace fingerprint?" *The Education Forum,* retrieved 28 May 2013:
educationforum.ipbhost.com/index.php?showtopic=4966

[635] Ibid.

CIA Officer E. Howard Hunt

Veteran operative Howard Hunt, in deathbed testimony, implicated Johnson as being at the operational top of the conspiracy to kill JFK. His "Chain of Command" diagram had "LBJ" as head honcho of the black op.[636]

Reduced Secret Service Protection

As I covered in the Evidence section, compared to other trips of President's Kennedy's, the Secret Service protection in Dallas was visibly reduced and a lot of those security reductions appeared to emanate from contacts of LBJ, like his aide Cliff Carter and Shift Leader of the White House Secret Service Detail, Emory Roberts.[637]

---

[636] Hunt, *Bond of Secrecy.*
[637] Palamara, *Survivor's Guilt.*

61

Complicity of H.L. Hunt and "Texas Oil"

Lyndon Johnson's benefactors apparently played a role in the assassination, too. "Texas Oil," as it was called, was a major supporter of Lyndon Johnson throughout his political career and it gave him a lot of clout. Men like H. L. Hunt (the richest man in the world at the time), Sid Richardson, Clint Murchison, and D. H. ("Dry Hole") Byrd had all made huge fortunes in the oil business and were busy buying influence with their profits. Byrd owned the building that Oswald supposedly killed Kennedy from. Murchison "owned a piece" of J. Edgar Hoover and used such friends for his political devices. Washington's infamous raconteur, Bobby Baker, put it like this:

> Clint Murchison owned a piece of Hoover. Rich people always try to put their money with the sheriff, because they're looking for protection. Hoover was the personification of law and order and officially against gangsters and everything, so it was a plus for a rich man to be identified with him. That's why men like Murchison made it their business to let everyone know Hoover was their friend. You can do a lot of illegal things if the head lawman is your buddy.[638]

---

[638] Anthony Summers, *Official and Confidential: The Secret Life of J. Edgar Hoover.*

Hunt was a rabid anti-Communist who despised the Kennedy Administration in general and John and Robert in particular. He was also quite possibly the person to whom Lee Harvey Oswald wrote the letter I showed you earlier in this book, asking for his "advice on how to proceed" before it was too late.

District Attorney Jim Garrison reportedly made a statement on September 21, 1967, that "the assassination of President Kennedy had been ordered and paid for by a handful of oil-rich psychotic millionaires."[639]

> It so happens that H. L. Hunt is also a longtime friend, admirer and financial 'angel' of the most prominent Texas politician of our time, Lyndon B. Johnson, the man who was destined to become President of the United States automatically the moment Kennedy died. Perhaps this is the reason why Garrison preferred not to be too specific.[640]

Dick Russell's research established a connection between H. L. Hunt and George de Mohrenschildt; the same de Mohrenschildt who also watched Lee Harvey Oswald.[641] Russell *also* established a connection between Hunt and Jack Ruby:

> More alarming was the Warren Commission's finding that on the day before the assassination, Jack Ruby had driven a young woman over to the Hunt offices for a job interview. After Ruby shot Oswald, Dallas police found two scripts from H. L. Hunt's *Life Line* radio program among his possessions. The FBI also reported that the telephone number of another son, Lamar, appeared 'in a book which was the property of Jack Ruby.' Questioned about this on December 17, 1963, Lamar replied 'that he could not think of any reason why his name would appear in Jack Ruby's personal property and that he had no contact whatsoever with Ruby to the best of his knowledge.'[642]

---

[639] Joachim Joesten, *How Kennedy Was Killed* (Dawnay, Tandem: 1968): spartacus.schoolnet. co.uk/JFKhuntHL.htm

[640] Ibid.

[641] Russell, *The Man Who Knew Too Much*, 173.

[642] Russell, *The Man Who Knew Too Much*, 375.

Maybe *he* couldn't think of any reason why Jack Ruby had his number, but I'm sure starting to see some.

Hunt seemed to have a lot of contacts in organized crime:

> The day before the assassination, Eugene Hale Brading, a Mafia man with a long arrest record, visited Hunt's office building in Dallas. Brading was arrested in Dealey Plaza on the day of the shooting when he was found to have taken an elevator to the ground floor of the Dal-Tex Building shortly after the shots were fired. Brading was released, however, because he gave the police an alias. While in Dallas, Brading stayed at the Cabana Hotel.[643]

The Cabana Motor Hotel in Dallas was also where Johnny Roselli and Chuck Nicoletti were supposed to be on the day of the assassination, as well as being where Brading (also known as Jim Braden) stayed, and where James Files was staying as well. Files said he had also seen Gary Marlowe there, the man who actually shot Officer Tippit, and that Lee Harvey Oswald had stopped at Files' room at the Cabana while he was staying there, too.[644] Mobster Chauncey Holt was supposed to take mobsters Leo Moceri and Chuck Nicoletti to the Cabana.[645] Another mobbed-up millionaire with connections to H. L. Hunt, named Morgan Brown, was also—*you guessed it*—staying right there at the Cabana.[646] There were, in fact, so many pre-assassination goings-on there that one researcher did a study specifically on the Cabana Motor Hotel![647] Jack Ruby was there at the Cabana also; now that was *quite* a popular place!

> Jack Ruby visited that hotel, and Hunt's office building, on November 21. Moreover, according to Hunt's former chief aide, John Curington, Marina Oswald met with Hunt two days before the shooting.

---

[643] Michael T. Griffith, "Suspects in the JFK Assassination," December 19, 2002: michaelgriffith1.tripod.com/suspects.htm

[644] Dankbaar, *Files on JFK.*

[645] William Kelly, "November 21, 1963—The Cabana Motor Hotel, Dallas, Texas," October 27, 1998: mcadams.posc.mu.edu/weberman/11-18-07.html

[646] Ibid.

[647] Ibid.

On November 23, Hunt asked his chief aide to see what kind of security the police had for Oswald. The aide reported that Oswald had very little protection and that security was very lax at police headquarters where Oswald was being kept. Hunt flew to Washington D.C., shortly after receiving this report. Oswald was killed on November 24.[648]

The above facts were confirmed in direct interviews with John Wesley Curington, who was chief aide to H. L. Hunt.[649] So Hunt obviously knew Jack Ruby and may have been involved in setting up the murder of Lee Harvey Oswald—as well as John F. Kennedy.

---

[648] Griffith, "Suspects in the JFK Assassination."

[649] Russell, *The Man Who Knew Too Much*, 376–377.

62

A CIA Plot Against Castro was Apparently "Hijacked" and Used Against JFK, which Explains the Perceived Need for a National Security Cover-Up

Historian Peter Dale Scott emphasized the importance of "the disturbing claim by John Roselli, the CIA's principal mafia contact, that a CIA hit team had been 'turned' and used to kill the President."[650]

The very same theme—a "hijacked" anti-Castro intelligence operation—was also later alluded to by the CIA Director, WHO (Western Hemisphere Operations), David Phillips:

> I was one of the two case officers who handled Lee Harvey
> Oswald . . . we gave him the mission of killing Fidel Castro in
> Cuba . . . I don't know why he killed Kennedy. But I do know he
> used precisely the plan we had devised against Castro.[651]

---

[650] Scott, *Deep Politics and the Death of JFK*.

[651] David Atlee Phillips, *The AMLASH Legacy* (unpublished manuscript), cited in Morley & Scott, *Our Man in Mexico*.

Author David Talbot observed the same demons at work, noting that "the assassination was probably the work of a conspiracy involving elements of the CIA, Mafia and anti-Kennedy Cuban exiles—a cabal that was working to terminate Castro's reign (by any means necessary) and turned its guns instead against Kennedy. This is precisely what Robert Kennedy himself immediately suspected on the afternoon of November 22, 1963 . . ."[652]

A "black operation" being hijacked by renegade members of our own intelligence community amounted, as writer Debra Conway put it, to a scenario in which the conspirators were "using the Castro plots for 'window dressing' for the true plot to assassinate President Kennedy. . . . These plots resulted in what I call a 'checkmate' situation for Attorney General Robert Kennedy, who we now know played a major role in rendering inaccessible much evidence in the case of his brother's murder. The deep remorse shown by RFK and his actions afterwards are only explainable when we allow that he believed—or was led to believe—he was somehow responsible for his brother's death through his continued encouragement—however innocent—of the Cuban exiles and their actions against Castro."[653]

The operation that killed the President apparently utilized direct components of the secret plans to assassinate Castro, which had to be kept secret.

Bobby Kennedy immediately called the CIA Director:

One of the first things Robert Kennedy did after learning of his brother's death was to immediately call the Director of the CIA and scream into the phone:

Did the CIA kill my brother?[654]

Bobby said that 'at the time' of JFK's death, he 'asked (CIA Director John) McCone . . . if they had killed my brother, and I asked him in a way that he couldn't lie to me, and they hadn't.' This statement is important, because Bobby said he asked McCone 'at the time' JFK died, meaning something about JFK's murder made him quickly suspect that the CIA might have been involved.[655]

---

[652] David Talbot, "Case Closed? A new book about the JFK assassination claims to finally solve the mystery," December 1, 2005, *Salon.com*: salon.com/2005/12/01/review_161/

[653] Debra Conway, "US-Cuba Relations: Castro Assassination Plots," November 2007:jfklancer.com/cuba/castroplots.html

[654] Waldron & Hartmann, *Ultimate Sacrifice*.

[655] Ibid.

Second, how could Bobby ask McCone 'in a way that he couldn't lie to me' unless there was some particular operation both men knew about? Clearly, Bobby was asking McCone if a plan meant for Castro had been used on his brother instead.[656]

Asking (CIA Director) McCone if the CIA was involved in such a way that 'he could not lie' suggested Kennedy thought the CIA operatives were acting at a deniable distance.[657]

RFK apparently recognized a relationship between anti-Castro intelligence operations and the murder of the President:

Robert Kennedy seemed to have immediately realized that the plot to kill President Kennedy was somehow a component of the CIA's anti-Castro operations.

He called up his contact with the anti-Castro Cubans in Florida and blurted the following into the phone:

One of your guys did it.[658]

That statement above was to his "anti-Castro" group in Florida and was verified and witnessed by both Harry Ruiz Williams and Haynes Johnson.[659] "Robert Kennedy was utterly in control of his emotions when he came on the line and sounded almost studiedly brisk as he said, 'One of your guys did it.'"[660] Historians interpret that remark as meaning that Robert Kennedy "clearly was referring to embittered Cubans deployed by elements in the CIA."[661]

At 9:20 a.m. on November 23, 1963—the morning after the assassination— CIA Director John McCone briefed the new President Lyndon Johnson:

---

[656] Richard D. Mahoney, *The Kennedy Brothers: The Rise and Fall of Jack and Bobby* (Skyhorse Publishing: 2011), 178.

[657] Ibid.

[658] Mahoney, *The Kennedy Brothers*, 178.

[659] Talbot, *Brothers*; David Talbot, May 26, 2007, "David Talbot: The Kennedy Family and the Assassination of JFK," *The Education Forum*: educationforum.ipbhost.com/index. php?showtopic=10049

[660] Mahoney, *The Kennedy Brothers*, 178.

[661] Ibid.

The CIA had information of foreign connections to the alleged assassin, Lee Harvey Oswald, which suggested to LBJ that Kennedy may have been murdered by an international conspiracy.[662]

A CIA memo written that day reported that Oswald had visited Mexico City in September and talked to a Soviet vice consul whom the CIA knew as a KGB expert in assassination and sabotage. The memo warned that if Oswald had indeed been part of a foreign conspiracy, he might be killed before he could reveal it to U.S. authorities.[663]

The name of the Russian KGB agent who supposedly met with "Oswald" in Mexico City was Valeriy Kostikov. FBI Director Clarence Kelley:

The importance of Kostikov cannot be overstated. As FBI agent Jim Hosty wrote later:

'Kostikov was the officer-in-charge for Western Hemisphere terrorist activities—including and especially assassination. In military ranking he would have been a one-star general. As the Russians would say, he was their Line V man—the most dangerous KGB terrorist assigned to this hemisphere!'[664]

So there was evidence of a communist conspiracy, even though a communist conspiracy had not actually transpired, because that evidence indicating a communist conspiracy had been deliberately planted in CIA channels prior to the assassination. This is a conclusion reached after extensive and highly professional examination of the inconsistencies in the evidence of Oswald in Mexico City and the CIA cable traffic.[665]

Two men who were intricately involved in the CIA-Mafia assassination plots against Castro—Johnny Roselli and John Martino—played a key role in

---

[662] Michael R. Beschloss, *Taking Charge: The Johnson White House Tapes, 1963–1964* (Simon & Schuster: 1997).

[663] Ibid.

[664] Newman, Ph.D., *Oswald and the CIA*, emphasis in original.

[665] Newman, Ph.D., *Oswald and the CIA* and John Newman, Ph.D. "Oswald, the CIA, and Mexico City," 2003: pbs.org/wgbh/pages/frontline/shows/oswald/conspiracy/newman.html

the quick dissemination of information falsely linking Oswald to Communist Cuba:

> For both men told the FBI that the assassination of John F. Kennedy had been Castro's retaliation for Kennedy's CIA-Mafia plots against himself, even to the point of Castro's having 'turned' an assassination team and sent it back to Dallas.[666]

> We now know that Lyndon Johnson himself, despite his public lip service to the Warren Report's verdict of a lone assassin, believed in fact that the killing was the work of a 'conspiracy,' a 'retaliation' for 'a CIA-backed assassination team . . . picked up in Havana.'[667]

It's, of course, impossible to really know if President Johnson actually believed those intelligence reports about a plot, or if he may have been "crying wolf," so to speak, to cover his own involvement. In any case, he certainly acted, behind-the-scenes, as though it were a matter of the utmost national security.

A top aide to President Johnson wrote that the Johnson Administration was aware that "a CIA-backed assassination team had been picked up in Havana. Johnson speculated that Dallas had been a retaliation for this thwarted attempt . . ."[668]

So issues of "national security" immediately played a major role in the post-assassination cover-up. As news columnist Jack Anderson wrote:

> When CIA chief John McCone learned of the assassination, he rushed to Robert Kennedy's home in McLean, Virginia, and stayed with him for three hours. No one else was admitted. Even Bobby's priest was turned away. . . . Sources would later tell me that McCone anguished with Bobby over the terrible possibility that the assassination plots sanctioned by the president's own brother may have backfired.[669]

---

[666] Scott, *Deep Politics and the Death of JFK.*

[667] Ibid.

[668] Leo Janos, "The Last Days of the President: LBJ in Retirement," *The Atlantic Monthly*, July 1973; Volume 232, No. 1; 35–41: theatlantic.com/past/docs/issues/73jul/janos.htm

[669] Jack Anderson & Daryl Gibson, *Peace, War, and Politics: An Eyewitness Account* (Forge: 1999) 115.

Imagine the shock waves in the corridors of power when it became known that the accused assassin of the President of the United States was associated with U.S. intelligence—and was using the "legend" created for him by U.S. intelligence. That makes it highly plausible that, as John Newman so aptly put it: ". . . when Oswald turned up with a rifle on the president's motorcade route, the CIA found itself living in an unthinkable nightmare of its own making."[670]

> A few key officials—like Bobby Kennedy, Richard Helms, and others—would also believe that Oswald had done it [at least initially], but not for the reasons most others did. They would think that a US asset like Oswald had 'turned,' for some reason. Yet that reason couldn't be publicly revealed—or even fully investigated . . .[671]

> In a memo kept classified for ten years, the Warren Commission lawyers wrote that 'the motive of' the 'anti-Castroites' using Oswald 'would, of course, be expectation that after the President was killed," that 'Oswald would be caught or at least his identity ascertained. Law enforcement authorities and the public would then blame the assassination on the Castro government, and the call for its forcible overthrow would be irresistible.'[672]

So it looks like CIA contract agent Robert Morrow—himself a veteran of many anti-Castro operations—nailed it exactly right when he said the following:

> The assassination of President Kennedy was, to put it simply, an anti-Castro 'provocation,' an act designed to be blamed on Castro to justify a punitive American invasion of the island. Such action would most clearly benefit the Mafia chieftains who had lost their gambling holdings in Havana because of Castro, and CIA agents

---

[670] John Newman, Ph.D., *Oswald and the CIA: The Documented Truth About the Unknown Relationship Between the U.S. Government and the Alleged Killer of JFK* (Skyhorse Publishing: 2008).

[671] Waldron & Hartmann, *Ultimate Sacrifice.*

[672] Ibid.

who had lost their credibility with the Cuban exile freedom fight-
ers from the ill-fated Bay of Pigs invasion.[673]

And, as Peter Dale Scott concluded from all the false linkages to Oswald,
"one can see the abundance of reasons behind the consensus, apparently generated by Hoover, for establishing that Oswald was just a nut who acted alone."[674]

---

[673] Robert D. Morrow, *First Hand Knowledge: How I Participated in the CIA-Mafia Murder of President Kennedy* (S.P.I. Books: 1992).

[674] Scott, *Deep Politics and the Death of JFK.*

63

The True Facts Concerning the Conspiracy and Cover-Up Have Still Not Been Revealed to the American Public

Eighty percent of the American people *still* refuse to believe the Warren Commission's conclusion that President Kennedy was murdered by one "lone nut" gunman.[675]

Because—to put it bluntly—*we're not stupid!*

I've made this point before as I've gone around the country speaking and teaching, and it bears repeating:

> During my first year as governor, I caused a pretty big stir when I told an interviewer from *Playboy* that I did not believe the official conclusion on Oswald. I think I may have been the highest-ranking official who ever said that, at least publicly. I started by simply applying common sense. If Oswald was who they told

---

[675] William E. Kelly, "Playing Politics with History—The Still Secret JFK Assassination Records 20 Years After the JFK Act," October 24, 2012: jfkcountercoup.blogspot. com/2012/10/playing-politics-with-history-still.html

us he was—a Marine private who gets out of the Marine Corps
and decides to defect to the Soviet Union at the height of the
Cold War, then comes back home with a Russian wife and does
minimum-wage jobs—why would any records need to be locked
away in the National Archives because of "national security" for
seventy-five years? As a Navy SEAL, I had to have Top-Secret
clearance. That was higher than Oswald's, and I know a few
secrets, but not enough to endanger national security.[676]

But in Oswald's case, thousands of documents are still being withheld.

My point is this: It's now fifty years after the assassination and the story is
still suppressed! WHY?

Here's a recent example of what I'm talking about:

On January 11, 2013, Robert Kennedy Jr. told Charlie Rose in
front of a large Dallas audience that his father, Robert F. Kennedy
(brother to JFK), privately believed the Warren Commission was 'a
shoddy piece of craftsmanship,' and that 'the evidence at this point
I think is very, very convincing that it was not a lone gunman.'

Kennedy said his father had 'asked Justice Department investigators to informally look into allegations that the accused assassin,
Lee Harvey Oswald, had received aid from the Mafia, the CIA or
other organizations. He said the staff members found phone lists
linking Jack Ruby, Oswald's assassin, to organized crime figures
with ties to the CIA, convincing the elder Kennedy that there was
something to the allegations.'[677]

Now get a load of *this:*

The Rose interview was taped but not broadcast by the media,
which evidently does not 'go there.'[678]

---

[676] Ventura & Russell, *American Conspiracies*, 25.

[677] Elizabeth Woodworth, "JFK, MLK, RFK, 50 Years of Suppressed History: New Evidence
on Assassination of John F. Kennedy, Martin Luther King and Robert F. Kennedy," April 5,
2013, *Global Research*: globalresearch.ca/50-years-of-suppressed-history-new-evidence-on-the-
assassination-of-john-f-kennedy-martin-luther-king-and-robert-f-kennedy/5329847

[678] Ibid.

The presentation was apparently taped at a public "town hall" presentation in Dallas, but was not actually aired on television.[679] In fact, a transcript of the presentation was apparently never made available either.[680]

And don't think for a second that you'll actually be seeing everything the government has been hiding all these years, because they're *still keeping crucial documents sealed*!

> You may think the November 22, 1963, assassination of President Kennedy is ancient history, but as we approach the fiftieth anniversary of the murder of the president, there are still government administrators who actively oppose the idea of the full truth being known today.

> To high level officials, some government records on the assassination are still a matter of national security, and many thousands of historical records are so sensitive that they won't allow you to read them nearly a half-century after Kennedy was killed.[681]

Researcher William Kelly notes that "we know that records have been intentionally destroyed, some gone totally missing and others are being wrongfully withheld, without any enforcement or oversight of the law."[682]

Now I ask you, *ISN'T THAT OUTRAGEOUS?*

> The National Archives and Records Administration[NARA] estimates that one percent of the records still remain classified, which would mean there are still an estimated 50,000 still-secret records.[683]

And, as investigative researcher Russ Baker points out, the loopholes are right there for them to continue hiding them for as long as they like:

---

[679] Ibid.

[680] Citizens for Truth about the Kennedy Assassination, "The MSM and RFK Jr.: Only 45 years Late this Time," February 3, 2013: ctka.net/2013/The_MSM_and_RFKJr.html

[681] Kelly, "Playing Politics with History—The Still Secret JFK Assassination Records 20 Years After the JFK Act".

[682] Ibid.

[683] Ibid

Release of the remaining documents, under the President John
F. Kennedy Assassination Records Collection Act of 1992, can be
postponed until October 26, 2017. Not so bad, you say? Actually,
the Act further states that even in 2017, the president may decide
to drag this on further, by withholding records indefinitely.[684]

Author Jefferson Morley knows this sad state of affairs better than most, as
a result of years of litigation with the CIA to try to get a judge to force them to
release specific records that it's known the CIA has in their possession.

Morley filed a lawsuit against the CIA, demanding the release of records
pertaining to CIA Officer George Joannides. Joannides was called out of his CIA
retirement in the 1970s and served as the CIA's liaison with the Congressional
investigation of the House Select Committee on Assassinations.[685]

Neither Joannides—nor the CIA—informed Congress that Joannides had
been the CIA case officer for a major Cuban exile group, the DRE, that Lee
Harvey Oswald had been involved with. That just goes to show you the *disdain* that they have sometimes for our Democratic processes. Can you *freaking
believe that*? This guy was *directly involved* with Oswald's intelligence actions,
and they don't even bother to mention that to Congress!

So Jefferson Morley—who has a long and distinguished career as an investigative reporter—knew that the CIA had records on Joannides and sued the
CIA to get those records released. To make a long story short, he's *still suing
them*. In October of 2006, a federal judge upheld the CIA's right to block disclosure of records about Joannides' operational activities in August of 1963.[686]
Morley is still suing them and that's a lawsuit that every one of us should follow.[687] You can keep track of that lawsuit at his website, JFKFacts.org: jfkfacts.
org/assassination/morley-v-cia-waiting-for-judgment-day/#more-4190.

So at least Morley is battling it out with the white shirts in Washington, I'll
say that for him! We'll see if he gets them to release the records. I don't know
about you, but I'm not holdin' my breath on that one!

---

[684] Russ Baker, "Is The Government Holding Back Crucial Documents?," May 30, 2012:
whowhatwhy.com/2012/05/30/is-the-government-holding-back-crucial-documents/

[685] John Simkin. "Jefferson Morley: Biography," *Spartacus Educational*: spartacus.schoolnet.
co.uk/JFKjeffersonmorley.htm

[686] Ibid.

[687] Jefferson Morley, "Oswald's handler? What Morley v. CIA clarified," April 15, 2013:
jfkfacts.org/assassination/morley-v-cia-waiting-for-judgment-day/#more-4190

William Kelly summed up the whole situation beautifully:

> In 1962, on the twentieth anniversary of the Voice of America, President Kennedy said, 'We seek a free flow of information. . . . We are not afraid to entrust the American people with unpleasant facts, foreign ideas, alien philosophies, and competitive values. For a nation that is afraid to let its people judge the truth and falsehood in an open market is a nation that is afraid of its people.'

> Today, the American government is afraid of its people, afraid to enforce its own laws and afraid to allow its citizens to know the complete truth about the assassination of President Kennedy.[688]

Man, you got that one right . . .

---

[688] Kelly, "Playing Politics with History—The Still Secret JFK Assassination Records 20 Years After the JFK Act."

Conclusion

've proved some very important points in this book:

- The official government version of the JFK assassination was—and still *is*—more full of holes than Swiss cheese;
- President Kennedy was <u>killed by a conspiracy;</u>
- The CIA and the FBI lied to us;
- There was a huge government cover-up;
- Lee Harvey Oswald was operational with U.S. Intelligence.

The U.S. Secret Service basically kidnapped the President's body from Texas authorities—even though Texas had full legal jurisdiction. That was the same Secret Service agency that Attorney General Robert Kennedy had been attempting to wrestle out of the control of the Treasury Department and get placed under the jurisdiction of the Department of Justice so that he could be in direct control of his brother's security protection.[689] Robert Kennedy clearly had some suspicions in that regard; he even investigated whether the Secret Service had

---

[689] Talbot, *Brothers*, 5, 21–22.

been "bought off" for the assassination and why they had failed to protect the President.[690]

The autopsy of the President's body was kept under the strict control of high-ranking military officers—two Navy Admirals and one Army General—none of whom had medical credentials but were "running the show" nonetheless.[691] The results of that autopsy directly contradicted the evidence of wounds from frontal gunshots that had been clearly documented by the doctors in Dallas.[692]

The best sense we can get of the real reason for the gigantic cover-up comes straight from the national security reasons that President Johnson gave when he twisted the arms of key national leaders like Chief Justice Earl Warren and Senator Richard Russell, who were at first unwilling to serve on the Warren Commission: "this is a question that has a good many more ramifications than on the surface and we've got to take this out of the arena where they're testifying that Khrushchev and Castro did this and did that and kicking us into a war that can kill forty million Americans in an hour."[693]

That was the larger drama at work and it was point-blank and dangerous:

> Johnson knew that he was being hustled into war with Cuba by
> forces within his own government. The Warren Commission
> would become his way of heading off this military showdown,
> which he realized could lead to nuclear war.[694]

President Johnson even saw fit to document some of the components of that cover-up, probably for the purpose of protecting himself. After speaking to Acting Attorney General Ramsey Clark about how the details of the cover-up were proceeding, Johnson even made it a point to "memorialize" that conversation in document form, in which he quoted Clark:

> On the other matter, I [Ramsey Clark] think we have the three
> pathologists and the photographer signed up now on the autopsy
> review and their conclusion is that the autopsy photos and x-rays

---

[690] Ibid.

[691] Talbot, *Brothers*, 15–17.

[692] Horne, *Inside the ARRB*.

[693] *American RadioWorks*, "The President Calling (November 28, 1963, at 8:55 p.m.)," retrieved 12 June 2013: americanradioworks.publicradio.org/features/prestapes/b4.html

[694] Talbot, *Brothers*, 285.

conclusively support the autopsy report rendered by them to the
Warren Commission . . .[695]

The plain fact of the matter is that the United States of America never admits
it when we've done something wrong; never admits that we've made the wrong
decision. But think about that. We know that decisions are made by people, and
people *do* make wrong decisions. The fact that we won't ever admit it—that we
were duped or wrong or did the wrong thing—is really very childish behavior,
grade-school stuff. We have to get over that or we're not going to survive, and I
believe that with all my heart. We need to come to grips. History is not history
when it's fabricated. And it also isn't history just because the winners write it, as
the old cliché goes. Because we all know that the people who write it don't always
report the truth.

But there's even *more at stake here* than all that. As I mentioned in the
Introduction, we don't even seem to actually be in control of our own Democracy
anymore. We elect a President who promised to get us out of a war, and *he can't
do it*! So who's running things? Who is really steering the ship of this Republic?
If it's not the President, Congress, or the Judiciary branch, then who?

Has the military-corporate complex already taken over this country? I'm
dead serious! I think that's a serious question that really needs to be asked at
this point. I love this country; I've served this country and I've risked my life and
dedicated many years of public service for this country.

But it's not the country I grew up in. It's no longer the "Land of the Free."
It's not *"Of* The People, *By* The People, and *For* The People." Something happened. It's now the home of the rich and the privileged. It's a country that goes
to war when war is clearly avoidable. It's a nation that has taken away rights
from the citizens it was sworn to protect and instead makes life more livable for
the corporations and for the wealthiest one percent of its citizens. What kind of
Republic does that?

America is a nation that is now virtually in a perpetual state of war around
the globe. Think about that for a moment. That's what we have become.

It wasn't always that way. In the 1960s, it seemed we were clearly headed in
precisely the opposite direction. We were on course to be the *hope* of the world.

695 President Lyndon Baines Johnson, "President Johnson's Notes on Conversation with
Acting Attorney General Ramsey Clark - January 26, 1967 - 6:29 P.M.," January 26, 1967:
history-matters.com/archive/jfk/arrb/master_med_set/md68/html/md68_0001a.htm

It may shock you to hear this, but as shocking as it is, a lot of people agree with it, and it may surprise you to learn that *PBS*'s Charlie Rose is among them.[696] So listen up!

> There's absolutely no evidence to support the statement that we're the greatest country in the world. We're 7th in Literacy, 27th in Math, 22nd in Science, 49th in Life Expectancy, 178th in Infant Mortality, 3rd in Median Household Income, 4th in Labor Force, and 4th in Exports. We lead the world in only 3 categories: Number of incarcerated citizens per capita, number of adults who believe angels are real, and Defense Spending—where we spend more than the next 26 countries combined, 25 of whom are allies.[697]

What happened? Why have we fallen back so far compared to the world leader that America used to truly be? Maybe the evidence tells us.

Eisenhower's warning about the military-industrial complex went unheeded. As we've recently witnessed in the Middle East, Afghanistan and Pakistan, the U.S. military now seems to be on a completely "different page" than the elected leaders who supposedly shape U.S. foreign policy. It's not clear at what exact point the U.S. military came to dominate foreign policy, but in my opinion, they now do. Here's my *Exhibit A*: President Barack Obama was elected on a platform clearly mandating a quick withdrawal of our troops from Iraq. Rather than being able to actually meet that pledge after being elected, as he no doubt personally wished, he was instead somehow forced to *expand* military actions, stalling the Iraq withdrawal for years, going "all-in" in the War in Afghanistan and *escalating* a covert—but *very* real—war in Pakistan as well.[698]

Were these conflicts avoidable, at least to such a large and destructive extent? *You bet they were.*

---

[696] Geoffrey Dickens, "Charlie Rose Endorses America is 'Not Greatest Country' View of Aaron Sorkin Show," June 22, 2012: newsbusters.org/blogs/geoffrey-dickens/2012/06/22/charlie-rose-endorses-america-not-greatest-country-view-aaron-sork

[697] Aaron Sorkin, *The Newsroom*, June 24, 2012, HBO: youtube.com/watch?v=16K6m3Ua2nw

[698] Adam Martin, "The C.I.A.'s Silence on Drone Strikes Is Getting Awkward," *The Atlantic*, February 6, 2012: theatlanticwire.com/global/2012/02/cis-silence-drone-strikes-getting-awkward/48328/

So why did we "rush in where angels fear to tread"[699] in direct violation of what was promised? Is it because Obama is a bad person?

I don't think so. I actually think that Barack Obama is a pretty decent human being who would keep us out of wars if he was able to. But *that's exactly my point!* He wasn't "able" to.

Which leads us right back to that all-important question: *Who the hell is actually running this country?* Because it obviously isn't the President any more, as evidenced above.

It isn't the Judiciary branch of government.

And it sure as heck isn't Congress—at this point, I don't think they can even manage to figure out how to *follow*, let alone lead.

Our civil liberties are disappearing, too: teenagers are being hauled in by the police for ridiculous "crimes" like posting a rap video on social media.[700] And then the cops who arrested and jailed the poor kid have the nerve to defend making the arrest even though they *openly admit* that there was no real substance to the so-called "terror threat."[701] Whatever happened to *our rights?* And under the insidiously-named Patriot Act, Americans who get arrested are not even technically entitled to legal representation because they are being accused of "terrorism."

And the fact that it's illegal doesn't seem to stop them from continuing it—or from lying about the fact that they do it! Edward Snowden, the NSA whistleblower who risked his life to let us know about the "massive surveillance machine they're secretly building," and that "The NSA routinely lies in response to congressional inquiries about the scope of surveillance in America," also had this to say:

> The NSA has built an infrastructure that allows it to intercept
> almost everything. With this capability, the vast majority of
> human communications are automatically ingested without

---

[699] Alexander Pope, *An Essay on Criticism*, 1709.

[700] Tim Cushing, "MA Teen Arrested And Held Without Bail For Posting Supposed 'Terrorist Threat' On Facebook," May 3, 2013, *Overhype*: techdirt.com/articles/20130502/18364622931/ma-teen-arrested-held-without-bail-posting-supposed-terrorist-threat-facebook.shtml

[701] Philip Caulfield, "Massachusetts teen charged with making 'terror' threats mentioning Boston Marathon on Facebook," May 3, 2013, *New York Daily News*: nydailynews.com/news/national/teen-faces-terror-charges-boston-marathon-facebook-post-article-1.1334038#ixzz2VerYsDsP

targeting. . . . The NSA specifically targets the communications
of everyone . . . I, sitting at my desk, certainly had the authority to
wiretap anyone, from you or your accountant, to a federal judge
or even the president if I had a personal email . . . I don't want to
live in a society that does these sort of things. I do not want to live
in a world where everything I do and say is recorded. That is not
something I am willing to support or live under.[702]

It's extremely noteworthy that former U.S. President Jimmy Carter came out
and told the press that it was good that those secrets on the extent of NSA spying
on U.S. citizens were revealed to the public! But was that story covered on your
nightly news broadcast? *No way!* And when a former President of the United
States says that "America does not have a functioning democracy at this point in
time" then that *should* be a real eye-catcher.[703] I implore you to read that article:
thenewamerican.com/usnews/constitution/item/16043-jimmy-carter-defends-
snowden-says-u-s-has-no-functioning-democracy. If mainstream media doesn't
cover a story that significant then, once again, we should be asking ourselves an
important question: *Why not?*

So let's remember the wise words of Benjamin Franklin. After leaving the
secret deliberations of America's Constitutional Convention in 1787, he was asked
by anxious citizens outside the proceedings, "Well, Doctor, what have we got, a
republic or a monarchy?" And without hesitation, Franklin responded:

A republic, if you can *keep* it.[704]

I'd like to say something else about the "War on Terror." I think it's really a
war on ourselves; please allow me to explain what I mean by that.

After World War II, the United States and the Soviet Union evolved into
the world's two great superpowers; each holding one side of a "nuclear balance
of terror," a protracted struggle for decades known historically as the Cold War.

---

[702] Thomas Gaist, "NSA Whistleblower Reveals Identity, Exposes US Government's
'Architecture of Oppression'," June 10, 2013, *Information Clearing House*:
informationclearinghouse.info/article35233.htm

[703] Jack Kenny, "Jimmy Carter Defends Snowden, Says U.S. Has No 'Functioning
Democracy'," July 20, 2013, *New American:* thenewamerican.com/usnews/constitution/
item/16043-jimmy-carter-defends-snowden-says-u-s-has-no-functioning-democracy

[704] Benjamin Franklin, "Constitutional Convention of 1787 in Philadelphia," September 17,
1787: ourrepubliconline.com/Author/21

The United States eventually defeated the Soviets; not with guns but with *money*. We outspent them militarily and the Soviets simply couldn't keep up; in trying to keep up, their economy crumbled. So I will concede that, up until that time in history, it was at least logically arguable that a huge defense budget may have made some sense. The key phrase there is not "defense budget"; the important part of that statement is "up to that point."

After that point in history, there was no real rationale or justification for spending more on weapons than almost the entire rest of the world combined, especially when our leaders were telling our people at home that there was no money for education, no money for jobs programs, no money for the elderly, and no money for much of anything except their lavish Washington parties and an unlimited defense budget.

After the Soviet threat receded, people anywhere close to my political persuasion started thinking, *"Hey, great! We're the world's only superpower. Now, finally, there'll be some serious money for programs that actually help people here at home."*

But the high levels of military spending continued. In the meantime, in other areas in which we had been world leaders, we experienced sharp declines compared to other countries.

The problem at that point in our history was "defense" from whom? We no longer had a Superpower enemy. So who were they protecting us from?

Then quite conveniently, along came the War on Terror. It was so convenient, in fact, that it brings to mind the expression that if it hadn't come along, it would have had to be invented. And some people think it may have been invented. Some think it was largely a manufactured conflict that was created to provide us with an invisible enemy that required insane amounts of spending and sacrifice to keep us safe. I can't prove that. I don't really want to believe that. I'm just saying we should be thinking about that—it's a question we should be asking. Because—as Benjamin Franklin also wrote:

> Those who would give up essential Liberty, to purchase a little temporary Safety, deserve neither Liberty nor Safety.[705]

---

[705] Benjamin Franklin, "Pennsylvania Assembly: Reply to the Governor," November 11, 1755: ushistory.org/Franklin/quotable/quote04.htm

Which leads us to what we have now—perpetual war. We spend more every year on weapons of death than almost the whole *rest of the world combined*—and then the politicians whine that there just isn't any money left for social programs.

But whether we're talking about the Cold War against Communism or our current War on Terrorism, the end result is the same. The products of destruction are paid for by mortgaging our country's hopes for the future. Every new weapons system actually represents a theft: it robs a school of a new library; prevents health care from reaching seniors who desperately need it; and makes universities unaffordable for our most gifted youth. As President Eisenhower noted:

> Every gun that is made, every warship launched, every rocket fired signifies, in the final sense, a theft from those who hunger and are not fed, those who are cold and not clothed. This world in arms is not spending money alone. It is spending the sweat of its laborers, the genius of its scientists, and the hopes of its children. This is not a way of life at all in any true sense.[706]

We, The People are now barely allowed the privilege of asking how come? But it <u>needs to be asked</u>. We *should* be asking! *How come?*

How come there's always money for another war but never enough money for jobs programs that millions of Americans really need, that could rebuild our breaking bridges and the rest of our infrastructure?

How come we give billions to defense contractors for new bomber programs and take money from the teachers who are preparing our children for their future?

How come? If we ask that too aggressively these days we're told we're being unpatriotic, possibly even a "terror threat!"

What happened? Where is that *Democracy* we all grew up believing in? *The Land of the Free.*

Representative Cynthia McKinney grilled Secretary of Defense Donald Rumsfeld a few years ago over the fact that the Comptroller General of the United States determined that 3.4 trillion dollars was "missing" from the Pentagon

---

[706] President Dwight D. Eisenhower, "The Chance for Peace," March, 1953: usnews.com/opinion/blogs/robert-schlesinger/2011/09/30/the-origins-of-that-eisenhower-every-gun-that-is-made-quote

budget in fiscal years 1999 and 2000. That's right, I said **3.4 trillion dollars**—I'm not making this up, it's Congressional testimony.[707]

Isn't that *insane*? Why on earth are we still we putting up with insanity like that? Shouldn't these maniacs be locked up in a nice little home somewhere to prevent them from sabotaging our children's future?

JFK faced that same type of political insanity and stood right up to it. At a meeting of the National Security Council in 1961, the Joint Chiefs of Staff presented President Kennedy with their plan for a surprise nuclear attack on the Soviet people.[708] They were dead serious.

JFK stood up from the table and walked out in disgust, right in the middle of the meeting. The President's disgust "was in response to a more specific evil in his own ranks: U.S. military and CIA leaders were enlisting his support for a plan to launch a nuclear attack on the Soviet Union."[709] As JFK walked away, he shot a strong look at his Secretary of State and snapped:

And we call ourselves the *human* race.[710]

That's the kind of leader we were blessed with in President Kennedy. And I think that "blessed" is really the right word.

What we can learn from that is that our problems are really nothing new. JFK had to fight the same demons that we're now faced with. Russian Premier Khrushchev and Kennedy secretly worked together through back channels to avoid war by going *behind the backs of their own generals*—because they both knew that was the only way that war could be avoided!

That secret strategy succeeded. In the Berlin Crisis in 1961 and the Cuban Missile Crisis in 1962, it was only by clinging to the hope of those secret negotiations that the peace was kept.[711] Had either leader actually listened to their own

---

[707] U.S. Representative Cynthia Ann McKinney, March 11, 2005, "U.S. House of Representatives Hearing on Fiscal Year 2006 Budget for the Department of Defense and Military Services": fromthewilderness.com/free/ww3/031505_mckinney_transcript. shtml and youtube.com/watch?v=Aupqwx6vaCs and Vince Gonzales, "Vince Gonzales investigates the Pentagon's inability to account for trillions of taxpayer dollars," *CBS News*, January 29, 2002: 911research.wtc7.net/cache/sept11/cbs_waronwaste.html and youtube. com/watch?v=LJmS_92Oo9I

[708] Douglass, *JFK and the Unspeakable*, 236.

[709] Ibid, 237.

[710] McGeorge Bundy, *Danger and Survival*, 354; Dean Rusk, *As I Saw It*, 246–247.

[711] Douglass, *JFK and the Unspeakable*, 237–243.

military advisors, this planet would have been incinerated with nuclear madness and its fallout.

That was an incredible moment:

> The two most heavily armed leaders in history, on the verge of total nuclear war, suddenly joined hands against those on both sides pressuring them to attack. Khrushchev ordered the immediate withdrawal of his missiles in return for Kennedy's public pledge never to invade Cuba and his secret promise to withdraw U.S. missiles from Turkey—as he would in fact do. The two Cold War enemies had turned, so that each now had more in common with his opponent than either had with his own generals.[712]

The Joint Chiefs of Staff, in a letter to JFK's Secretary of Defense on November 20, 1962, stated the following:

The Joint Chiefs of Staff consider that a first-strike capability is both feasible and desirable . . .[713]

That was a *nuclear* first-strike they were talking about. And it got even worse. The Chairman of the Joint Chiefs of Staff delivered a top-secret memo to JFK's Secretary of Defense on March 13, 1962. That memo urged the Kennedy Administration to create a number of "shock incidents," in the form of fake attacks on U.S. soldiers stationed in Cuba and other Central American countries and also in Miami, other Florida cities, and "even in Washington."[714] The plans even included blowing up an American ship in Guantanamo Bay. The purpose of the proposed "false flag" attacks was to create a backlash—referred to in the memo as "a helpful wave of national indignation"—that would provide a rationale for invading Cuba.[715]

The stakes were higher than most people even imagine; then or now. That national security structure firmly believed that <u>nuclear war was winnable</u>. As former Secretary of Defense Robert McNamara put it, "They were certain of

---

[712] Ibid, 382–383.

[713] *Foreign Relations of the United States, 1961–1963, Volume III: National Security Policy* (U.S. Government Printing Office: 1996), 388.

[714] Talbot, *Brothers*, 106.

[715] Ibid.

that. There were men in power who believed that America could claim victory even if the country lost 20 or 30 million people."[716]

President Kennedy was totally committed to *drastic* reductions in the arms race:

> On May 6, 1963, President Kennedy issued National Security Action Memorandum Number 239, ordering his principal national security advisers to pursue both a nuclear test ban and a policy of general and complete disarmament.[717]

And I want to now end this book with an extremely important point. JFK won that war against his own national security structure. And so can we. Join me in that effort online at "Jesse Ventura—The Official Facebook Page": facebook.com/OfficialJesseVentura.

I aim to make our so-called leaders once again responsible to the people they are supposed to represent. I want your input on a pledge I'm drafting that we are going to send to every member of Congress and request that they sign.

That pledge will include the following:

- Immediately release all documents related to the JFK assassination that are currently being withheld;
- Repeal provisions of the "Patriot Act" which are contrary to the historically established rights of American citizens as set forth in the United States Constitution and Bill of Rights;
- Any act of warfare against another people or nation must be justified by formal declaration and ratified by the United States Congress;
- Reduce "defense" spending to a level that actually reflects the level necessary for our defense;
- Use the resources from spending reductions and a more just system of taxation to benefit our citizens through increased access to quality health care, a massive public works jobs program that rebuilds our nation's infrastructure at the same time that it creates employment, the rescue and funding of the Social Security retirement system, and creating quality education through valuing the teachers of our children the way they should be—with our thanks, our vision, and with ample reward.

---

[716] Talbot, *Brothers*, 221.

[717] Douglass, *JFK and the Unspeakable*, 326.

All those Washington politicians can decide as they wish; either to sign it or to not sign our petition—but I'm gonna put it right into every single one of their laps and they're gonna have to go on public record of either supporting those principles or opposing them.

I taught at the Harvard University Kennedy School of Government and I've learned that innovation is the key to problem-solving. As Margaret Mead, a cultural anthropologist who was way ahead of her time said, "We are continually faced with great opportunities which are brilliantly disguised as unsolvable problems."[718]

That translates like this: We're *not* powerless! I'll give you a specific example of the type of catalyst change that I'm talking about. Take the gigantic "immigration problem" in this country right now that no one wants to address. We can change the whole paradigm on immigration and here's how. We grant long-term permission to stay in this country—"green cards"—to the best foreign students. In exchange for giving them their education, we actually *encourage them* to stay here in the U.S. and practice the skills that they learned in our universities. We keep the *fruits* of their education. That's how we can *immediately* enrich our U.S. labor pool, by keeping the cream of the crop—the best and brightest academics at the top of the most important fields. Right now, after getting educated here, most of them have to leave the country. It makes no sense.

Meanwhile, we increase teacher salaries and innovate change throughout our school system to make that job worthy of a career in education and gradually that will provide huge future benefits to our economy and our country. That's how to revitalize our educational system and begin coming to terms with the issue of immigration at the same time; by looking at our problems as *opportunities*. I don't believe in problems—I believe in *solutions*. We can mobilize a political force of concerned citizens that has to be reckoned with simply by caring and getting involved in the future course of our country. We can use that power to turn negatives into a positive. We can energize that knowledge to revitalize our Republic.

Take strength from the fact that others have gone before you, and still more will follow. Join me in standing strong on these issues and promoting that petition to the so-called leaders in our government. Because it's still *our* government. They just need to be reminded of that.

---

[718] *Geniuses*, "Margaret Mead—Anthropologist, psychologist, activist," retrieved 16 June, 2013: geniusrevive.com/en/geniuses.html?pid=73&sid=235:Margaret-Mead-Anthropologist-psychologist-activist

Stay vigilant! **Let's take back our country!**

I will end with a little story, and it's an important one, too.

It may shock some to learn that, long before President Nixon's Watergate tapes conspiracy in the 1970s, JFK secretly taped events like his National Security Council meetings with the Generals and Admirals who were his war-mongering adversaries.[719] And unlike President Richard Nixon, Kennedy knew how to keep a secret. Even among the White House inner circle, only he and—one would guess, his brother, the Attorney General—knew of the secret taping system.[720] Also unlike Nixon, Kennedy used it to protect the common people from the evil designs of their leaders.

What those tapes revealed when they listened to the recordings of those Generals and Admirals must have scared the *hell* out of them, too. The tapes were eventually released, and as soon as the President leaves the room, the Joint Chiefs of Staff all start squawking with profanities about what a chicken the President was.[721]

Listening to those tapes would reveal that even the Joint Chiefs thought to be most loyal to the President and Commander-in-Chief were also viciously opposed to what they saw as his "pacifist" policies. It was no laughing matter.

So JFK would marshal together his forces, telling his real team of advisors that they had better develop a consensus for peace—*and fast*. He explained why with a simple gesture toward the Joint Chiefs of Staff and one short and scary sentence:

"They all want war."[722]

That's what JFK was up against.

Well, guess what? They *still do* want war! War has become a very important "business" to the military and corporate Powers That Be who purport to be our masters.

So we, as a nation, must now develop a consensus for peace, because anything less than that is our *de facto* acceptance of the perpetual war state of that military-corporate complex.

---

[719] Talbot, *Brothers*, 166.

[720] Ted Widner, "JFK's Secret White House Recordings Unveiled," September 5, 2012: thedailybeast.com/articles/2012/09/25/jfk-s-secret-white-house-recordings-unveiled.html

[721] Talbot, *Brothers*, 166.

[722] Talbot, *Brothers*, 166.

I continue to seek your support for *rebuilding* America back into a country that again invokes the words spoken by President Kennedy shortly before his murder:

> I am talking about genuine peace, the kind of peace that makes life on earth worth living, the kind that enables men and nations to grow and to hope and to build a better life for their children—not merely peace for Americans but peace for all men and women—not merely peace in our time, but peace for all time.

> No problem of human destiny is beyond human beings. . . . So let us persevere. Peace need not be impracticable, and war need not be inevitable. By defining our goal more clearly, by making it seem more manageable and less remote, we can help all people to see it, to draw hope from it, and to move irresistibly toward it.

> So, let us not be blind to our differences—but let us also direct attention to our common interests and to the means by which those differences can be resolved. And if we cannot end now our differences, at least we can help make the world safe for diversity. For, in the final analysis, our most basic common link is that we all inhabit this small planet. We all breathe the same air. We all cherish our children's futures. And we are all mortal.

> The United States, as the world knows, will never start a war. We do not want a war. We do not now expect a war. This generation of Americans has already had enough—more than enough—of war and hate and oppression. We shall be prepared if others wish it. We shall be alert to try to stop it. But we shall also do our part to build a world of peace where the weak are safe and the strong are just. We are not helpless before that task or hopeless of its success. Confident and unafraid, we must labor on—not toward a strategy of annihilation but toward a strategy of peace.[723]

---

[723] President John F. Kennedy, "Commencement Speech at American University," June 10, 1963.

It's time to put an end to the influence of special interests that pollutes our political process. It's also time to put an end to the two-party dictatorship sponsored by those special interests that are *not* in the People's interests.

When I was Governor Jesse Ventura in Minnesota—as an Independent—I ran and was elected governor with *zero* PAC money (political action committees). I took no special interest money, and I would not even allow those people into my office—for four years in office I never once met with a lobbyist. I literally banned them from the Governor's Office. So for four years the state of Minnesota was not run by special interests.

Would you like to know what happened? My state ran budget surpluses, and I returned that money to the taxpayers every year. That's how it *should* be— because that's the People's money!

It's time to do the same thing on a national level. Our current system of "politics as usual" has got this country in a chokehold, and we're pinned down on the mat. As I said in my book, *Don't Start the Revolution Without Me!*, if we would have had the money that we spent in the whole fiasco of the Iraq War, we could have worked wonders:

> *The New York Times* recently noted that, for what the war is costing, we could've instituted universal health coverage, provided a nursery school education for every three and four year old, and immunized kids around the world against numerous diseases— and still had half the money left over.[724]

My point is this: That was *our* money, and it should've been *us* who decided how it was spent, not Pentagon war-mongers, not corporate fat cats, and not special interest lobbyists.

Peace,

Governor Jesse Ventura

---

[724] Jesse Ventura & Dick Russell, *Don't Start the Revolution Without Me: From the Minnesota Governor's Mansion to the Baja Outback: Reflections and Revisionings* (Skyhorse Publishing: 2008), 263.